Stringtown To The Kokernot

Recollections of a wildlife biologist, outdoor writer, hunter and gun collector

By Horace Gore

Texas Trophy Hunters Association

Stringtown To The Kokernot

By Horace Gore

Recollections of a wildlife biologist, outdoor writer, hunter and gun collector

"Home is the sailor, home from the sea, and the hunter home from the hill."
— *RLS*

◇◇

Copyright © 2024 Horace Gore

All rights reserved. No part of this book may be reproduced or used in any manner without the prior written permission of the copyright owner, except for the use of brief quotations in a book review.

ISBN 978-1-7349970-5-7

Copy-edited by Debbie Keene and Martin Malacara

Layout by Todd and Tracey Woodard, Dust Devil Publishing

Edited by Mark McDonald, Dust Devil Publishing

Cover photo by Marty Berry

All live deer photos by Marty Berry

With contributions from Donna Athey and Barry Gore

Printed in South Korea

Texas Trophy Hunters Association — An SCI Organization
654 Richland Hills Dr., Suite 160
San Antonio, TX 78245
210-523-8500
www.ttha.com

Dear Friends,

I am delighted to extend my warmest greetings to you as we celebrate a significant milestone in the illustrious history of Texas Trophy Hunters Association (TTHA) – our 50th anniversary. Join us as we proudly embody the "Voice of Texas Hunting."

Fifty years ago, TTHA was founded with a bold vision: To unite and celebrate the passion of hunters across Texas, while fostering conservation efforts and preserving our rich hunting heritage. As we reflect on our journey, we take immense pride in the countless memories made; friendships forged, and accomplishments achieved along the way.

During the last fifty years, TTHA has grown from strength to strength, evolving into a beacon of excellence within the Texas hunting community. Our continued success is a testament to the unwavering dedication of our members; the tireless efforts of our team, and the enduring support of our partners and sponsors.

As we mark this significant milestone, we also look to the future with great optimism and excitement. The next chapter of TTHA promises even more memorable events; an expanded membership base, and an array of new initiatives to enrich the hunting experience for enthusiasts across Texas.

(210) 523-8500 • 654 RICHLAND HILLS, SAN ANTONIO, TX 78245 • www.ttha.com

In commemoration of our 50th anniversary, I am thrilled with the release of "Stringtown to the Kokernot." This book stands as a tribute to the countless individuals who have contributed to our success and will inspire future generations of hunters to carry forth our legacy with pride.

On behalf of the entire TTHA family, I extend my heartfelt gratitude to each of you for your unwavering support and dedication. Together, we have achieved incredible milestones, and we will continue to shape the future of hunting in Texas for generations to come.

Here's to fifty years of cherished memories, and to many more decades of adventure, camaraderie, and conservation.

With warm regards,

Christina Pittman

Christina Pittman
President & CEO
Texas Trophy Hunters Association

(210) 523-8500 • 654 RICHLAND HILLS, SAN ANTONIO, TX 78245 • www.ttha.com

DEDICATION

To Jim Tiller, who taught me to hunt

To Newton Lewis, who guided me to Texas A&M

To Clyde Holt, who was a surrogate father and mentor

To Jerry Johnston, who gave me a second career

INTRODUCTION

Horace Gore is a longtime friend, professional wildlife biologist, hunting companion, gun collector, journalist, deer, quail and turkey expert, and fellow Aggie, class of 1960.

Horace and I first met at Texas A&M in 1958. We attended numerous classes together in our junior and seniors years, majoring in Wildlife Management. He was a veteran attending A&M on the GI Bill, and I was in the Corp of Cadets. Horace drove a county school bus as part-time work, and I cut hair for several students with a pair of hand clippers. Money was tight! Once a month, I would go to Horace's small apartment, and cut his hair, son Joey's hair, and trim his daughter's bangs—all for a fried chicken supper.

Just prior to graduation, Horace, Don Frels and I went to Austin to be interviewed by Al Springs for a job with the Texas Game and Fish Department. We filled out the necessary papers, and Horace and Don took field biologist jobs. I was obligated to two years in the military, but Al suggested that I write him a few months before discharge. Out of the military, I went to work for the department in South Texas, as a field biologist.

Horace began his wildlife career with Charlie Winkler in Mineral Wells, but soon moved to Brownwood. Working under Clyde Holt of Decatur, he was elevated to Regional Wildlife Supervisor in 1965, and worked in the Waco office. Later, he left Texas to become the Game Chief of the Oklahoma Game and Fish Department. After a short stay in Oklahoma, Horace returned to the

Texas Parks and Wildlife Department as Wildlife Chief of the Wildlife Division. He survived a department reorganization, and served as Upland Game and White-tailed Deer Leaders for 20 years.

After a divorce in 1992, Horace lived in a south Austin apartment and kept his bird dogs in the back yard. He retired from Texas Parks and Wildlife in 1993, and spent two winters guiding quail hunters at a hunting lodge on the Clear Fork of the Brazos in Shackelford County.

In July of 1995, Horace met me and Dr. Brian Denman at the Kokernot Ranch in Gonzales County. Brian was leasing out the ranch for hunting, and wanted our advice on several matters. Brian was looking for someone to live on the ranch, and I had suggested Horace as the perfect person. While on the ranch, Horace and Brian came to agreement about Horace moving to the ranch, and the move was made in September. I took my truck and cattle trailer up to Austin, and helped him move into the Fred Kokernot ranch house. That was one of the smartest moves Horace Gore ever made, and he lived on the Kokernot Ranch for 22 years.

Horace killed his first whitetail buck while attending Texas A&M. One of the boys who rode his school bus agreed to take Horace deer hunting if he could borrow a deer rifle. Horace agreed, and that season Horace killed a yearling buck with his war-relic Enfield .30-06, that he had converted to a sporter rifle. The 10-acre oats patch was in the Navasota River Bottom near Bryan, and Horace shot the buck while perched on a live oak tree limb.

Through the years, Horace and I have squirrel hunted a lot, and I must admit that I am a better shot with a .22. We may have set a state record when we killed 42 squirrels in two consecutive mornings in the Guadalupe River bottom. Mine were mostly head-shot, while his were shot all over!

Read on in Stringtown to the Kokernot to learn more about an iconic character who has had two eventful careers and a full life as an Arkansas "Hillbilly" who turned True Texan. —**Al Brothers Class of '60, 2022**

PREFACE

"A man should never lose his hand at hunting." —**Ernest Hemingway**

"Stringtown to the Kokernot" is a long look from a high hill, and is my pseudo-autobiography. I could have included other people, but I wanted to write a book about my life. I'm a wildlife biologist, hunter, writer, editor and gun collector. I was born to Morris and Nettie Gore on October 21, 1933 on the Walls Place, a small rental on the Stringtown Loop, about six miles east of Horatio, Sevier County, Arkansas. Stringtown Road started at the Dilworth Cumberland Presbyterian Church, and ran east across the Cossatot River to Highway 71.

There is a dirt loop that leaves and comes back to Stringtown Road that I refer to as the Stringtown Loop. On that loop, most of the three of four families were Gores, or kin to Gores. In fact, the entire area between De Queen, Horatio, and Lockesburg were Gores, or relatives of Gores, until World War II.

According to my Brother Bill (six years older), my life was almost cut short at six weeks, when I got some kind of fever and almost died. In those days, sanitation was poor; water came out of the well; everyone drank from the same dipper at the water bucket; went to the same outhouse, and doctors were scarce. I recovered, and the Gore family moved from the Walls place to Horatio when I was 3 years old.

The Great Depression was in full swing, and if you could get a job the pay was about $1 per day in cash or more often in trade. Everyone in rural areas lived off the land, had hogs and a milk cow, and hardly ever saw any cash money. Farmers traded work and food, and much of the meat came from hogs, chickens, rabbits, squirrels, and an occasional coon. Folks ate a lot of fish and watermelons in the summer, augmented by cornbread and milk and an occasional blackberry cobbler.

My days with the family at the Stringtown Loop, and later at Horatio, where I started to school, were cut short when Morris abandoned Mother, Bill and me in 1938. Mother managed to keep us for a while, but after my second grade, Bill and I went to live with our grandmother, Maude Gilmore at Briggsville, Arkansas. I lived with Maude for about four years — a very important time in forming a young adolescent through the fifth grade.

My school years at Hooks, Texas — sixth grade through high school — were good years for one who loved sports, hunting, and managed to be a "C" student. When you have a lot of outside interests, school seems to come last! I had a paper route that kept me in pocket change through the eighth grade, but there were too many sports and hunts to keep the route in high school.

Hooks, Texas was a "boom town" that sprang up at the beginning of WWII. A large war effort arsenal, along with an ammunition manufacturing depot — all on the south side of Highway 82. The north side became the town of Hooks, which had been a small farming community until the war. Our high school was 2A, and had an excellent school system. The small number of juniors and seniors allowed me to take part in everything from school plays to athletics. When we started football in 1949, I played left halfback and was in the band. After high school, I spent several months enrolled at Draughon's Business College in Dallas.

The Korean War had an enormous affect on my future after high school. I worked at both Red River Arsenal and the ammunition depot, but all jobs were contracted, and jobs would come and go. Finally, in March of 1954 I volunteered for the army and was inducted in November. My basic training was spent at Fort Bliss, Texas and Fort Leonard Wood in Missouri. The rest of my two years was spent at Fort Hood in the 36th Ordnance Battalion Headquarters, where my association with college graduates led me to Texarkana Junior College and Texas A&M University.

I had a very productive life as a wildlife biologist for 33 years, and another 27 years as editor of *The Journal of the Texas Trophy Hunters*. The first career involved quail, turkey, and white-tailed deer. The second career involved editing, writing, TV shows, Extravaganzas, and a few fascinating hunts on two continents.

My 22 years on the Kokernot Ranch in Gonzales County started in 1995 and ended in 2017 when the old diabetes took my right leg, and I went to live with Bubby and Donna in Lorena. The Kokernot years were some of the best—just me and the dogs on the best 2,200-acre cattle and wildlife ranch in Gonzales County. My present life is very regimented, but good as I write this book of my various memoirs.

"Stringtown to the Kokernot" has been a thought process that finally ended as this book, which covers my personal endeavors from birth to the present. It is meant to be somewhat of a history of my life, to be enjoyed by my future relatives and friends who can read. **—Horace Gilmore Gore, 2023**

CONTENTS

SECTION 1: GOOD START

Chapter 1: From Arkansas to Texas — My Formative Years 14

Chapter 2: Hunting is in My Blood 48

Chapter 3: The Army — 1954 to 1956 54

Chapter 4: The Making Of A Wildlife Biologist 58

Chapter 5: My Long Quest For Whitetails 70

Chapter 6: Mule Deer In The High Country 76

Chapter 7: Rifles for Texas Hunters 81

Chapter 8: Spring is for Gobblers 86

Chapter 9: *"What a Shot!"* 94

Chapter 10: Aoudads: Texas' Most Bizarre Trophy 98

SECTION 2: DOWN THE STRETCH

Chapter 11: The Quintessential Quail Hunter 103

Chapter 12: Little Jack 118

Chapter 13: Guns: 75 Years of Buying, Selling,
            Trading and Collecting 122

Chapter 14: An Aggie Discovers Country Skeet 127

Chapter 15: Make the First Shot Count 132

Chapter 16: My Days with James A. Michener 137

Chapter 17: The Unique American Pronghorn 142

Chapter 18: From Wyoming to Argentina: Hunting Two Americas . 147

Chapter 19: Texotics 152

Chapter 20: Dogs and Doves 157

SECTION 3: FAST FINISH

Chapter 21: Twenty-Two Years On the Kokernot 163

Chapter 22: Texas Trophy Hunters: A Second Career 208

Chapter 23: Ducks, *"Doc,"* And December 214

Chapter 24: Two Celebrated Squirrel Hunters. 218

Chapter 25: Russian Boars of the Guadalupe 223

Chapter 26: A Half Century of Texas Trophy Hunters 228

Chapter 27: Hunters Extravaganzas 233

Chapter 28: Trophy Hunters TV: A Memorable Video Experience . 238

Chapter 29: The .224 Texas Trophy Hunter 242

Chapter 30: The Kokernot Mockingbird 246

Chapter 31: The Boar of Long Lake 250

SECTION 4: EPILOGUE

Chapter 32: Was That Trip Necessary? 267

Chapter 33: My Last Whitetail 272

Chapter 34: The Kokernot Finality 276

Chapter 35: Requiem for a Tiger in a Cage 280

Acknowledgments 283

Author's Note: What is a "Goreism?" It can best be defined as a proposition that states Horace Gore's views and opinions on society, accumulated through decades of observation and experience.

SECTION 1
GOOD START

CHAPTER 1

From Arkansas to Texas — My Formative Years

The Post Office doesn't show a "Stringtown", Arkansas. It doesn't even show a "Dilworth". Both are Route 2, Horatio Arkansas. But in 1933, Stringtown was an active rural area on the watershed of the Cossatot River, where Nettie (Gilmore) Gore gave birth to her second son. She, husband Morris and son, Billy Wayne lived at the Walls place, a little four-room house just off the dirt road of the Stringtown Loop. Billy was six, so my arrival filled up the little Walls house.

The entire country was in the middle of the Great Depression, and Morris Gore was a dirt farmer, who lived in that area where everyone was a Gore or kin to a Gore. A full day's work would bring a dollar, but Morris liked to play the piano and drink. My first three years were spent on the Walls Place, and then Morris and Nettie moved to Horatio, about six miles west toward Little River, near the Oklahoma state line.

I remember my Dad as being popular. People came to get him to play for weddings, or funerals or a dance — no matter if music was required. A glass of "shine" usually sat near on the piano. He never did own a piano, but other people did, and I can remember him playing the "Maple Leaf Rag." For a short time, he demonstrated pianos for the Beasley Music Company in Texarkana.

The Gore Clan in Arkansas

While the Hatfields and McCoys were feuding back and forth across the Tug Fork of the Big Sandy from 1863 to 1881, the Gore Clan came peaceably to Sevier County, Arkansas from Irondale, (Jefferson County) Alabama in the 1870s.

Great Grandfather Thomas Silas Gore was born in Spartanburg, South Carolina on March 28, 1813, and came to Arkansas with his third wife. He died in the Dilworth Community, Sevier County, in 1892. His second wife was Rebecca Coker, and they had several children, one of which was James Thompson Gore. Rebecca died in Irondale, Alabama in 1861, when only 42 years old. James was six years old.

Grandfather James Thompson "Pood" Gore was born in Jefferson County, Alabama in 1855, and came to Arkansas with Thomas Gore and his third wife. James died in 1931 in the Dilworth Community (Stringtown) of Sevier County, Arkansas. His wife, Isabel Elizabeth "Belle" Wilson Gore died in the same community in 1933. They had six children: Charlie, Joe, Dewey, Alice and twins, Morris and Horris. Horris died as an infant.

Nettie Vinson (formerly Gilmore, formerly Gore) Horace's mother

My father, Morris Gore grew up in the Dilworth community (Stringtown Loop) in a rural family with little entertainment. His mother, Belle had a foot-pump organ, which apparently gave Morris something to do on rainy days. The whole family was music-minded; all could sing; and Morris taught himself to play the organ at an early age. From the organ, he advanced to the piano, which he played by ear (couldn't read music) and very well.

"Truck-patch" farming on small acreages was common in Sevier County, and the Gore clan raised corn, watermelons, cucumbers, peanuts, and every family has a big garden. Women canned winter food from the summer gardens, and folks generally lived off one-another. Cash money was about a dollar a day, the Great Depression was on, and everybody was poor, but they didn't know it. President Roosevelt and Congress passed the "New Deal" to help people in poverty, but it wasn't working. Soup lines in big cities were long!

Morris Gore married Nettie Gilmore in 1925, and their first child, Billy Wayne was born in 1927. The Stringtown Loop was a hopeless place to live during the Depression, and Morris took his family to the nearest town, Horatio, in 1937. The small, one-street town was more to the liking of Morris, who worked when he could, and played the piano. He was popular at country dances, weddings and other parties. Both Morris and Nettie made a dollar anyway they could.

Horatio was a small 900-resident town in Sevier, County, Arkansas, about 45 miles up the Oklahoma line from Texarkana. De Queen was the County Seat, lying on the drainage of the Cossatot River, which flowed into the Little River, which flowed into the Red River, which flowed into the Mississippi, which flowed into the Gulf of Mexico.

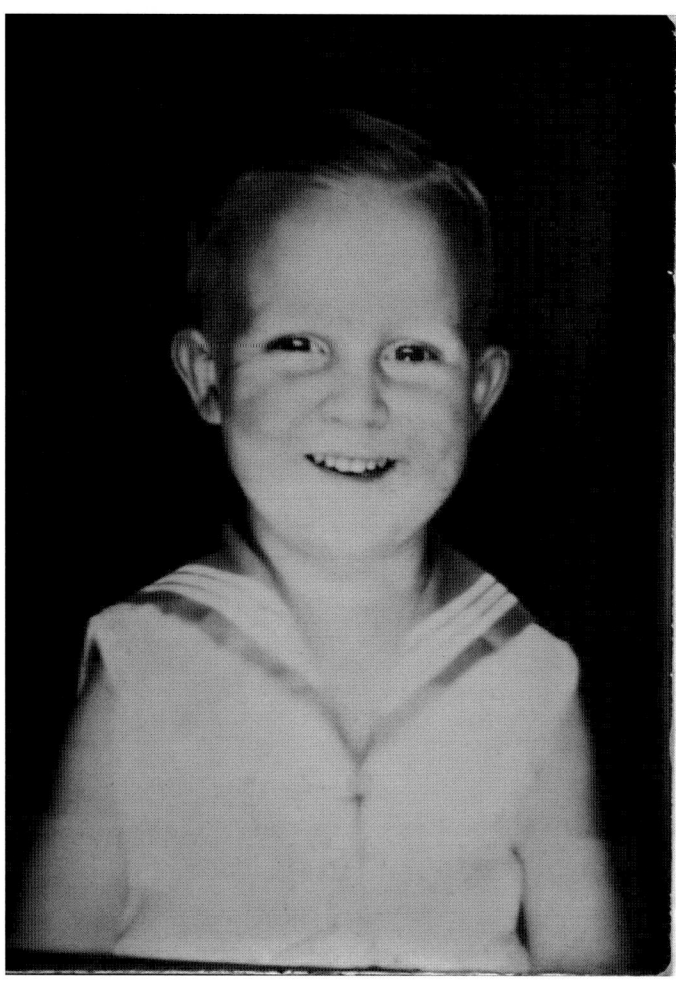

Horace Gore, age 3,
Stringtown Community, Arkansas 1936

Sevier County, established in 1828 in the Arkansas Territory, was the "wettest" county in Arkansas to be classified as a dry county for alcohol. Sometime in 1938, Morris walked away from Nettie, Bill and me. He couldn't make a living for us, so he just went away, leaving mother to hustle a living for us any way she could. I was five years old that October.

Hard Times For All

1933 was not the best time to enter this world, for several reasons. Everyone was poor as a snake; the Depression had destroyed all hope for a lot of rural people in Arkansas; FDR's "New Deal" had not brought any relief from the Depression, and Bonnie Parker and Clyde Barrow were killing, pillaging, and robbing banks and gas stations all over North Texas and as far north as Chicago and East to Arkansas and Louisiana. Their outlaw ways would last about 18 months, ending in Northwest Louisiana in May of 1934.

Prohibition was over — that is, the law was passed, to be effective on December 6, 1933, but you couldn't buy any liquor or beer until December 15. It didn't matter that store-bought whiskey was legal — you could buy all the "shine" you wanted for fifty cents a gallon. People in Sevier County used to say that they had to wear moonshine buttons to keep from selling whiskey to each other!

The few lucky people who had jobs were working, and hobos were riding trains and coming to back doors, asking for a handout. It was not uncommon for a stray dog to get rabies, and a "mad dog" could scare the neighborhood until it was dispatched. I remember seeing one or two at Horatio before I started to school. Times were not good.

On October 21, 1933 (according to a local fortune teller) I was born at 5:30 on Saturday morning on the Stringtown Loop. I was Morris and Nettie's second child — Billy Wayne was six years older.

A local midwife named Granny Manning delivered me. The Walls place where I was born was on a gravel and dirt road that made a half-mile circle toward the river and back. The three or four families on the loop were all Gores. The center of activity in the community is the Dilworth Cumberland Presbyterian Church on the west end of Stringtown Road. The local cemetery is the Millwee Cemetery where most of the old Gore clan is buried.

In 1933, transportation in Sevier County, Arkansas was more likely walking, horseback or wagon, rather than automobile. There were many more gravel than paved roads, and most folks lived and died less than 20 miles from where they were born. A few people had automobiles, and the Model A Ford was popular.

The area between Horatio, De Queen, and across the Cossatot River to Lockesburg on Highway 71, was full of Gores, and it stayed that way until World War II, when folks all over the U.S. were transformed into the war effort. New jobs and the Armed Forces caused men and women to move away from home for the first time, and the Gore Clan was dissolved for good.

I was named after my Dad's twin brother, Horris, and my maternal grandfather, William Horace "Buck" Gilmore. Life started off hard for Horris Gilmore Gore. I got a fever at about six weeks, and nearly died. Life on the Stringtown Loop was hard — no screens on windows, and lots of mosquitoes! The nearest doctor was six miles away in Horatio, or eight miles in De Queen.

My mother had a breast problem, and couldn't nurse me, so a cousin (Cleo, Uncle Charlie's daughter), who was breastfeeding her son, kept me alive for a while. She demanded a family favor, and wanted to change my name to Ralph Lynn, but my father wouldn't have it, and I kept the name of his deceased twin brother. When I went to the Army, and was cleared for Top Secret, I had to explain why my birth certificate spelled my name "Horris" rather than Horace, the name I used.

Buck and Maude Gilmore moved from Yell County to Sevier County in the '20s, and lived in Pond Creek Bottom where the mosquitoes were thick, and the dollar was thin. Nettie was the second girl, and she married Morris Gore while the Gilmores lived on Pond Creek. Later, in 1927 Buck Gilmore died from a fever carried by the mosquitoes, and Maude took the family back to Yell County, Arkansas.

A Single Mother With Two Boys

After she was abandoned, Mother (nee Nettie Gilmore) lived with Roy and Hattie Carpenter in Horatio, when I started 1st grade in the fall of 1939. Roy had an A Model Ford sedan, and they sold magazine subscriptions for anything (gold teeth, chickens, eggs, garden vegetables, etc.) that they could get.

We all lived in a little house that rented for $6, or the equivalent of goods, per month. Rent, food and gasoline were the main expenses for Mother and the Carpenters, and they got by somehow. Bill and I were a burden to Mother, and she had to make hard decisions about us, and what she was going to do in a poor and resentful society.

When I was about 5 years old, my close friend was Peggy Haynes. Her dad, Bill Haynes was the local pseudo-cowboy in Horatio. He had a '37 Chevy pickup with wooden sideboards that he used to buy and sell cattle and hogs. I liked Bill Haynes because he reminded me of all the cowboy heroes in the black and white, two-reel movies. Four and five were the years for my stick horses, which were usually a cut-off broom handle with some kind of cord for the reins. I rode a stick horse a million miles in 1937-1938.

Maude Gilmore, Horace's maternal grandmother

Bill Haynes carried a lariat rope twisted into a circle on the extended rear-view mirror. His dress was khaki shirt and pants, tucked inside his cowboy boots, a big felt hat, and red kerchief around his neck. At hog killing time, Bill Haynes showed me how to measure a hog's tail, but that's another story.

Bill liked to tease me, and would give me a nickel to sing, "She'll be coming around the mountain, when she comes," He called me "Red Rooster" and got a kick out of pulling pranks on me. He was married to Juanita Vassar, and their one child was Peggy, but they used their original sir names, and hardly ever socialized together.

Juanita worked in Fred Sharp's drug store and lived most of the time with her mother. I played a lot with Peggy, and Mrs. Vassar had a piano that Morris played before he left Horatio. At that young age, I couldn't understand why Juanita's daddy had taken a pistol and shot himself in the head!

I saw my first silver dollar when my brother went to caddy for Fred Sharp at the Little River Country Club. Billy Wayne was about 12, and Fred Sharp, who owned the local drug store, took Billy Wayne with him to the golf course, in that day, eight holes of walking was a full morning of golfing, and Billy Wayne carried Fred's clubs. For his caddying work, Fred gave Billy a silver dollar.

My birthday is October 21, and Arkansas law permitted kids to enter the first grade if they were 6 years old on September 1. Mother got me into the first grade in September before my sixth birthday in October. An incident happened in first grade that has lingered in my mind all these years.

I found a nickel on the school ground and carried it in my pocket for a few days. Martha Sue Montgomery was a blonde-haired girl in my class, and I was high on her. She found out that I had the nickel, and wanted it. We cut a deal, and I gave it to her when she agreed to be "my girl" for a day. That was an early example of how easily I could be charmed.

I finished the first grade and half of the second in Horatio, but mother moved to Central (Called "Frog Level"), east of Horatio and I went to the second half of 2nd grade at Central School, being taught by my cousin's wife. The Central School house had been built as a WPA project during the depression. I remember it as being only a grade school — the high school was in Horatio.

I was a rascal at early age, and I got in trouble in second grade, when I drew a picture of a boy peeing in a flower bed. My teacher put me in the cloak closet (where we hung our coats) and forgot about me when school was out at 4 p.m. I didn't say anything, and they all came and got me about dark. Of course, mother gave me a thorough whipping!

Briggsville, Arkansas

That fall (1941) I was due to go to the third grade, so Mother got her sister (Aunt Ruby) to take Bill and me to live with our maternal grandmother, Maude Gilmore on a sharecropper farm at Briggsville, Arkansas.

Bill and I lived with Maude and three of my uncles, starting in early summer. I started third grade at Briggsville school (1-12) with Grace Weems, my teacher, who was the sister of Ode Weems, who was married to Aunt Sybil. If I remember right, there were about six of us in third grade, and about that many in the fourth grade, and Ms. Weems taught both classes in the same room.

Grace Weems was about 30 years old — an "old maid." She roomed at home with her father, along with Dura Lasenby, another old maid teacher who also taught at Briggsville school, which was the only high school in Fourche Valley. Plainview, a town at the east end of the valley, was the only town of any size, and most folks went to Danville (Yell County Seat) for their serious buying.

The Fourche La Fave River starts in western Arkansas and flows through a valley between the North and South Ouachita Mountain range eastward to the Arkansas River. The river got its name from a French family (Fave) who lived near its source in Scott County (Fourche means Fork in French, so Fourche La Fave means the Fave Fork). The river caught wet-weather water from both sides of the valley, and was a steady flowing stream.

The land originally belonged to France, and was called the Louisiana Territory before Thomas Jefferson's Administration bought the Territory from France in 1803 for $15 million (2 cents per acre) and Arkansas was formed as a state in 1836.

Arkansas Highway 28 runs about 35 miles East and West through Fourche Valley from Needmore (Hwy 71) to Ola, and crosses the Fourche La Fave River four times. The road was gravel before it was paved after WWII. The small villages and communities on 28 through the valley include Parks, Harvey, Gravelly, Bluffton, Briggsville, Rover, and Plainview.

All of the school-age kids in Fourche Valley went to the Briggsville school, which had been built as a WPA government project in the early 1930s. Most of the outer structure was made of rock, as was a 3-foot-high rock border fence on the south side of the school ground that faced Highway 28, a gravel road.

The students and teachers all used a big outdoor privy on the north side of the school ground — the boys on one end; the girls on the other. As I recall, in 1941 there were about forty students in the lower grades, and another 30 or so in high school. The older boys would cut peep holes between boards with their pocket knives, but the girls would cover every hole as fast as it was cut. The girls acted like they didn't like the boys peeking, but the boys thought different.

The Gilmore Clan

I had a lot of aunts and uncles on my mother's side of the family. Maude and Horace (Buck) Gilmore had 10 children — five boys and five girls. Mother was No. 2 of the girls. Buck had died at 49 (1927) from a fever when they lived in Pond Creek Bottom near Horatio, leaving Maude to take the family that was still living at home, back to Yell County, Arkansas to a share-cropping farm near the community of Briggsville.

The boys were Cecil, J.K., Theo, R.L., and Don. The girls were Viola, Nettie, Ruby, Amy and Sybil. By the time I got to Yell County in 1941, Cecil and all of the girls were married and gone. R.L. had left home for the Civilian Conservation Corps (CCC), and Theo, J.K., and Don were still living with Maude at home.

Maude's family made a living sharecropping with Homer Lofland, a landowner at Briggsville, and lived in a log house with a "dog trot" between two big rooms with a fireplace on each end. Homer was a privileged landowner, and in the standard arrangement, his share was ⅓ of the cotton, ¼ of the corn, and ¼ of the hay.

Homer had cattle; the local dipping vat (to dip cattle for ticks, etc.), and a Ford tractor and pickup. His son, Billy Seth, was my age, and we played together a lot, and rode his Shetland pony. Theo and J.K. helped Homer dip his cattle, and Theo would throw his German shepherd dog "Major" in dipping vat with the cows. Ticks were a real problem to every warm-blooded creature in Yell County. The Loflands were the "haves," and the Gilmores were the "have nots," and it was good for me to recognize that difference at an early age.

Through the years, a kitchen and back bedroom had been added to the back of the log house, along with a long, narrow porch. Bill and I slept in the bedroom (we called it the "junk room") on a feather bed, and that room is where we took a bath in the washtub. The wood floors had sizable cracks, and I remember watching the chickens under the house, through the cracks. It didn't matter if we spilled water on the floor — it just ran through the cracks!

The underpinning put the house off the ground high enough that chickens, dog (Major), varmints, and snakes could take shelter there. I can't remember any kind of poisonous snakes, but black racers and "spreading adders" (hog nose) were common and often got into the hen house and swallowed the eggs. Of course, all snakes found in hen nests met their demise.

Maude didn't want snakes in the hen nests — she wanted all hens to lay eggs in the hen house, and not somewhere around where we couldn't find the nest. Sometimes a hen would lay a dozen eggs somewhere, set on them for 21 days, and come up with a brood of little "bitties."

Our two-hole privy was out back of the house, just far enough away to be private and down wind. It had a cob box and a Sears Roebuck catalogue for wiping, and reading. I never could figure out why the privy had two holes — nobody went to the privy with anybody else!

The first winter we lived in the log house with Maude and our uncles, Bill and I got the "itch," scabies, that probably came from wearing long handle underwear for several days at a time. Or, we may have caught the mites that cause the rash from kids at school.

I don't recall a doctor of any kind in Fourche Valley. Maude had a large "Doctor Book" that had a remedy for everything, and she sent Bill out behind the "privy" to pull some polkweed stalks that always grew behind the toilet. Bill brought back an arm load, and Maude boiled the polkweed with roots in the wash pot with water. The water came out blood red, and Maude made Bill and me take a tub bath in the polkweed water.

Maude's "cure" on our rash-infested skins was so painful that we could hardly stand it. We kept the water in the wash tub in the back room, and warmed it up for several baths, until the itch rash was cured — a week or two. I remember that incident as one for the ages!

At Christmas time in 1941, Aunt Ruby Baber and her family drove up from Ozan, Arkansas (near Hope), and Amy and her family drove over from Oklahoma City. We all had a good Christmas dinner and shot firecrackers and Roman candles. I played with Jimmy Dan Baber and Aunt Amy's son, Jimmy Lane Woolbright. It was a fun time, even though we had declared war on Japan on December 7 after they bombed our ships in Pearl Harbor in the Hawaiian Islands. I wasn't old enough to get the full meaning of war.

I remember that Christmas because my dad had sent me a pair of high-heeled cowboy boots through the mail. We opened the box on Christmas Day, and found out that the boots were too big for me. Maude put some cotton in the toes to take up the space, but it didn't work — the boots were still too big! Jimmy Dan was younger than me, but he had big feet. Maude tried the boots on him, and they were a perfect fit.

My grandmother took me off in a corner and suggested that we give the boots to Jimmy Dan. I didn't want to, because they had come from my Dad, but Maude convinced me by promising to take me to Danville on the Cook bus, and buy me a pair of boots that would fit. I agreed, and Jimmy Dan got the boots for Christmas. We never did have enough money to buy me a replacement pair of boots, and I continued to wear my brogan "stronger than the law" ankle-high shoes.

Life On The Farm

When we lived in the Lofland log house on the farm, a peddler came down the gravel road about twice each month, in a covered flat-bed vehicle that contained such things as salt, sugar, candy, snuff, tobacco, baking powder, soda, coal oil, horseshoe nails, needles, thread, etc. We were always anxious to see the peddler. There was hardly any cash money, so the peddler would take pigs, chickens, eggs — practically anything you could eat — in trade for his goods.

I was about eight years old — old enough to outwit a peddler. I had found a hen "setting" (incubating) on a nest full of eggs, so I ran her off and took all the eggs. They were very slick and shiny, because she had been setting on them for several days. Fresh eggs had a dull look, so I took some dirt and sand and carefully rubbed the eggs to make them look fresh. When the peddler came by, I traded the eggs to him for candy. Somebody, somewhere, ended up with a dozen rotten eggs!

The third grade went by without incident, and I learned what, and what not to do around my uncles (Theo, J.K., and Don), who were still at home. Cecil was married and lived down the road near Briggsville school. R.L. was in the C.C.C. (Civilian Conservation Corps). Theo was the oldest at home, and made a living cutting 52-inch barrel staves (white oak for making whiskey and syrup barrels). On a good day, he and his mules would make about $2.

J.K. farmed for a living, raising enough corn to feed his horses; Theo's mare and mules, and the milk cow, with some left over for the hogs and the corn meal that we had ground. His three bales of cotton brought about $125 cash. The hay he bailed was used for everything from feeding the livestock to winter shelter for the potatoes that we kept covered in the barn.

Don was a senior at Briggsville High School, and made extra money as school janitor. The school burned coal in pot-bellied stoves, so Don was responsible for getting fires started in the winter, and plenty of coal for each stove in the "coal box."

The log house was about a mile from school, so Don rode his Schwinn bicycle back and forth to school. I thought the bike was neat, with a siren attached to the front wheel that was activated by a chain that was pulled by hand. Why the siren? I guess it was just a gimmick, but it sounded "cool" to a third grader!

There were no wasted days on the farm. If it was raining, Theo and J.K. would kill rats in the corn crib. Rainy days were good for rat killing, because the rats wouldn't leave the crib and go into the rain. So, my uncles, aided by Theo's German shepherd named "Major," would simply move the corn (ears in the shuck) from one side of the crib to the other. With every move, the guys with clubs, and Major would kill several rats. In a half day of moving corn and killing rats, the rat problem was solved for a while.

Another rainy-day session at the barn was "nail straightening." Nails on the farm were scarce, and when a piece of wood was discarded, any nails in it were pulled out and thrown in a bucket. Most of the nails were bent, so on rainy days the guys would use a hammer and a flat surface to straighten the nails, and put them in the "good nail" bucket. Nothing was wasted on the farm.

J.K. did all the horse and mule shoeing. About every six weeks, he would shoe Theo's mare (Lula Belle), Theo's mules (Dick and Nina), and his horses (Bill and Choc). It was an all-day affair, and sometimes got a little rowdy. Theo's mules were feisty, and didn't want their back feet shod. I remember J.K. getting their attention by clubbing them in the head with a hammer. Even a mule understands a lick from a hammer, and it usually settled them down, and allowed J.K. to finish the job.

Maude was stern, but fair. At the time, she was about 60 years old, and tough as a boot. She dipped Sweet Garrett snuff and could get riled when she ran out of snuff and her Cherokee heritage came out. I was glad to go horseback the four miles from Briggsville to Bluffton and get her another jar of Sweet Garrett — anything to improve her temperament. She was hard on me, but I'll have to admit that the years I spent with her were probably the most important years of my young life.

The gravel road crossed the Fourche La Fave (we called it the Fourche) river between Briggsville and Bluffton, and the old steel bridge had a plank floor. Many of the old planks were broken, and a few were gone, leaving large holes in the floor. I was afraid to ride a horse over the broken plank holes, so I got off and led the horse across the bridge. I didn't make the 4-mile trip very often horseback, and I was scared of the 15-foot-high bridge.

There was no refrigeration in the log house, so we kept the milk and butter in the water well. The water was about 12-fcet from the surface, and the glass jugs were covered with gunny sack material and held on the end of a rope. One day I tried my hand at pulling up the milk. The jar began to swing around, and finally hit a rock on the edge of the well, spilling all the milk in the well water. That was my first whipping from Maude — the first of many during the next four years.

World War II Brings Changes

Bill and I had been with Maude and my uncles about six months when the Japanese bombed Pearl Harbor, and World War II began. I remember President Roosevelt giving his famous speech, "This Day in Infamy" on the battery radio. After December 7, 1941, things were never the same at the log house.

Theo and J.K. joined the Army. Don finished school and joined the Army Paratroops. This left Maude, Bill and me on the farm, keeping up with the war by listening to Gabriel Heater on the radio. We felt safe with "Ol' Major," Theo's German shepherd that he had left behind when he joined the Army. Major would be with Maude and me for the rest of my time in Arkansas.

> "Rebel steak in Dallas is bologna in Hooks." — Goreism

When Theo, J.K. and Don left home for the Army, Maude depended on me and Bill to do what was necessary for us to live in the log house. Theo had sold his mules (Dick and Nina), but J.K. had left his horses (Bill and Choc) at home. Ol' Bill was a good riding horse, and he was our transportation to Bluffton. I can remember us going to the corn crib and picking out white corn and shucking it for corn meal. My brother didn't like horses, so it was my job to take the corn to the gristmill at Ferguson's store.

We would fill a tow sack with ears of white corn and take it to the house where Maude had a hand-turned corn sheller. The ears of corn were pushed into the sheller, which was turned by hand, to shell the corn from the cob. Maude would go through the shelled corn and pick out bad corn or trash. The white corn cobs were saved for the privy "cob box." Unlike yellow corn cobs that were rough, the white corn had a soft, fuzzy cob that was easy on the rear.

I would ride Ol' Bill and carry the sack of shelled corn to Bluffton to Lex Ferguson's store. He had a grist mill that would grind corn into meal. I would wait for the meal at the store, and when it was ready, I would go back to the log house with a sack of white corn meal. We ate cornbread nearly every day, and this is how we got the cornmeal. Maude could do wonders with meal, eggs, milk, butter, sorghum syrup, and potatoes. We had it all, right there on the farm.

Hooks, Texas

In 1942, Mother went to Dallas to a training school for wartime work, and met Earl Vinson, a train engineer from Missouri, who was in Texas driving a locomotive at Red River Arsenal near Hooks, Texas. They were soon married, and living in a little makeshift house in Hooks. Nothing in that day was considered permanent, and everything centered around winning the war.

Hooks was a boom town with no water or sewer except in the downtown area. Rex Poe had a water-delivery service, and filled a 55-gallon wooden barrel with water once a week. A No. 2 washtub was a necessary household item for taking baths. We had a government-issued outhouse until 1947, when a city sewer system was completed, along with water. It was the first time I could remember running water or an inside toilet. Mother thought it was nice to go to the bathroom in the house during the cold winter.

Mother cooked on a kerosene stove, and carried water in a gallon bucket. The small house had a wood-burning stove in the living room, and one closet. After we got running water, the pipes froze every winter. It was a hard way to live, and what everyone thought to be a temporary war effort became permanent. I spent late summer of 1943 with mother and Earl, and went back to Arkansas to live with Maude.

When Bill was 14, he left Bluffton in June of 1942, and went to Hooks to live with Mother and Earl, and finish high school. I stayed with Maude, but when all the men went to the war, we couldn't farm anymore, so we moved from the farm and the Lofland log house about two miles down the road to the Bogle House near Briggsville school.

The Bogle Place

The Bogle house was located near Hopper creek, and had a small acreage for a garden and corn patch. I think there had been a previous house, that probably burned down, because the water well was a long way behind the present house that was close to the gravel road. Maude's oldest son, Cecil lived about half a mile down the road from us.

I didn't like carrying a bucket of water from the well all the way to the house. We fed a hog to butcher, and Maude canned a lot of vegetables out of the garden. We also had a good-sized white corn patch that we used for meal and hog/cow feed when Uncle Cecil would bring us a milk cow.

While we lived on the Bogle Place, my uncle Cecil gave Maude a pregnant sow, and for a time we had about eight little pigs running around the place. They would get out of the hog pen, and wander about. When they were about a month old, I kept noticing hair in the water that I drew from the well.

We didn't think much about the hair, until I pulled up a bucket of water with a dead pig. One of the small pigs fell through a hole at the bottom of the wooden well casing, and was in the well water. We lived over it, and Maude made me draw about fifty buckets of water until we couldn't see any more hog hair.

There were good times at the Bogle place. I found an old, rusty .22 single-shot rifle in the barn that wouldn't shoot, but gave me something to chase Indians and outlaws with. I also enjoyed playing in the creek, and taking care of my pet gray fox that Uncle Cecil has brought me before its eyes were open.

I soon found that I couldn't eat lunch, run a trotline in the creek, stake out the fish (to clean after school), check on my fox, and get back to school by the time the noon bell rang. It was a big load for a 9-year-old, and I got into a lot of trouble. My teacher was an old maid named Jesse Buford, and she was exceptionally ornery!

I learned that foxes are smart — sometimes too smart! The Bogle house had a rock pinning around the base of the house, and I found a hole through the rocks as a place for my fox to go under the house. It was his den. I had a collar and long, slender chain on him, situated so that he could go back and forth under the house. Old Major, the German shepherd paid no attention to the fox and they got along just fine.

Maude made a lot of cornbread — practically every day, and I learned that the fox liked cornbread. There was no such thing as dog feed in those days, so my fox basically lived on cornbread. I would give him a piece as big as my hand, and he would eat it quickly, always leaving some large crumbs on the ground near his den.

I kept seeing chicken feathers where he ate his cornbread, and I checked his den under the house. It was full of feathers, and I knew that the fox was catching chickens when they came to the breadcrumbs. Maude knew it, too. The jig was up — no more fox. Uncle Cecil came and took him off to the Fourche River bottom — far enough away that he wouldn't come back. That was my last, and only, pet fox.

I got my first cash-paying job while we lived in the Bogle house. Chester Williamson, who had moved into Fourche Valley from Arizona and married Bead Briggs, granddaughter of the Settler of the Briggsville area, had some registered hogs. I think they were Chester Whites, and the sows were very big, and normally had about 10 pigs.

Williamson raised hogs for sale, and during the summer he had a sow that was about to have a litter of valuable pigs. He was concerned that the big sow might smother the little pigs when she laid down in her small pen, and he hired me at 25 cents a day to sit in the pen on a stool and make sure that all the pigs were clear when the sow laid down.

The job lasted for about two weeks until the pigs got old enough to take care of themselves, and I made about $3, which was a lot of money for a 9-year-old in the Fourche La Fave River valley of Arkansas.

The Phillips House and My First Horse

We had lived in the Bogle house for about a year, when Aunt Amy and her husband, Jim Woolbright bought the Phillips Place in Bluffton. We moved to the Phillips house, and Maude bought me a bay mare named "Pokey" from Odell King for $50. Mr. King drove the school bus from Bluffton to Briggsville school, and I rode the bus.

Horace Gore, age 11 on "Pokey." Bluffton, Arkansas 1944

Every young boy needs a horse. Pokey was my transportation, and I rode her bareback (or saddle blanket) everywhere within two or three miles of home. I would have to find an object high enough to get on Pokey — stump, wagon wheel, porch or deep ditch. I always had to look around for some way to get back on, before I got off.

When Maude bought the mare, she got a bridle and that was all. In the western movies, I had seen Indians ride their ponies with a long leather string tied through the horse's mouth, so I substituted baling wire for string, and rode Pokey everywhere with nothing but a long piece of wire twisted around her bottom jaw. It sounds cruel, but it worked just fine. Someone gave me an old, dilapidated saddle, but a kid doesn't have time for a saddle. I rode bareback most of the time.

The Phillips place had a big house with wrap-around porch and two fireplaces, a big barn, a small chicken house with a tin roof, and 3-4 acres for the horse and milk cow. It was close to town; about ¼ mile to the four stores and post office (in Daniel's store). We lived there until the War was over, and I moved to Hooks to live with Mother while Bill was in the Army Air Corps.

While we lived in the Phillips house, Yell County got one of the biggest snows I've ever seen. Actually, it snowed about three times over a 10-day period, and the snow reached a depth of sixteen inches. Schools closed; activities around Bluffton came to a halt, and I enjoyed the whole thing! In case you're wondering, a 16-inch snow in that day was over knee deep to me!

My horse was shod on only the front hooves, and when it snowed, I had to have her shoes removed; otherwise, ice from the snow would build up on the iron horseshoes so much that Pokey couldn't walk. I left her shoes off during the winter, because we always got two or three big snows.

Maude and I enjoyed the Phillips house; it was big, with open fireplaces, and I enjoyed playing in the barn. Of course, we had chickens, a big garden, a very good peach tree, and some Concord grape vines on a fence. Uncle Cecil would bring us a fresh milk cow about twice a year. Ol' Major was the watchdog, and I learned that a 10-year-old kid couldn't keep a fireplace and a wood stove going at the same time! I did all my traveling to Bluffton; to visit my cousin, Charles Daniel, and the swimming holes on the bay mare.

Bluffton, Arkansas

The only way for folks like Maude and me to get out of Fourche Valley to any sizable town was to go east on Cook's Bus Line. A Mr. Cook lived on the west end of Hwy 28, and had an old, renovated school bus with a luggage rack fixed on top. The Cook bus ran east on 28 once a week, all the way to Rover, then north on Hwy 27 to Danville — about 20 miles.

Danville was the county seat of Yell County, and a good-sized town of about 2,000. We could get things to live on at Bluffton, but if we needed anything special, or wanted to catch a Greyhound bus, we had to take the Cook bus to Danville. From Bluffton to Danville and back was always a one-day trip.

When Maude and I lived in Bluffton, Earl Vinson died at Hooks, and I started getting an $11 check every month from his railroad pension. That money gave me and my grandmother an economic jump, and I remember Maude splurging for a Sunday *Arkansas Gazette* newspaper and a loaf of Wonder Bread (not sliced) once a week. I'm not sure what day we got the paper and bread, bit I think it was Sunday. The delivery station wagon would drop the paper and bread off in a sack on the side of the gravel road, and I'd go pick them up.

One or two of the cows that Uncle Cecil brought us were very wild, and I would have to chase them down, put shackles on their back legs, and milk them in the pasture. One of the cows was a little Jersey with a small bag and little teats. I would chase her down, put on the shackles, and clean her bag and teats with the warm water that I had in the bucket. She was a real pain, but her milk was rich, and made good butter.

I hated it when the weather was cold, or when the cow's tail was full of cockle burs, and she would swat me on the head with her tail. Chasing down a cow and milking her in the pasture without a stool was not fun, but such was the life of a 10-year-old living with Maude Gilmore in Bluffton, Arkansas, with a bay pony and an old German shepherd dog.

There wasn't much entertainment to be had in Bluffton. The game of croquet was big in 1944, and the town men had built a croquet court on a vacant lot — no grass; all smooth dirt with the wire hoops, goal posts, wooden balls, and mallets that go with croquet. The court had about two hanging light bulbs, so the game could be played at night.

In the summer, someone might drive to Rover and bring back a 25-pound block of ice on the vehicle bumper to make ice cream at Ferguson's store. Or, maybe the guy from Gravelly, about four miles to the West, might bring his projector and a movie (usually a two-reel western, black and white), tack up a sheet on the side of a building, and show us the movie on Saturday night.

The picture shows cost a dime, and a two-reeler would have to be changed between reels. Everybody took their own chair and drink. Speaking of drinks — you didn't have to go any farther than Daniel's store (the post office) to get a quart jar of "shine." It was supposed to be a secret, but everybody knew it.

One Saturday I was late getting my chores done, and Maude declared that I would not get to go to the picture show that evening. We had heard that a good western, featuring one of the heroes of the day (Tom Mix, Buck Jones, or Tex Ritter) would be showing. As the day went by, I knew that Maude wanted to go, but she had laid down the law to me — no picture show!

About 5 p.m., Maude called me in and said, "There's going to be a good picture show this evening. Would you like to take about three licks, so we can go?" I thought about it, and decided to take the licks. Maude bent me over, and hit me three times on the rear with a stick of stove wood from behind the wood stove; we washed up, got our chairs, and went to the picture show. Maude was very stern, but fair.

Bluffton to Hooks For Good

The war with Germany and Japan was nearing the end in the summer of 1944, and Ode and Aunt Sybil and their two girls moved into the Phillips house with Maude. In August of that year, I moved to Hooks in East Texas to live with Mother and Bill. I started the sixth grade at Hooks Elementary just a couple of blocks from the house, and my teacher was Ms. Reitz.

I set a record for the sixth grade by getting four spankings in one day, but Ms. Reitz liked me. She sent me to the woods north of Hooks with Billy James Hitchcock to cut our sixth grade Christmas tree with a hatchet that Mother had given me for my birthday.

Ms. Reitz knew that I spent a lot of time in the woods and could easily find a good head-high cedar to decorate in the school room, and we did. We could have brought a Christmas tree back in a couple of hours, but we took the whole day off from school, and enjoyed the woods.

The one thing that I remember about that Christmas tree trip to Ms. Wilder's oak flatwoods in December 1944 was the couple of hours that Billy James and I spent enjoying a fall day under a group of tall longleaf pines that were as out of place as a fly in the punch bowl.

The trees were in a corner of the oak woods, and I always guessed that they had been planted there when Hooks was a young community. They were the only pine trees in that part of Bowie County, and four or five were at least 100 years old.

I've remembered those trees through the years. I was high on a girl in our class named Jean Jones, and I took my pocketknife and cut deep into the pine bark, "HG + JJ." The cuts were about an inch deep in the thick pine bark, and through the next few years when Jerry Barrow and I would pass the trees on our quail hunts, I would inspect the initials in the cuts.

My First .22 Rifle

In October 1945 when I turned 12, and the war was over, Maude visited us at Hooks, and told me that she had sold the mare for $50. While she was there, she ordered me a new Sears Roebuck .22 rifle for my birthday. It was a model 15 Springfield single shot, ($6.15), and I loved it. Later on, I spent a lot of time on my paper route (*Texarkana Gazette*) making money for a bicycle, .22 shells, and the 12 cents to go to the Lone Star Theater on Saturday evening.

Getting a rifle of my own at 12 started me on a learning curve about shooting, and being responsible for where each bullet went. I learned quickly that a .22 long rifle really would shoot a mile, and that knowing my target was no more important than knowing where the bullet would go if I missed the target!

Maude laid down the law on birds — no wrens, redbirds, mockingbirds, or even robins, unless I was going to eat them. No red-headed woodpeckers, but sparrows, blackbirds, blue jays and meadow larks were all fair game, as were cottontails and squirrels. I ate every robin, rabbit and squirrel that I killed, and Mother would just turn the kitchen over to me. It was usually meat, gravy and light bread (that came in a solid loaf, unsliced).

Mother was working in the school cafeteria when I moved to Hooks, but she later got a job keeping a used furniture store open in Hooks, and selling when customers came in. The store was next to J.R. Guinn's General Store, and Mother would visit with Mr. Guinn once in a while. One day J.R. asked Mother how I was doing, and where I spent my time. "He's about 13, isn't he?" Mother replied, "Yes, and I guess he's in the woods. He has a .22, and likes to hunt."

J.R. Guinn was a "retired" quail hunter, and had just sold his bird dog and 16-gauge Remington shotgun to my friend, Jerry Barrow (Jerry's Uncle Jess furnished the money). "Don't worry about the boy," said J.R. "Kids don't get in trouble when they're hunting." Mother told me the story, and I've thought about it many times — kids don't get in trouble when they're hunting!

The Phantom Killer

In early 1946, a series of murders in and around Texarkana had the general area terrified. From February to May, double homicides occurred in the Texarkana area. Eight victims were attacked in Lovers Lanes and other places, and five were murdered.

The acts of the "Phantom Killer" attracted both national and worldwide attention. Texas Ranger M. T. "Lone Wolf" Gonzaullas was called in, as well as dozens of law enforcement personnel. On weekends, local citizens would hole up, firearms close by, scared to go outside at night.

Bill was in the Army Air Force, so it was just Mother and me. I was 12 years old, and mother's little man. We were there in Hooks, just 14 miles from all the murders, and I could tell that Mother was worried. She told me to keep my .22 loaded and handy. We didn't dare go out after dark.

Sometime in April, after several attacks and murders by the Phantom Killer, we heard a noise well after dark outside in the direction of the freshly plowed garden. "Get your .22," Mother directed, and I got it from behind the kitchen door. "Shoot at the noise," she said. "Are you sure? I might hit somebody," I replied. "That'll be just fine. Shoot." With that, I opened the kitchen door and fired into the dark in the direction of the noise. All hell broke loose when I hit a stray mule that was in the garden. It bolted, and left in a hurry.

Mother gave a sigh of relief, but I worried that somebody was going to come collect for a dead mule! That summer was filled with fright for everyone in the Texarkana area and beyond. The killer was never caught, but a verified suspect was caused to leave Texarkana from pressure of law enforcement. After that, things settled down by the time school started in September.

On With Grade School

My seventh-grade teacher was Mrs. Canady, a pretty blonde woman about 30 years old. The year went smoothly, except for the time I borrowed a Case Trapper pocketknife to make a boat out of some balsa wood. I was pulling the blade toward my wrist when I cut my arm pretty bad. Ms. Canady called the principal, Mr. Chism, who took me to the New Boston Clinic for an 11-clip metal closure of the wound. I remember Mr. Chism saying, "Boy, you need to pay attention to what you are doing. Push the knife from you — not toward you." I took his advice, and never cut myself again.

One of my favorite classes in grade school was Choral Club, where about 15 of us learned to sing all classes of music, led by the cutest and greatest music teacher that ever lived. Marvalynn Stubbs (everybody called her Lynn) was about 25, and knew music from front to back. She played the piano and we sang at different occasions — school functions, funerals, celebrations, church, and wherever. I loved choral music — in fact, I still like all kinds of music.

While I was in high school, Lynn Stubbs married a businessman from DeKalb named Bluett Cotton, and moved to live with him at DeKalb, about 20 miles west on Highway 82. We all loved Miss Stubbs, and hated to see her go.

My eighth-grade teacher was Mrs. Hill, a stern woman, about 40, who rarely smiled. I don't think Mrs. Hill was happy — if she was, she didn't show it. The only thing about the eighth grade that I remember is getting interested in baseball. It was also a time when I discovered girls, and took a great interest in watching the girls and throwing the ball. During the next four years, baseball would be very important in my high school days, and would follow me into the army in 1954.

Halloween In Hooks

October 31 was a special day in Hooks when me and my buddies were in our early teens. We planned Halloween pranks long before that night arrived, and until I was 16 and chasing the girls, Halloween was our greatest night of the year. It was usually Jerry Barrow, Allen Reed, James Henson and me, and we reveled in the tricks we pulled on people.

If the weather was good, we would go to the Lone Star Theater and push a red potato over the tail pipe of cars we knew. Back then, all vehicle tail pipes were sharp and angled on the end. We knew that the engine had to "breathe" by emitting exhaust out the pipe, and a potato on the end prevented the engine from breathing — they wouldn't start! When the movie was over, all manner of folks couldn't figure why their cars and trucks wouldn't start!

Another prank that we loved was to put some fresh cow manure in a small paper sack, and twist the top shut. We usually used this trick when everyone was sitting in the living room (no television) listing to the radio or whatever — about 9 p.m. We would slip up to the front porch, light the top of the paper sack with a match, and knock on the door. Someone would always come to the door, and see the burning sack on the porch. They would always try to stomp out the flame. Of course, they got cow shit all over their feet, while we watched from the darkness. It was a hoot!

Back then, no one locked their cars at night, and many cars were parked close to the house — no garage. We would go to people we knew, and put a stick under one wide of the steering wheel, over the vehicle horn, and under the other side of the wheel. The horn would blow until someone got up at midnight and removed the stick (all while we watched).

A standard on Halloween night was to turn over a few outhouses in the neighborhood. Everyone had an outside privy, and we usually managed to turn over a few. One Halloween night, some local guys picked up a privy with a truck, and took it to town and placed it at the front door of Guinn's General Store.

One of our most hilarious tricks was to wrap an old tire with brown paper, to look like a brand-new tire. All new tires at that time were wrapped in brown paper. We would tie a long cord to the tire and place it on the edge of Highway 82 that ran from Texarkana to Paris (100 miles of highway). Traffic was usually thin, but regular from midnight to morning.

Cars would pass the tire, and invariably a car or truck would stop, reverse the vehicle to go get the "new" tire. While this was happening, we would pull the tire off of the road with the cord, and the traveler would look and look — finally driving away, while we giggled in the roadside weeds.

Our one-and-only bad trick occurred about 2 a.m., on a cold Halloween night in 1947. Three of us knew of a corn patch just out of town near the highway. We gathered corn stalks and stacked them near the two-lane pavement. On Halloween night, when there was a lull in traffic, we quickly pilled the corn stalks on the highway from side to side, making a barrier. We then poured kerosene on the stalks and set the whole line of stalks ablaze.

Traffic piled up for half a mile while the corn stalks were burning, and we were all off in the bushes laughing at the turmoil. However, we all got scared when a highway patrol car came up the side of all the cars to the burning barricade. The officers got out, and we scampered away. That was our only bad, dirty trick in all of our Halloween tricks at Hooks.

High School

My first year in high school as a "Hooks Hornet" was quite exciting. All of my classes were in the rather new high-school building, across the school yard from the old grade-school building, where I had spent my sixth through eighth grades. The high school building had long, oak floor halls with many rooms and a cafeteria. All of this was attached to a new gymnasium.

Hall Griffin was the superintendent; D.L. Conner was principal, and my favorite teacher was William Villa, who grew up in Rosebud, a small community south of Waco. Mr. Villa (we called him "Pancho" behind his back) was a bachelor, about 40 years old, who enjoyed carousing around on weekends. We soon found that it was best to steer clear of him on Monday, after a weekend of beer and bluster! He taught math and biology, and I thought he was a grand fellow.

Bill Villa always wore a little Dobbs felt hat that he tipped to the ladies, and he liked to quail hunt. I had a bird dog, and hunted every weekend during quail season. Mr. Villa would join me on several hunts, and would quietly inform me when he was going to give an unannounced quiz on Monday morning. I was usually the only one in class that was prepared for the quiz. Mr. Villa influenced me a great deal, and his biology classes were a true inspiration for my future years as a wildlife biologist.

Another high school teacher that had a very important part in my formative years was Mrs. Mary Reed Moore Reed. She taught me four years of English, from sentence structure to Chaucer. She was about 60 years old when I started high school, and was married to Spencer Reed, the local Justice of the Peace, and Allen Reed's grandfather.

Ms. Reed's maiden name was Mary Reed Moore, and she married Judge Reed, so her name was Mary Reed Moore Reed. She was a "tough old bird," but her stern teaching had a strong bearing on my future in college, and my second career as a hunting-magazine editor and outdoor writer. Hooks high had a lot of good teachers like Mr. Villa, Ms. Reed, and Ms. Morrow who made good citizens out of us rowdies.

I think I loved my typing teacher, Virginia Morrow. I took typing for two years, and I'm so glad! The old Underwood typewriter had hard keys, and how many times did I write, "Now is the time for all good men to come to the aid of their country."? Ms. Morrow was about 35, pretty, kind, and gentle, and I can remember her bending over to help me, and I could smell her sweet perfume. I think I loved her, but then, I didn't know what love was!

The Horatio Shootout

In my young teens, I spent a couple of summers with my first cousin, James T. Tompson on Stringtown Loop, just east of Horatio, Arkansas. Stringtown Road started at the Cumberland Church, and ran east for several miles across the Cossatot River to Highway 71. James T. lived on the Stringtown Loop (where I was born), and was the youngest son of Aunt Allice and Uncle Harve Thompson.

James T. and I were the same age, but my life in Texas was quite different than his in rural Arkansas. I was as straight as a string, and James T. was wild as a Comanche. We roamed the entire countryside during my visits, and he taught me how to be rowdy and drink whiskey.

On one visit in July 1948, James T. taught me how to dance. We were about 15, and he had found out the American Legion Hall in Horatio was having a dance on Saturday night. James T. was a good two-stepper, and wanted us to thumb a ride to Horatio for the shindig. I couldn't dance.

We decided to go when James T. and I were standing in the middle of the dirt road on the Stringtown Loop. At the time, I sang a lot in church and Choral Club in school, and James T. said, "Hum a little of "Walking the Floor Over You" (an Ernest Tubb song) and I'll be the girl. I hummed, and James T. spun me around in the dirt road. After a while, I got the dance rhythm down, and soon we were dancing like Fred Astaire and Ginger Rogers! I was ready for Saturday night.

We thumbed a ride into Horatio on Saturday evening, and I went to Obe Shull's store and bought a new yellow short-sleeved shirt made of polyester. We both knew people in Horatio, and at the dance,

I ran into Julia Ann Pickett, the only daughter of Joyce Pickett, Aunt Ruby's first husband. "Judy Ann" was 15, and a good dancer, and we danced every set together. It was hot, and we both sweated like Louisiana Democrats. We just danced and danced in the July heat, while our clothes stuck to us, and we stuck to each other!

Judy Ann was cute as a bug's ear, even though she had a wandering eye — one eye would look straight ahead, while the other wandered. She never did look at me with both eyes, but that was fine — one pretty eye was enough.

I knew the Pickett family very well, and I was definitely high on Judy Ann. I remember her brother getting killed in a logging accident, leaving Judy Ann the only child in the family. My times with her was short and sweet, but hot as a firecracker in more ways than one!

The only people sober at the dance were the band and the law. Those standing around or dancing were pretty tipsy. Both Sevier County and all of Oklahoma were "dry," but you'd never know it. A quart of "shine" could be bought almost anywhere, and the dance hall was as wet as a spring rain. Judy Ann didn't drink, but it didn't take much to get me high, and the tighter I got, the better she looked.

Just before midnight, three Choctaw soldiers from Tom, Oklahoma, (10 miles away) on furlough, entered the dance hall and began to dance with the local girls. They were all drunk, and soon a fight started between one of the soldiers and a girl's husband. While the fight was on, one of the soldiers pulled out a pistol and started shooting. The dance floor cleared, and James T and I dove under a nearby pickup. No one was hit by the flying bullets, but we weren't ready to get killed by lead poisoning!

The local constable tried to stop the fight, when one of the Choctaw intruders grabbed the lawman's .45 pistol and emptied the automatic into the air and elsewhere. The law finally prevailed and took the three soldiers to the Horatio jail house behind Brinkley's store. The crowd had split up, and Judy Ann was nowhere to be found. It was about 1:30 in the morning when everything quieted down, and James T. and I were stranded in Horatio.

We knew Joyce Pickett, Judy Ann's father who owned the "Blue Room" recreational hall (gambling, drinking, whoring, etc. behind closed doors), and there were about four rooms upstairs. We climbed up to the upper floor, found one of the rooms vacant, and quietly went to bed with our clothes on.

We awoke to a quiet Sunday morning, and James T. and I went downstairs and out on the street. No one was around, and we started the six-mile walk back to Stringtown, hoping to catch a ride. Going through town, we noticed a crowd at a small café made from a railroad passenger car. We found that they were gawking at a juke box in the café that had been hit by a stray bullet from the shootout the night before. The stack of 78 rpm records was shot all-to-hell, and record pieces and broken glass were everywhere! We just smiled and kept going toward Stringtown.

The Dallas State Fair

As a freshman in high school, I joined the 4-H Club, and my project was 12 Rhode Island Red laying hens. I got them as chicks, and built a chicken yard out back of the house. They got old enough to lay eggs during the school year, and I was proud to say that I got 12 eggs a day from 12 hens. I got to be a good shot shooting blackbirds off the feed trough with my .22 rifle. I'd go home for lunch and shoot blackbirds until a few minutes before the school bell rang.

One of the reasons I joined the 4-H Club was to be able to go the State Fair of Texas in Dallas. On the annual "school day," Hooks always took about two buses of high school kids who earned the trip. I went to the fair every year that I was in high school. It was the highlight of the year for out-of-town trips.

On my second trip to the fair, I rode the bus with Jerry Barrow and James Henson. We toured the fair together and had a big time. I remember us walking up to a floor show featuring Sally Rand, a noted fan dancer fresh down from New York (so the Barker said). We walked up, and the barker asked, "You boys 18 years old?" I was 15, and Jerry and James were 16. James Henson looked older, and he said, "I'm 19 and they are 18."

The Barker looked us over, took our money, and we went in. It was a flashy stage with music, and Sally Rand put on a fan dance like we had never seen. She appeared to be completely naked. Of course, her fans got stuck together two or three times so that we could see her naked body! I hadn't ever seen anything like that in Hooks!

After the show was over, we stood up and looked around. Sitting right behind us was Coach Vernon, Robert Green, and Jack Hill — all close friends, and teachers and assistants at Hooks High. Mr. Hill and Robert had driven the buses. They all laughed, and asked how we had gotten into the adult show. When we got back to Hooks, they told everybody that we went to see Sally Rand's striptease show. We just smiled.

Drive-in Theaters and Hamburger Joints

After World War II, several new types of enjoyment came into being — skating rinks, hamburger joints, bowling alleys, and drive-in movies. All were well accepted by the busy towns and communities that were starving for something different. Driving up to a small café and having a young girl or boy come out with orange juice and peanuts, and place a tray on your car window was a treat for both young and old.

Ordering from a short menu, and getting "curb" service was the beginning that has developed into billion-dollar businesses today. At Hooks, "Catfish" Ford's little drive-in café was the gathering place for all us high school chums. We bowled a little, and skated at school events, but drive-in theaters were "the cat's meow."

Before, and even after, television, going to a drive-in theater with work clothes (or nothing) on; your own popcorn or soft drink brought from home, and watching a movie from the front seat (or back seat) of the car or pickup was exciting and convenient to a lot of working folks.

From about 1947 to the days of good TV, drive-in moves were exceptionally popular, and many guys got their first kiss while watching a drive-in movie. A folded blanket was common on the back seat of young folks' vehicles!

We all loved drive-in movies, and as 16-year-olds will do — we tried to get in free. Our first attempts involved the girls driving and us covered with a blanket in the back floorboard of the car. Our next attempts involved us guys getting in the trunk of the car, and the girls driving. This all ended one Saturday night when we were caught getting out of the trunk of the car, and led to the front gate. After that, we paid.

Horace played two years of football on Hooks' first team, 1949-1950

After about 20 years, nearly all drive-in movies were gone, as television took the stage for family entertainment. For years, old drive-in screens donned the landscape, and a few ticket booths and other remains were visible alone boulevards and country roads in Texas.

All High School Sports

As a freshman in high school, I played all the sports — basketball, baseball, and track. Football would come later when Hooks started its first band and football team, ever! I had developed a style of throwing the ball

*Hooks District-winning baseball team 1950.
Horace is third from right on the bottom row*

that made me a pretty good pitcher. During my four years in high school, our baseball team won district every year, and went to Regionals once.

Hooks high was a Class 2A powerhouse in basketball during those years, as well as baseball. We played schools like New Boston, Atlanta, James Bowie, Linden and DeKalb. When I was a sophomore, Mr. D.L. Connor called us all to assembly to make an announcement. Hooks would have a football team and a band the next year — the first time in school history. He introduced Mr. Norman White, the newly hired band director, and Jeff Addison, who would be our first football coach.

Mr. White spoke to all of us about the new band, and suggested that all students who patted their foot when they heard music, remain in the room to talk to him about being in the band. I stayed, because I loved music, and had been in choral classes with Miss Lynn Stubbs through both grade and high school. My choice of instrument was the alto saxophone, which I played in the band for two years.

Hooks High was a small school, and Jeff Addison had to scratch the bottom of the barrel to find an 11-man football team. I played right halfback for two years, but was never big enough, or mean enough, to play football. I was much more inclined to play baseball and chase girls, and good at both!

When Hooks started playing football, the other schools in our district saw a chance to get back at our school for beating them so bad in basketball and baseball, year after year. Our new football team was "fresh meat" for all the other teams, and we suffered a lot of defeats during my two years on the team!

Dekalb, 19 miles west on Highway 82 was our nemesis in basketball and baseball, and we beat them every year. They got back at us the first year of football by beating us 97-0 on our first football field full of weeds, rocks, and an occasional persimmon bush! It was a rough beginning, but 20 years later, a football star at Hooks went to Oklahoma and won the Heisman Trophy!

Baseball

I enjoyed playing baseball, and we had an outstanding team during my last three years in high school. I pitched most of the games, since we usually played only Tuesday and Friday of each week, and I was always fit and ready for every game. I remember a few incidents while playing ball, under the coaching of George Hubbert Vernon.

Coach Vernon was an excellent baseball coach, and had played many years of local ball as a catcher. We won district every year that he coached the team, and one bi-district game at Honey Grove comes to mind. But first, I recall a game when I was chewing Beech Nut tobacco, and trying to keep it a secret from Coach Vernon. He noticed me spitting on the mound, and came out for a talk.

"Are you chewing tobacco?" Coach Vernon asked. "Yes sir," I replied. "Why?" asked the coach. "It makes the home plate look about three feet wide, and the ball sails like a pigeon," I replied. In that game, I already had several strikeouts, and Coach Vernon leaned closer and said, "Well, fine. Keep chewing, but don't let anybody see you spitting. Just win the game." I kept chewing, and we won the game.

When I was a senior, we played Honey Grove, a small town on Highway 82 in Fannin County, for bi-district. Honey Grove billed itself as the "Sweetest Town in Texas," but we went over there for the district game and took the sweet out of their baseball. The game ended with an 8-7 score in favor of Hooks, and I struck out a player or two who were team favorites at Honey Grove.

The town was angry that Hooks had come to Honey Grove and beat them in the bi-district playoff. The locals were riled up, and the sheriff of Fannin County had to guard us as we got on the bus, for fear that someone would throw a rock or beer bottle and hit one of us in the head. All of the commotion from the community made the victory over Honey Grove even "sweeter."

Horace Gore, age 18, Draughon's Business College, Dallas, Texas 1951

High School Graduation, And On to a New World

Hooks High School had about 140 students in the four grades — usually about 25 to 30 seniors. When I graduated in 1951, we had 29 graduates, about half and half, boys and girls. G.L. Alexander was valedictorian, and Hazel Abercrombie put the yearbook together.

I was into a lot of activities, including all sports, band (alto sax), and the junior and senior plays. Our senior motto was "Damn the torpedoes; full steam ahead," and the entire class was as clean as a hound's tooth — no cheating, lying, stealing or drinking. Bowie County was clean and dry, and so were we!

> *"I hope I've left a good trail that others will follow."* — Goreism

Our graduation exercise was held at the football field in East Hooks, a government housing development built during the war to house people working at the two local defense plants, Red River Arsenal and Lone Star Ammunition Depot. With 29 graduates walking across the makeshift stage, it didn't take long. We played football on the "cow pasture" field until we got a new stadium and field in 1953.

As I walked up to Mr. Connor to receive my diploma, he handed me an envelope that contained a $300 scholarship to Draughon's Business College in Dallas. It was my only opportunity to further my education, so mother and I made plans for me to go to Dallas in the fall and take a business course. It would be my first time away from home in a big city, and mother and Bill spent $800 on a used '48 Plymouth four-door sedan — my first car.

I had no idea at the time that having Draughon's Business College on my resume would make such a big difference in my life. It gave me breaks in the Army, put me in headquarters of the 86th Ordnance Battalion at Fort Hood, among collegiate friends who convinced me to get an early discharge and go to college — Texas A&M — and get a degree in wildlife science.

My opinion is skewed, I'm sure, but through the years I have been a respectable wildlife biologist, focusing on deer, quail and wild turkey. In 1969, I became a certified big game scorer for the Boone and Crockett Club. Since 1995, I have edited *The Journal of Texas Trophy Hunters*. It all started at Stringtown in 1933, and a .22 rifle that Maude Gilmore gave me when I was 12. The future led me to Texas A&M University and 64 years as a biologist, hunter, editor, writer, and gun collector. I'm the product of many varied experiences, which makes me who I am.

CHAPTER 2

Hunting is in My Blood

The Beginning

I've been a hunter since I was 12; when my grandmother bought me a single shot .22 out of the Sears Roebuck catalogue. My paper route in Hooks, Texas (Texarkana Gazette) made enough for a bicycle; Saturday movies, and .22 shells through the eighth grade. I traded for a 16-gauge shotgun and got a bird dog in the ninth grade—on my way to being a lifelong hunter.

Squirrels, Quail, And Ducks

With no deer or other big game, squirrels were an important spring and fall species for Bowie County hunters. The creek and river bottoms had both fox and gray squirrels, and the optimum weapon was a full-choke shotgun. Fox squirrels could be taken with a .22, but gray squirrels were always moving, and required a shotgun when hunting favorite places like Barkman Creek and the Red and Sulphur river bottoms.

Although I was shooting my .22 regularly, I learned to hunt squirrels at 13 with a retired farmer Jim Tiller and his squirrel dogs. I turned the treed squirrel so Jim could shoot it out with a .22, and later, a shotgun! I went from hunting squirrels with a dog to "still-hunting" at 15, and have been a devout squirrel hunter ever since.

I got an English setter bird dog when I was 15, and Jerry Barrow and I hunted quail regularly before, during, and after quail season. "Corky" was a good dog, and so was "Mike," Jerry's English pointer. I also

> *"A trophy was any animal that fitted my fancy! My best hunt was my last hunt."* — Goreism

traded a bicycle for my first shotgun, a Winchester pump Model 1912 16-gauge.

Ducks were also a regular fall hunt, and not all hunts were in season. Jerry Barrow and I would go to the Red River bottom in wet weather on a John Deere tractor. We felt safe from the game warden because he couldn't drive the wet terrain in his car. Some of the best hunting was late January and February when mallard drakes were going back north.

Just out of high school, I had a new Browning "Sweet Sixteen" auto, and was hunting quail in the last week of January with Corky in the Red River bottom. I heard a lot of quacking in a nearly slough, so I took off my belt and tied Corky to a bush, and crawled up to the slough to see the water covered with greenhead mallards.

I always carried five "duck loads" when quail hunting, so I removed the quail loads and put in five high-load No. 6 and leveled the 16-gauge at the biggest concentration of mallards. The first shot killed three greenheads, and crippled two more. As the birds rose off the slough, I shot four more times and got two more greenheads. When the smoke cleared (no pun) Corky had caught the two cripples, and I had seven greenhead mallards.

My hunting was put on hold in 1954, when I joined the Army for two years. I hunted squirrels a time or two on Fort Hood's Cow Creek, but nothing else until I returned to Hooks in Bowie County to attend Texarkana College on the GI Bill. I got Corky back, and took up quail and squirrel hunting again. This lasted for two seasons, when I transferred to Texas A&M University in January 1958.

White-tailed Deer

During my first spring semester at A&M, I began driving a school bus and met a boy whose grandmother owned 10 acres in the Navasota River bottom. He agreed to take me deer hunting if I would loan him a deer rifle and shells.

I had two rifles: a Japanese 7.7 caliber war relic and a $40 Enfield .30-06, both converted to hunting rifles with cheap scopes. On the hunt, we both shot at a young buck in an oats patch. The boy took a long shot and missed, while I was much closer to the buck and killed my first whitetail!

The next season I went back to the 10 acres and got another yearling buck. After I graduated and took a job with Texas Game and Fish Department in the spring of '60, my field work as a wildlife biologist took me to the Brownwood area where I became acquainted with a local rancher who managed a 4,200-acre ranch that had a lot of whitetails. Treldon Cutbirth ran the family ranch, and invited me to go deer hunting.

First Trophy Whitetail

On a Saturday evening in November 1961, Treldon was putting out mineral blocks for the cattle and I was toting my Enfield .30-06. As we rounded the Texas tank on the west side of the ranch, a buck and four does were feeding about 100 yards away. Treldon gave me the go-ahead, and I quickly exited the truck and shot the buck.

The buck was a long-tined 10-pointer with antler spread just over 16 inches — my first trophy whitetail! Treldon had a '58 version of the Boone and Crockett Record Book, and we scored the buck at 149 5/8—a good buck for the time! I became good friends with the Cutbirth family and spent a lot of time hunting and fishing on the ranch.

Quail Hunting

I had been living in Brownwood for about six months when I went back to Hooks on a business trip. While there, I found a 3-year-old "drop" bird dog — a cross between a pointer and setter — that I bought for $60. The dog's name was "Jack," and I hunted him for eight years. Jack was the best bird dog I ever owned! I was working on a quail research project which required me to census and hunt bobwhites about three days each week during fall and winter, and Jack and I got pretty good at quail hunting.

I was promoted to a supervisory job in Waco in 1965, but I continued to deer and dove hunt on the Cutbirth Ranch. My hunting and shooting at Waco included quail and skeet. I had two good quail dogs, and contin-

Horace carrying his Winchester shotgun and a spring gobbler, Cutbirth Ranch.

ued to hunt with Clyde Holt at Decatur, while also hunting a lot around Waco. In 1971, I left Waco for a jaunt in Oklahoma as Game Chief.

While in Oklahoma, I hunted deer, doves, and pheasants. In January 1972, I got a call from Austin offering me the job of Wildlife Chief, and I returned to Texas Parks and Wildlife. After one year, the Department went through a reorganization, and I became State Wildlife Projects Leader. The next year, I became Upland Game Leader for six years, then I became White-tailed Deer Leader for 11 years.

Spring Turkey

During my 1971 stint in Oklahoma, I was acquainted with a fellow biologist who hunted spring turkey. He had developed a small mouth call that fit on the tongue and sounded exactly like a turkey hen! He gave me a couple of these unique calls, and I learned to imitate a lovelorn hen with a call that left both hands free — important to a turkey hunter.

I used this call, or ones like it, to take one or two turkey gobblers every spring for 30 years. I still have the old Winchester model 1897 pump 12-gauge that caused the demise of about 40 Rio Grande gobblers in both North and South Texas, and one Eastern gobbler in Louisiana!

Pronghorn (antelope)

In 1975, a young man came by the Austin office inquiring about a good bird dog. He knew I quail hunted, and after talking quail dogs for a while, the subject turned to pronghorn antelope. His uncle had a ranch near Roswell, New Mexico, with a lot of pronghorns, and after I gave him a good tip for a dog, he invited me to go pronghorn hunting as a guest. I accepted.

The pronghorn season opened in late August, and I was in Roswell the evening before the hunt started on Saturday. Charlie Martin told me where to hunt, and I had a nice 14-inch heart-shaped buck by late Saturday evening — the first of several pronghorns I would take in West Texas and New Mexico.

I took my last pronghorn buck while hunting mule deer in Wyoming. The local game warden, Bill Backer, asked me to go with him to visit a landowner. "Bring your rifle — we might see a pronghorn." I replied, "I don't have a permit!" Bill winked at me and asked, "Do you question the authority of your game warden?"

I caught his drift, and during the trip I killed a young buck running full-tilt in 4-inch snow. We took the pronghorn back to deer camp and ate everything but the hide and horns during the next few days — no questions asked!

Multiple Hunts Out of Austin and Beyond

During my 23 years in Austin, I hunted whitetails, mule deer, exotics, doves, ducks, quail and squirrels from the Rockies to Mexico. There was always something to hunt, and I didn't pass up any invitations.

When I retired from TPWD in 1993, I guided quail hunters for two winters in Shackelford County. I had three good quail dogs when I moved to the Kokernot Ranch in east Gonzales County in the fall of 1995. I continued to hunt quail in both North and South Texas, but my Gonzales

> "Man has walked on the moon, but he has yet to tame the coyote." — Goreism

County hunting also included hogs, ducks, doves, and squirrels. Deer and turkey were verboten since the ranch was leased to hunters.

The Kokernot is a haven for wildlife, and I enjoyed hunting year-around. I called up a spring gobbler for a family hunter on the Kokernot. On another hunt, Bill Booth invited me to take Dean Davis for his first spring gobbler. Later, I hunted on the same ranch and killed a strutting gobbler with my Winchester model 1897 pump 12 gauge — the last of about 40 gobblers with that old gun.

During my 22 years on the Kokernot I had two of the best black lab retrievers a hunter could want for waterfowl and doves, and the ranch had the best squirrel hunting I've ever seen. Example: Al Brothers and I killed 42 fox and gray squirrels during two consecutive fall morning hunts — some kind of a Texas record!

In 1997, two Argentinian ranchers paid my way to recommend hunting and management of eared doves and red deer. I spent a month traveling Argentina, studying the eared doves and red stags that were bringing hunters to the Pampas and Patagonia from all over the world.

I could write about hunting eared doves on the Pampas, and hurrying to the birds before the hogs got them, or chasing red stag in Patagonia with a borrowed .300 Weatherby! Then, there was the big bull elk in Colorado's Black Canyon of the Gunnison, and many trophy exotics — aoudad, nilgai, and sika deer, but those are stories for another time.

CHAPTER 3

The Army — 1954 to 1956

The Korean War was coming to a close, and agreements had been signed in 1954. I was 21 years old, 1A in draft status, and couldn't get a job. 1A meant I could be drafted any time, and no one would hire me for that reason. I didn't have any qualifications other than bookkeeping from Draughon's Business College and the situation was bleak.

One day, I decided to volunteer for the Army. The term of service would be two years, and I didn't have much of a future at the time. I went to the draft board in March and signed up as a volunteer. The board said I would be notified when my time came around. I expected to be called any day, and made arrangements to go to the Army.

Spring and summer passed with no word from the draft board. I was working part time at a local grocery store — waiting to go to the Army. The grocery store was near the high school, and when school started in September I was working every day. We served hot dogs and cold drinks to the students, and I was in charge of this assignment. Squirrel season opened on October 1, and I did a lot of hunting — still waiting for the Army.

Fort Bliss, Fort Leonard Wood, and Fort Hood

On November 1, I received a letter giving me directions for being in Texarkana on November 4 to be sworn into the military. I was there, and after a full day of getting ready, I was put on a C-3 two-prop plane, and sent to Goland Heights at Fort Bliss, El Paso as a private in the U.S. Army.

The first eight weeks was served in basic boot camp in an area of Fort Bliss that had been used to house prisoners of war in World War II.

The "village" consisted of several small huts that slept four people. I remember the floors being loose boards about 4-feet long, and instead of sweeping, we simply turned all the boards over. After two weeks, we were allowed off base, and I learned a lot about Juarez, Mexico — just across the river. Two things I remember was my first taste of tequila and a silver belt buckle that I bought — and still have — from a Mexican street vendor.

Boot camp lasted until Christmas time, when they let us go home for one week. I had to report to Fort Leonard Wood, Missouri in early January to be a student in a clerk typist school that would last about two months. My time at Draughon's Business College in Dallas put me in with college-educated soldiers, and I studied the ways of the Army, and how they operated in headquarters situations. The fort, near Waynesville, Missouri, was a dismal place — cold, wet, and the coal-burning stoves were dirty, and not enough heat for the hills of Missouri.

Horace in Class A Army uniform, Fort Bliss, Texas 1954

On about April 1, I was assigned to the 86th Ordnance Battalion at Fort Hood. I lived in a barracks for a while with about eight other clerk typists who worked at various jobs in battalion headquarters, and then moved off base with the family. One of my duties was driver for Col. Clayton's Jeep, and I took him to various places every day. It was a good position, and I learned a lot about military officers, and how they connected with each other.

My baseball pitching in high school paid off in the Army. Col. Clayton was a baseball fan, and he wanted to win a big trophy in Third Corps baseball. The 86th Ordnance had a team in the Third Corps League, and I volunteered as pitcher for the team. We practiced a couple times each week, and played on Friday night. I was pitching pretty good, and we had a good team. The catcher's name was Yoder from Ohio, and he was good. Our 86th Ordnance team won the summer games, and a 3-foot-high trophy that Col. Clayton placed in his office. As pitcher, I was in good graces with the Colonel, and set my own schedule for work and baseball.

In the Fall of 1955, Col. Clayton transferred to another unit, and I was asked to go to Third Corps and pick up the new Colonel that would head the 86th. I shined the Jeep, picked up the new Colonel, and introduced myself. On the way back to 86th, Col. Paul W. Sadler made acquaintance with me, and by the time we got back to 86th, we were becoming good friends. I could tell that he wanted me to take care of him, and be on hand when he needed something.

I became "The Colonel's Orderly," which meant driving him around the fort, writing personal letters, caddying for him on the golf course, drinking his beer and whiskey, and assisting his two daughters in mowing the yard with an electric, self-operating lawn mower. I considered it a choice position, and took good care of the Colonel.

In the Fall of 1955, the 86th was part of a large military maneuver in Louisiana called "Sage Brush." The entire battalion went to Louisiana for three months, bivouacking in several rural areas of Western Louisiana. The Colonel had an office and sleeping quarters in a "Deuce and a Half" trailer, and I had my little Jeep trailer with canvas top for sleeping. I also carried the Colonel's whiskey in my Jeep trailer.

The three-month maneuver went off without a hitch, and by the time we got back to Fort Hood, Col. Sadler and I were very good friends. I had learned how to set up his "pottie" in the brush, how he liked his boiled

"It is better to chase than be chased." — Goreism

> *"A democratic society works best in times of plenty."* — Goreism

peanuts, survived the theft of his Jeep and radio, survived his wrath when I set his trailer on fire while boiling peanuts, got his blessing when I thumbed back to camp from Bossier City with a case of whiskey, and enjoyed going to the Bonnie and Clyde ambush spot 8 miles southwest of Gibsland, Bienville Parish, Louisiana on Highway 154.

I worked every day with about four or five guys who were graduates of major universities. In our daily communication, college came up quite often, and they usually asked me if I would take advantage of the new GI Bill and go to college. I had no idea what they were talking about, but they soon filled me in.

The GI Bill, ratified in Texas by Sen. Ralph Yarborough, gave Korean veterans 36 months of college tuition, books, a small monthly check, and more. My buddies at Fort Hood thought I should get discharged early and go to college. The more we talked about it, the more interested I got.

I was scheduled for discharge on October 4, 1956, and when that time got nearer I approached Col. Sadler about an early discharge so I could enter Texarkana Junior College as a "general education student" in September. The Colonel commented I would go back to Hooks and starve to death, but he gave me the early discharge and wished me well. I entered TJC in September and the rest of my college career at TJC and Texas A&M is history.

CHAPTER 4
The Making Of A Wildlife Biologist

The reason why I'm starting with my time in the Army is because my contacts in the headquarters of 86th Ordnance Battalion at Fort Hood, which were mostly college graduates, were the main reasons why I went to college on the GI Bill. When I graduated from Hooks High School in 1951, I got a chance to go to Draughon's Business College in Dallas. Those months at Draughon's put me in with the college graduates at Fort Hood, who influenced me to go to college.

The law was new when I was assigned to Fort Hood in March 1955, and I didn't know anything about it. The headquarters staff coached me about the opportunities afforded in the new bill, and I took advantage of it by leaving the Army one month early in September 1956, and entering Texarkana Junior College as a "general education" student.

Texarkana Junior College

Mary worked at Red River Arsenal while I attended college, taking the usual classes of a freshman. I got a break during my third semester, when I took an agriculture class under Mr. Newton Lewis. Newt, as everyone called him outside of class, was a Texas Aggie, and had worked at several high-level jobs before taking the teaching job at TJC. I made friends with Newt, and found that he liked to quail hunt.

During our quail hunts, Newt and I talked about college, and he asked what I going to major in after I left TJC. I told him that I wasn't sure, but I liked wildlife and hunting. "You need to go to A&M and take wildlife science," he said. I didn't know what he was talking about, and he explained that a wildlife student studied all manner of wildlife and worked with state and federal agencies. It sounded good to me, but I knew nothing about Texas A&M.

"I can help," Newt said. "I know the Brazos County school superintendent, and I think I can get you a part-time job driving a school bus." He gave me a phone number, and told me to call as soon as possible. "You need to get in line for one of the bus driver jobs." The quail hunts with Newt Lewis paid off.

Baghdad On The Brazos

I was a full-time student — spring, summer, and fall — so I finished TJC during the fall of '57 and planned to transfer to Texas A&M for the spring semester of '58. We moved to Bryan and I entered A&M in January 1958, transferring 68 hours. After the spring and summer of '58, I got my Aggie ring, an important stage of any Aggie's coursework. I was proud of it, and knew that I was on my way to graduation.

In the summer of 1958, we moved to an apartment in some old army barracks that A&M reserved for married students. The rent was $27 per month, bills paid. I went to classes all year — fall, spring, and summer — but took time out to do some deer and dove hunting.

I killed my first white-tailed buck during the fall of 1958. I had made acquaintance with a school kid who rode my bus, and he wanted to go deer hunting on his grandmother's 10 acres, if I would loan him a deer rifle. He said that there were deer in the area of the 10 acres that had been planted in winter oats.

I had two war-relic deer rifles—a 7.7 Japanese with a 4-power Weaver scope, and an Enfield .30-06 with a 2½ power scope. We climbed up in some big oak trees on each end of the oats patch one Saturday evening, and about dusk a deer came into the field. I couldn't tell if it was a buck, but when the boy shot at it and missed, I figured that it must be a buck.

Texas A&M University, Wildlife Science Dept, College Station

I took a quick shot with my .30-06, and knocked the buck down. The yearling buck had small five-point antlers that would go into a baseball cap. It was the first of many bucks that I would get in the ensuing years. In fact, I killed another three-point yearling the next fall on the same 10 acres.

Game And Fish Commission, Mineral Wells

I graduated in June 1960 with a B.S. in wildlife science, with my happy mother and brother Bill looking on. I was fortunate to have two jobs to choose from — a Fish and Wildlife Service job on an island of the Louisiana Coast, and a job with the Texas Game and Fish Commission. The Texas job involved some quail research, which pulled my attention in that direction. The pay was not as much, but the quail and deer work had my interest, and I took the state job in Mineral Wells, working under Clyde Holt in the Possum Kingdom Regulatory District. Clyde was headquartered in Decatur, and I was assigned to work with Charlie Winkler for a year.

Horace ages quail wings, during a five-year quail research project from 1960-1965.

Clyde was 46 and I was 27, so he became a kind of surrogate father to me. He knew all the people that we needed to know, and Clyde had three of the best bird dogs (pointers) that I've ever hunted with. We followed Heck, Harriet, and June over a lot of quail country between Decatur and Albany, and I was fortunate to get a pup from Clyde's pointer blood lines.

One of the first research projects that I got into was a five-year study of bobwhite quail population turnover, with emphasis on age, weight and food habits. The important project eventually affected changes in Texas quail seasons and bag limits. Charlie Winkler transferred to Pearsall, and Clyde gave me the job of writing all of the quail project annual reports, as well as the final report. With some experience under my belt, I moved to Brownwood. In September 1963, the Game and Fish Commission merged with the Parks Board, creating the Texas Parks and Wildlife Commission.

Parks And Wildlife, Brownwood (Bangs)

My work on the quail project, along with the work I did with pronghorn census and voluntary reports given at staff meetings, gave me the opportunity to fill a vacancy in Waco as the Region 2 Wildlife Supervisor in 1965. I was the third choice, after two senior biologists turned the job down. Jack Thomas was going back to college, and Bob VanCleave didn't

Horace Gore, Field biologist, Texas Parks and Wildlife Brownwood, Texas 1963

want to work with Capt. Allie Lewis, the Regional Director. Capt. Lewis had a reputation of being a tough, cigar-chewing individual, having come up through the ranks as a long-time game warden.

I was headquartered in Brownwood, working out of an office with Capt. John Wood, supervisor of a game warden district that extended down into the Edwards Plateau. Capt. Wood was a close friend, and he helped me get a good start in my job in the Brownwood area, that extending west to Abilene and Midland.

Our first house in Brownwood in 1962 was the Locker Place, a nice old house on 10 acres near the east end of Austin Avenue. Donna started to school that year, and the twins, Barry and Garry, were born on July 13. The next year, we moved to Bangs, a small town nine miles west of Brownwood. The Bangs house was brand new, and we enjoyed it, the neighbors, and the town. We lived in Bangs about two years, and Joey started school there.

Region 2 Wildlife Supervisor, Waco

Gene Walker, the wildlife director in Austin, called on a Sunday evening in August 1965 and asked if I could come to Austin for a visit. I was stage-struck by the invitation because I never got calls from Austin. I reported to Gene on Monday morning, wondering why I was being called in. He hadn't told me why. When I entered his office, he immediately took me to the executive director, Weldon Watson.

"Sit down, Mr. Gore. I want to talk to you about a wildlife supervisor job in Waco. Gene tells me that you are a capable young man, and we need someone who can work with Capt. Allie Lewis in the Regional office. Do you know Capt. Lewis?"

Mr. Watson's comments settled me down a bit, and I told him I not only knew Capt. Lewis, but I hunted dove and quail with him. Clyde Holt, Allie Lewis and I hunted together every quail season. "Do you think you can work with Mr. Lewis," was the next question. I thought about it a few seconds, knowing how tough Capt. Lewis could get at times, and replied, "If I can't work with him, nobody can." With that, Weldon Watson looked at Gene Walker and said, "Gene, I think Mr. Gore can handle the job. Send him to Waco." I reported to the regional office in Waco, and worked — and hunted — with Capt. Lewis until 1971.

Oklahoma Game Chief

Things got a little hectic around the Austin office in 1971, and I became disgruntled with the way the wildlife division was being run. Capt. Lewis was nearing retirement, and I was looking for a promotion to Austin that never came. In the spring of '71, I got an offer from the Oklahoma Game and Fish Department for a job as Game Chief. I didn't think much of the Oklahoma Game Department, but I was ready for a change and the salary was satisfactory.

I took the job with Oklahoma, and drove back and forth during the summer of '71. We sold the house in Woodway in August, and moved to Edmond in time for the kids to enroll in school. I took the job of Game Chief in stride, finding that I was in over my head with regard to Oklahoma politics and fighting within the department.

Fire the Director!

At every Commission meeting, there was a motion to fire Ferral Copeland, the executive director who hired me. Every meeting had a 5-3 vote to keep Copeland, but it was a scary situation. One of the commissioners had quietly asked me if I would accept the executive director job, and I quickly informed him that I was not ready for that job, especially in Oklahoma. By winter, I had decided to stay, regardless of the internal turmoil, and put money down on a nice house in Edmond.

The people in Oklahoma are "country," and a little backward compared to Texas. I enjoyed my time there, doing some trotline fishing with a fellow biologist who also took me deer hunting. I got in some dove and snowy pheasant hunting in the Panhandle. Mary and the kids got involved with the folks at the First Baptist Church, and we liked Edmond. But that didn't help the tension in the headquarters office.

I got my first taste of district court when I was called to testify about our proposal to hunt deer at Robbers Cave State Park in Eastern Oklahoma. The large park had a lot of whitetails, and we proposed a short season to control the deer herd. Some local people who were probably hunting the park took us to court. It was an uncomfortable situation, but we won the case, and had the hunt. I found that there wasn't a dull moment as Game Chief in Oklahoma!

Back to Texas

Sometime in late December 1971, I got a call from Pierce Uzzell, an old friend in the Austin office, who told me that there had been a re-organization of the department, and that Gen. James U. Cross, retired from Bergstrom Air Force Base in Austin, was the new executive director. Gen. Cross had flown Air Force One for President Lyndon Johnson, and I'm sure that connection got him the TPWD job.

Wildlife Chief, Austin

In the new organization, there was a job of Wildlife Chief, under Pierce's direction, and he said that I could have the job if I wanted to move back to Austin. The call was a big surprise, with an offer that was hard to refuse. Mary and I discussed a move back to Texas, and also the $1,500 I had put down on the house. We both wanted to go back to Texas, and I made arrangements to get back $1,200 of the escrow money.

In early January we moved to Austin and I took the job of Wildlife Chief in the newly organized Texas Parks and Wildlife Department. There were a lot of new people in the re-organization, but there were a few of my

Trapping turkey: Horace Gore with rare black Rio Grande hen in 1967.

> *"There is seldom a situation when 2 and 2 won't equal 4."* — Goreism

old friends. We bought a two-story house in the Manchaca area, and got the kids in school. Everything went well for a year when we had another political shake-up, and another re-organization. The three-man commission had gotten crossways with Gen. Cross, and he decided "to go fishing."

New Job as Statewide Projects Leader

Gen. Cross resigned under pressure, and when the smoke cleared, I had been replaced by an old friend who had been booted out of his job when a planning division was abolished. I ended up, luckily, as supervisor of all statewide projects: doves, endangered species, and special projects. A year later, one of our commissioners from East Texas wanted me to take the job of Upland Game Leader, and place emphasis on restoring Eastern turkey to the Pineywoods.

Upland Game Program Leader

Clayton Garrison, who had been the finance officer, was the new executive director, and we hunted quail together. I felt good with him in the CEO job, and things went well for a few years. I did all I could to stock Eastern turkey in East Texas, and headed up a research project involving the use of wild Rio Grande hens and eastern turkey poults hatched from eggs we got from Georgia and South Carolina. The project worked well, and we established a large flock of eastern turkey on the Engling Wildlife Area near Palestine, where the study was conducted.

White-tailed Deer Program Leader

My job title changed in the fall of 1979 when Bob Cook left the department for a job in the private sector. I replaced him as White-tailed Deer Program Leader when he left. This job involved supervision of white-tailed deer research and management programs across the

> *"Political candidates get richer, whether they win or lose."* — Goreism

state. I kept that position for 11 years, until a disruption involving elk made some big changes in the Wildlife Division.

One achievement that I was proud of in 1991 was the development of the Texas Big Game Awards. The system involved Texas' big three — whitetail, mule deer and pronghorn. I had been a Boone and Crockett scorer for years, and when one of my fellow biologist suggested we have a big-game awards, I liked the idea.

The program involved B&C scores for typical and non-typical deer, and a reasonable awards score for pronghorn. Biologists and a few game wardens across the state were trained to score big game animals, and the program was initiated in 1992. The leadership in Austin did not like the idea of promoting "trophies," and sat on the program for about six months. Chairman Chuck Nash of San Marcos heard about the program, and insisted that it be initiated. After a couple of years, I suggested to David Langford, president of Texas Wildlife Association, that TWA take the program. During the last few years, TWA has administered the popular Big Game Awards program, and added javelina to the list of species.

The Elk Fiasco

Gib Lewis, Speaker of the House, and a longtime friend and politician, owned a 400-acre high-fenced place near Bertram, north of Austin. Our new Wildlife Division director, Charles Allen, was a good friend of Gib, and arranged for the transfer of some elk from a South Texas ranch to his property at Bertram, a move that would disrupt the Wildlife Division.

I was directed to find a department trailer big enough to haul several head of elk, and I found one on a project near Alpine. The trailer was delivered to South Texas, and 10-12 adult elk were captured and hauled from Webb County to Bertram. The news media got wind of the deal, and the headlines of the *Austin American-Statesman* showed a cartoon of an 18-wheeler full of elk, and a windup Volkswagen ahead with a sign reading, "Bertram or Bust."

Special Projects Leader

The entire escapade turned into a political football, and several heads rolled, including mine. Although I had done as directed, the ax fell just the same. I was replaced as white-tailed deer program leader, and given an assignment of special projects leader (symposiums, speaking engagements, wildlife expo, etc.). I was nearing retirement, and I told all my friends of my plans to retire in October 1993.

Sexual Harassment

For a period of time, Texas Parks and Wildlife Department went through a series of changes which were part of the federally imposed Title IX, sexual harassment, and discrimination in the workplace. I liked to joke with the girls, call the ones I knew well "darling" on occasion, and was generally unaccepted by a few new female employees. I was more than 60 years old, ready for retirement, and didn't really care what they thought of me. However, my character didn't fit the occasion.

I had played a part in the Wildlife Expo that the department put on in front of the headquarters building each October. Bob Cook had seen a similar event in Montana, and came back to Austin with a suggestion to Chairman Chuck Nash that we put on the same kind of event.

The Wildlife Expos

I was special events coordinator after the demotion from Whitetail Program Leader, and the chairman asked me if we could do it. I assured him that we could, and after a lot of work and coordination we put on the first Wildlife Expo in the early '80s. It was a big-tent affair, with other tents, trailers and accommodations for a big wildlife event. The biggest party of each expo was a Friday night steak dinner to invited guests under the big tent. The shindig was funded by Toyota, and free wine was endless.

On one occasion, Governor Ann Richards was the speaker, and she gave a talk on turkey hunting, which had the crowd laughing. It was well known Gov. Richards was "on the wagon" and didn't drink a drop.

I was at a table with Gib Lewis and several others, and Gib saw the governor sitting by herself with a couple of bottles of wine on her table. He motioned to her about the wine. She smiled and motioned to "come and get it." Gib said, "Hoss, go and get Ann's wine for us."

I went to her table to get the wine, and she struck up a conversation. I squatted down on the asphalt floor, and talked to her about spring turkey. After a few minutes, I tried to get up, and she tried to help me. I put my hand on her knee and pushed myself up. We talked some more, and she handed me the wine and I went back to Gib's table.

In a few minutes, two game wardens came to the table and proceeded to gather me up and haul me out of the tent to my pickup. They didn't say much, and neither did I, but I wondered what all the commotion was about. Later, I thought about it, and figured that Ann didn't appreciate me using her knee to get up from the floor. Regardless, it was an affair to remember, and may have been the straw that broke the camel's back.

Fired and Re-hired

One day I was called in and told I was under investigation for sexual harassment. My office phone was bugged, and a female game warden was sent across the country to interview all of the women that I had worked with over the years. She was reported to have said to interviewees, "We're going to fire Horace Gore, and we need your help." Of course, the women she interviewed called and told me all about it.

Well, I was eventually fired, and I immediately contacted one of my dove hunting lawyers. He directed me to do several things, and before long we were in a grievance court. They produced two witnesses and my lawyer produced four, and could have called in more. One of their witnesses had already left the department and was living in Albuquerque. My attorney, who was working *pro bono* for me, showed his opponent how the "cow ate the cabbage" and the harassment charge was reversed.

Retirement

In the end, we won the case, although my attorney said TPWD would sweep it under the rug. I was absolved of all wrong-doing, and shortly afterward I retired in October 1993. The entire fracas was uncalled for, and was caused by a couple of females who had problems of their own. I came out of it smelling like a rose, but it was a time when males

> *"Never let the truth interfere with a good story."* — Goreism

were liable, and some females had a chip on their shoulder. You were simply guilty as charged, and the recourse was a grievance hearing.

John Jefferson, Glen Boydston, and Joe Pierce arranged a superb retirement party that had to be postponed until January. I was up to my old tricks, and got with my friend, Arvin Harrell, who owned a funeral home. I dressed in my cowboy tux, starched and ironed Wranglers, with a new Stetson hat and alligator boots. He put me in the back of a hearse, and called to say we were on the way. At the party, I jumped out of the back of the hearse and yelled, "I'm not dead, yet."

The large crowd of guests roared, and we had a very lively belated retirement party. Jefferson took the item to the newspaper, which had a headline "Last Laugh Retirement Party." My 33 years with Texas Parks and Wildlife were enjoyable, and I hope, worthy of all of the effort that I put into the wildlife division through the years.

Little did I know that I would not be retired long. After moving to the Kokernot Ranch in Gonzales County, and settling in for a full retirement, Jerry Johnston called and wanted me to edit *The Journal of the Texas Trophy Hunters*, work on TV shows, and run the deer contest for the annual Hunters Extravaganzas. We arranged for me to take the job and live on the Kokernot Ranch. That was 27 years ago, and I'm still the editor of *The Journal* and working for Texas Trophy Hunters.

CHAPTER 5

My Long Quest For Whitetails

After 60 years of chasing whitetails from the North Texas to Mexico, I've killed a lot of bucks. However, I can think of at least eight whitetail hunts that stand out in my mind. I remember these bucks because they were unusual or because I made a good shot — or a bad shot!

I've taken more deer with a .30-06 and .270 than other rifles, but I liked a Model 70 .257 Roberts Improved about as well. I've had to shoot a buck or two the second time, but I can remember losing only one buck and two does in my long deer-hunting career. I waited too long to shoot the buck, and crippled him. The two does were shot with small-caliber rifles, and I made poor shots on both.

I've killed a lot of bucks since my first in the fall of 1958. I was a student at Texas A&M, majoring in wildlife science. As a county school bus driver, I met a boy on my bus that wanted to go deer hunting on 10 acres that his grandmother owned near the Navasota River. He agreed to take me if I would loan him a deer rifle.

We went to a small oats patch and climbed up in some large live oak trees, to wait for a legal buck. At sundown, a lone deer came into the oats, but I couldn't see any antlers with my J 2.5 Weaver scope. My friend shot at the deer and missed. I figured that if he shot, it must be a buck, so I pulled the trigger on my war-relic .30-06, and killed the yearling five-point buck with antlers that would fit easily in a feed-store cap. The next season, I got a three-point yearling on the same 10 acres.

My third buck was my best 10-point. I was invited to go hunting by my friend, Treldon Cutbirth on the family ranch south of Brownwood.

South Texas Trophy whitetail

He was looking at cattle and putting out salt and mineral blocks. I was looking for a buck that I hoped he would approve. About sundown we rounded the dam below the Texas tank, and ahead of us were four does and a good buck. Treldon gave me the go-ahead, and I put the buck on the ground with my war-relic .30-06. The 10-point was high and narrow, but he had long tines, and scored 150 B&C.

Another buck was killed on the Cutbirth Ranch while Treldon and I were driving in his Jeep on the south end of the ranch. As we rounded a curve in the ranch road, we came upon a buck and doe about 50 yards away. I quickly raised the old Enfield .30-06, but it wouldn't fire because of the freezing weather. I quickly bolted another shell as the buck broke into a run and jumped a brush pile. At the height of his jump, I put a bullet behind his shoulder. He collapsed behind the brush pile, and we went to look.

To our surprise, the 10-point had five long points on one side, and a handful of five points on the other. When I skinned the buck, I found a

.25 caliber lead bullet in his neck, capsuled in a gristle as big as a golf ball — hence, the deformed antler.

Another buck that I killed on the Cutbirth Ranch was from a 250-acre free lease I had for 18 years. On a hunt, I was looking down in a deep draw, cradling my .22-250 and waiting for a buck at sundown. A good buck came down the other side of the draw, and I took an offhand shot at about 125 yards. The buck wheeled around and ran back from where he had come. I was confident that he would be dead on the trail, but I couldn't find any blood or a dead buck.

The next weekend, I could hardly wait to go back and look for the "dead" buck. I looked all evening after reaching the ranch — but found no buck. The next morning, I decided to rattle about nine o'clock in the morning, and I set up in some cedars near where I had shot at the buck a week earlier. While I was rattling the antlers, I got a glimpse of a deer coming through the cedars. I quickly took a look through the scope and saw a nice buck. A quick shot put the deer down, and I went to look.

To my surprise, the antlers were broken up, with the only point left on the 20-inch right beam was the brow tine. The left beam had two points missing, with the brow and G-2 left on the long beam. I rolled the buck over and got another surprise. His brisket had a bullet hole through it that had festered up, but not enough to cause death. Then, it was clear to me — this was the buck that I had shot the week before. The wound didn't keep him from coming to rattling.

The longest shot on a buck came on a hunt with Jimmy Gallagher, Al Brothers and Tommy Kaye on Jimmy's ranch in Webb County. It was an annual hunt, and I was after a good eight-point. We hunted safari-style, corning the roads and going back for a look. On one tour of the corn, we spotted a nice eight-point on a long road some distance away. Jimmy said it looked like an eight-point, so I got out and took aim off the pickup mirror. The .224 TTH sent a 75-grain Amax to the buck's shoulder. Tommy counted the fence posts as we drove to the buck — 275 yards!

My widest and best whitetail came from San Patricio County. I was hunting with Marty Berry and Jerry Johnston on Marty's Gum Hollow Ranch north of Corpus Christi. Marty had called and invited me down to hunt a very wide eight-point he had seen on the ranch, and

Laura Berry with monster whitetail, 2023

Jerry wanted to see the "wide" buck. It would be simple — we would go to one of the feeders. The hunt would take a half-day — or so we thought. We hunted the wide buck for three days, and Jerry Johnston got weary of the hunt and went home.

On the fourth day of the hunt, we hadn't seen hide nor hair of the buck, and I knew Marty didn't have the time to stay with me another day. At noon on the fourth day, I decided to go home, but Marty didn't want to give up. So, I stayed, and we left camp about 3 p.m. to look for the buck again.

Shortly after sundown, Marty glassed a ridge and spotted the buck with another deer about 175 yards away. I told Marty I could kill the buck from that distance, and got my custom .25-284 Sako out the window of the truck. It was getting late, and the first shot missed. I hit a tall weed or something. Marty got excited as I quickly bolted another round and fired again. At the shot the buck's nose hit the ground first, and he didn't move. A tape on the antlers showed 29¾ inches, so we just rounded it off to 30 inches! He grossed 163 B&C — my best eight-point, ever!

My last buck was with Marty Berry and Jason Shipman on Marty's Gloriosa Ranch in Live Oak County. Marty had spotted a big eight-point — the kind of buck I like — and called with an invitation. The old diabetes was getting to me, so Jason drove me to the ranch. About 2 p.m., Marty showed up with a plan. We would corn some roads where he had seen the buck a few times, and get "old, crippled Gore" a shot at the buck.

Marty corned the roads as Jason and I stayed in camp and petted my new Jack O'Connor Commemorative .270. The Winchester Model 70 was a high-dollar rifle made in memory of the greatest outdoor and gun writer of our time. I bought it with a plan — kill the Texas Big Three with it — whitetail, mule deer and pronghorn — and write about the hunts. This hunt would be the whitetail.

An hour before sundown, we began driving the roads, hoping to see the big eight-point Marty was after. Before long, we spotted a huge buck with a basket full of antlers down by the lake. I suggested that we trade the eight-point for the huge non-typical, but Marty didn't agree.

An hour later, just at sundown, we spotted the buck we were after, but he was among a group of does and wouldn't give us a clear shot. We

> *"Why are we all compelled to chase that which runs away?"* — Goreism

waited — and waited — and waited. Finally, Marty glassed the buck alone in the brush. He thought that the buck would come out of the brush less than 100 yards away.

I was ready with the O'Connor .270 when the buck appeared. I questioned Marty's opinion of the buck, but he said, "Just shoot!" The .270 cracked and the buck fell like a sack of feed. We went for a look, and the eight-point had two short kickers on the base of the beams. He was an impressive buck — close to 160 gross — which turned out to be my last Texas whitetail.

CHAPTER 6

Mule Deer In The High Country

Each fall, deer hunters from all over Texas converged on the high country of Colorado, Wyoming and New Mexico in search of the long-eared mule deer. A group of us from Austin was in the mix for several years, hunting in Wyoming's Bighorn Mountains. I also hunted Colorado and Utah with Al Brothers (The Zachry Group) and the Panhandle with Brian Hawkins (Trophy Hunters TV).

I killed my first mule deer in the foothills of the Bighorns in about 1978. The buck was a 3-year-old four-pointer (western count). He fell to a 125-yard shot from my .270, on the first morning of a week-long hunt just northwest of Kaycee, and south of Buffalo. That first buck had me hooked on mule deer for about 25 years, from the Bighorns of Wyoming to Colorado and Utah, and the Texas Panhandle.

Through the years, I have taken mule deer with a variety of rifles, including .270, .257 Roberts Improved, .30-06, .264 Win. Mag. and .224 TTH. Mule deer are not hard to kill, but they sometimes offer long shots. Like all thin-skinned animals, they fall better to a lot of hydrostatic shock from smaller bullets at high velocity. Lung shots behind the shoulder are best, and offer a big target.

In all of my hunts, only one big 13-point buck ran more than a few yards, and he was about 300 yards away, going into dark timber when I hit him with the second shot. He disappeared, but we later found him about 30 yards in the timber. I got so excited that I left my rifle leaning against a tree, and we had to go back for it late that night.

There is hardly any similarity to hunting Texas whitetails and Rocky Mountain mule deer. Most whitetails are taken at feeders or water holes, or shot safari-style on ranch roads. Mule deer are usually killed on flats, where they come to feed in the evening, or are encountered in

Mule deer camp in Wyoming's Bighorn Range in 1985

the early morning when they leave the flats and go back to the mountains. Most mule deer are killed during walking and stalking hunts.

Even though I've killed about 10 mulie bucks, I cannot claim to be a good mule deer hunter. I simply go hunting and hope for the best. Of course, a good hunter will get more deer than a bad hunter, and knowing the daily routine of mule deer, as some hunters do, will help put a buck on the skinning rack. I have a few good tips for Nimrods, but people who live locally, and hunt mule deer regularly, are more knowledgeable of their habits.

Mule deer, like other deer are creatures of habit. They travel and feed in regular places unless they're disturbed. In general, mule deer stay high in the day and go low to feed. This means that deer travel during the very early morning, and also near sunset in the evening. The traveling deer can be intercepted going to feeding grounds.

Mule deer usually arrive on the flats just before sundown, and stay low in the good brush all night. The older bucks will leave the low areas

Utah mule deer hunt with Al Brothers and the Zachry Group in 2004.

well before daylight, and be high on the mountain by daylight. Younger bucks stay on the brush flats longer, and sometimes they are moving to the higher elevations as late as sunup. This habit makes them more vulnerable than the older bucks.

A deep snow can change a mule deer's habits overnight. He may be high, and stay high, even when he is feeding and resting. If a good snow comes during the night, he may be off the mountain and down in the willow glens by noon the next day. Once the deer are driven down by weather, they usually stay down until spring. So, in late fall and winter, look for mule deer down low.

Hunters after mule deer during the day are better off if they are high, looking down on the mountain side. Mule deer often reach a certain elevation and bed down for the day, and can be seen from above with the eye or with binoculars. Hunting high and looking down can give the hunter a good shot at a buck in his bed, or a buck standing in his favorite spot. I've known of several good bucks being killed this way.

When the weather is cold and windy, bucks will often leave their feeding areas on the flats, and go into protected places at the base of the mountain. Big boulders, brushy areas, and dense timber will often hold bucks during the day. My best Bighorn Range buck was jumped out of a group of boulders at early morning, and I was lucky to put two .257 bullets behind his shoulder.

If someone gives you a tip about feeding bucks, you can go to a flat and wait for the deer to come down from the higher elevations. I recall siting on the edge of some good brush, and watching two nice bucks feed until dark. I left and went back to camp. The game warden, Bill Backer, was feeding the campfire, and commented, "I watched you today with my binoculars, and those two bucks near you were as good as you will see in these hills." I took Bill's advice and went back and killed the best buck the next evening.

You'll get all kinds of opinions about guns and bullets that are best for mule deer. Take my advice: the best mule deer rifle is the one you shoot the best. I've seen mulies killed with .224 TTH, 6mm Rem., .25-06, .30-06, .270, .264 Win. Mag., and .300 Win. Mag. I killed my first mulie with a .270. and my best buck in the Bighorns with a .257 Rob. Improved (basically, a .25-06). Bullets ranging from 100- to 117-grain in the 6mm-25 calibers work well. I like 130-grain in .270 and 150-grain in 30 calibers. My .264 Win. Mag. was deadly with the 140-grain Nosler.

Weather in the Rocky Mountains can be cruel at times. The Bighorn Mountain Range has some winds that come at dusk, and sometimes blow everything away. I was in one such wind, and it demolished our Texas tents. We didn't find some items such as coats and hats for quite a while! I've gone to bed when everything was dry, only to wake up in a foot of snow. After October, you never can tell what the weather is going to do in the high country.

Eating mule deer is a touch and go proposition. We go to the high country to kill the biggest, oldest deer that we can find, and hardly anyone comes home with a good-eating, 2-year-old buck. If you kill an older deer with good antlers, I suggest you tenderize and fry the back straps, and make a lot of hamburger and sausage out of the rest. I don't think mule deer is as good as whitetail, and certainly not as good as axis or nilgai, because they are usually older and tougher.

> *"Man has an infinite appetite for distractions."* — Goreism

As a rule, mule deer hunting is not for the meek. Mulies can inhabit some very rough terrain, and sometimes the weather is bad. It is good to have help when a buck falls into a deep gorge, or is killed in faraway places. I was once hunting mule deer in the Bighorns and killed a nice bull elk that weight about 350 pounds. I was lucky to have some friends who helped me get him out. Texas whitetail hunters are in for some surprises when they hunt mule deer in the high country.

CHAPTER 7

Rifles for Texas Hunters

Hunters from Amarillo to Brownsville have used favorite rifles for years for two reasons — confidence and reliability. These two attributes in a rifle are most important, regardless of the caliber or model. If a rifle is not reliable, you lose confidence, and everything else is lost. Let's look at some of the things that give confidence and reliability to a deer-hunting rifle and caliber of bullet.

We will begin with caliber and what most hunters think is necessary to kill a deer. The amount of kinetic energy in a bullet to anchor a whitetail was established years ago at 1,000 ft.-lbs. at any given distance. Most Texas whitetails are taken at close range, so we will start with bullets capable of taking a mature whitetail at 100 yards.

My smallest caliber and bullet for whitetails would be a .22-250 or equivalent with 55-grain soft point. This combination has adequate energy and shock to kill a deer by placing the bullet in the largest vulnerable spots. These are where the neck intersects with the shoulder, or a lung shot directly behind the shoulder. Both are big targets and deadly. This caliber may be a little shy on bullet weight, but velocity takes up the slack and recoil-sensitive hunters take hundreds of whitetails each season with the .22-250.

Since 1956, the Winchester .243 with 100-grain bullets has been super-popular for medium-size game. This caliber was made famous in the Winchester Model 70 Featherweight rifle. Another good rifle is the Remington 6mm, which is excellent for deer-size animals, but has not been as popular at the Winchester .243. Both the .243 and 6mm have their limits, so choose a larger caliber for animals weighing 300 to 500 pounds.

For years, .25 caliber bullets have been desirable in deer rifles. The .250 Savage and .257 Roberts were especially popular for hunters who were recoil shy. Both are best with 100-grain bullets that open quickly and destroy a lot of tissue. At today's hunting distances (from the blind to the feeder) these calibers are very adequate. The same bullets used in a .25-06 or .257 Weatherby extends the range by another 200 yards for longer shots and bigger animals.

The 6.5 caliber has always been popular with Texans, but limited in use. The 6.5 Swedish Mauser is excellent on deer-size animals, and with 160-grain bullets, can do well on aoudad or even elk. Recent 6.5 cartridges like the Creedmoor have shown unusual long-range accuracy, and are expressly popular as close-range deer rifles. When used with dial in caliber/velocity scopes (and no wind) hunters can take deer and pronghorn at phenomenal distances with the 6.5 Creedmoor and several other 6.5 caliber rifles.

I must admit a lot of rifles in 6.5 caliber can surpass the Creedmoor — the 6.5 Swedish Mauser, .264 Winchester, and 6.5 PRC to name a few. However, if a deer hunter gets serious and uses the 120-grain GMX or 130 Barnes TSX in the Creedmoor, the caliber gets better for whitetails, pronghorn, and smaller exotics with well-placed shots.

The .270 Winchester was made famous by Jack O'Connor, and for good reason. The caliber and bullet weights are excellent for everything in Texas except nilgai. We won't argue about the merits of the .277 caliber, and I can attest to the use of the .270 on whitetails, mule deer, aoudads, elk, and hogs. Recoil is mild enough for the tender hearted, and velocity produces a lot of hydrostatic shock in 22-inch barrels. The .270 with proper bullets is a good choice.

I have shot some fine 7mm rifles, and all did well on deer, pronghorns, exotics and hogs with the 139-grain Hornady. Many hunters think the 7mm (.284) is the perfect caliber for American game (except the big bears). I tend to agree, having used a custom P.O. Ackley .284 on Texas game. This exquisite rifle was made by the "Master" and shoots like a dream! When handloaded with good bullets, the .284 is underrated as an all-around cartridge.

One of the finest rifles I've ever owned, and fit for a king, is a short action 7mm Mauser in "Premier Grade." My only other 7mm caliber is the custom P.O. Ackley .284 Winchester. The .284 case holds about 10 grains more powder and shoots the same bullet 150 fps faster than the 7mm

Donna Athey's 7mm-08 Winchester Featherweight.

Mauser. They both do a good job on medium-sized game, and I would recommend either one for Texas deer hunting, with the proper bullet.

The 7mm-08, which can be used in a short action rifle, shoots a 140-grain bullet 2,800 fps in a 22-inch barrel. Various 7mm-08 rifles have been highly successful, and are often referred to as the "Perfect Texas Whitetail Rifle." My experience on whitetails, exotics and hogs has been very good. My daughter, Donna has used a Winchester model 70 in 7mm-08 for years, and loves it!

Another 7mm caliber is the Remington .280, which is the .30-06 case necked down to 7mm (.284). The Remington people first named the cartridge 7mm Express and shooters rejected it. Later, they came out with the same cartridge, but called it the .280 Remington. It's an excellent hunting load with a variety of bullets, but never did past the acceptance test of American hunters. This is another caliber that is superb, and underrated as a deer rifle.

South Texas deer hunters have praised the 7mm Magnum — declaring that it takes a Magnum to killed south Texas bucks. The 7mm Magnum in Remington 700 kicks like a mule, and many hunters flinch at the recoil. The result is a lot of crippled bucks that have to be found/caught by the dog. I have a friend who uses dogs to regularly find wounded deer, and he says the 7mm Magnum is usually the culprit, but that the 6.5 Creedmoor is a close second! The reason — recoil in 7mm Mag, and low velocity in the 6.5 Creed.

But then, there is another side to the 7mm Magnum. I know several hunters who have used the 7mm Mag. for years, and they say good things about the cartridge. Apparently, some rifles express more recoil than others, depending on the stock. The Klienguenther rifle of Seguin kicks less than the Remington 700. For me — I've found that I can do well with

Tina and Clarence Kahlig with Tina's double-drop tined buck taken with her 7mm Mag.

> *"A problem can often be a cloaked opportunity."* — *Goreism*

milder cartridges with good bullets, like the 7mm Mauser, 7mm-08, .270 or .284, getting the same results with less teeth-rattling recoil.

The various .30 calibers from .300 Savage to .300 Weatherby Mag. have always been popular with American hunters. Although the Magnum craze of the '60s, '70s, and '80s is about gone, but one caliber — the .300 Win. Mag. — still holds firm with many hunters. Fact is, a Texas hunter with only one rifle would do well with a .300 Win. Mag. and good bullets. A soft recoil pad is essential, and a rifle weight of 8 pounds or more is best.

My hunting experience with .30 calibers has been mostly with .30-06 and the Weatherby .300 Mag. My first 15 whitetails were taken with a war-relic sporterized Enfield .30-06 — most one-shot kills. I've also taken whitetails, hogs, and bull elk with a custom .300 Weatherby (with muzzle brake). The big rifle was unnecessary except for the bull elk, but as Al Brothers says, "They don't run off."

We will end this dissertation with the big .375 H&H Magnum. I've never hunted with a .375, but I have owned and shot several Winchester Model 70s in that caliber, and I have hunted with friends who used a .375 on pronghorn, whitetails, and King Ranch bull nilgai. The 250-grain bullet is ample for almost anything, and I have seen several "Blue Bulls" bite the dust from this load. Nilgai are tough, but no match for the .375 with good bullets and a well-placed shot.

So, there you have it from someone who has used practically every hunting rifle and caliber on a variety of game. I have found that for most hunting, it is not the size or speed of the bullet, but where you put the bullet, that counts. Remember to "shoot the rifle that you shoot best," and you won't go wrong.

I forgot to mention the Wildcat .224 TTH (Texas Trophy Hunter) which has been a deadly caliber on everything from coyotes to big whitetails — one aoudad ram, and one bull elk. But that's another story.

CHAPTER 8

Spring is for Gobblers

During the last 75 years, I've hunted practically all of the game birds and animals in Texas, and some in other states. If I had to confess which species of game excited me the most, it would be a strutting turkey coming to my call in April. The loud ring of an old gobbler at daybreak literally makes the hair stand up on my red neck! To me, there's no other sound like it in the wild.

We all know hunting certain game birds and animals requires specific skills for success. A poor shotgun shot gets fewer quail or doves than an expert shooter. Deer hunting requires certain skills, but probably fewer than any other hunting sport. Hunting gray (cat) squirrels is demanding, and is a worthy sport in the east Texas river bottoms.

Shooting a turkey at 100 yards with a .30-06 requires very little skill or sportsmanship, but calling up a gobbler to shotgun range and making a clean head shot at 25 yards requires great skills and is above the ability of many hunters. The art of spring turkey hunting with a shotgun and call tops my list of hunts that require calling skill and patience, along with stalking, and hunting decisions.

Although spring turkey hunting has been popular in the southeastern states for 150 years, Texas was rather late in establishing such a season. We had, and still have, turkeys running out our ears, but the leadership in Austin was hesitant about a spring season. It took a few funerals and retirements to eliminate the resentment.

The truth was nobody knew how to hunt turkey in the spring. Their only turkey hunting was shooting a gobbler during deer season with a deer rifle. Few hunters knew how to use a turkey call, and fewer knew what it took to call up a turkey and shoot it with a shotgun at close range. Finally, reason and judgment prevailed, and the first spring turkey season was held in 1969.

Strutting spring turkey

The spring turkey seasons of 2023 marks the 52nd year for a spring season. The Texas Parks and Wildlife Commission canceled the 1976 season because of a poor turkey hatch the previous year.

Only one county in the state had the first season — Kerr County. Many landowners and hunters were opposed to hunting turkey during the mating season. Many felt such a hunt would annihilate the turkey population, which at the time was estimated at a million Rio Grande turkeys in the western two-thirds of the state.

Only gobblers were legal, and game wardens were called in to enforce the Kerr County season. When the smoke cleared, about 150 gobblers were killed from a population of 10,000 turkeys in the county, and the hunt was deemed a success.

In 1970, about 16 more counties were added to the spring season, but the Kerr County Commissioners Court vetoed the proposed hunt in Kerr County. However, the next (third) year of spring season, the Kerr County officials agreed with the season, and Kerr County.

Today, gobblers and bearded hens are legal in all counties with a spring season for Rio Grande turkeys. Bearded hens, which make up about 15 percent of older hens, were legalized several years ago because some hunters who use a rifle and no call can't distinguish between a gobbler and a bearded hen at rifle distance.

Because of the variations in weather and habitat conditions for turkey in Texas, a split season was established early on to satisfy both landowners and hunters who felt that turkey breed earlier in South Texas than in the rest of the turkey range. The result was an earlier season in South Texas.

My first spring turkey hunt was on Jim Ned Creek in Brown County. Larry Holland, a fellow wildlife biologist and close friend, invited me to go with him. We split up near the creek where he had heard several gobblers a few days earlier. Neither of us knew much about spring turkey or the art of calling. I was carrying a .22 Hornet because I figured on having to take a longer-than-shotgun-range shot at a gobbler — that is, if I got a shot!

About 8 a.m., I heard a gobbler down the creek about 300 yards away. He was yelling his head off, and I decided to give him a few yelps on a cedar box call. I would yelp and he would gobble. I got excited as his gobbling came closer and readied myself for a shot if he appeared, but he didn't show, and he quit gobbling at what seemed to be about 50 yards from me. He was close, but I couldn't see him.

It was at that moment that I learned my first lesson about calling turkeys. The word is patience, patience, patience. I would yelp on the call,

> *"You may not know it, but don't let anybody know that you don't know it." — Goreism*

but he wouldn't answer. I lost patience and crawled on my hands and knees to an embankment near me on the edge of the creek. As I peered over the embankment, I looked eye to eye with the gobbler about 20 yards away.

We eyed each other for about two seconds, and before I could get my gun up, he was gone. Had I been more patient, and been ready to shoot when he came over the embankment, I probably would have gotten my first spring gobbler. First lesson: Patience.

Since that first hunt, I have learned a lot about spring hunting — enough to get a gobbler, or call up a turkey for someone else, nearly every year for about 30 years. Actually, after all those years of hunting and learning the dos and don'ts of calling and shooting turkeys, it now seems rather easy to call and kill a gobbler with a shotgun.

In my early days of turkey hunting, I always hunted alone. Even though I called up and killed at least one gobbler every season, I didn't think I knew enough about turkey to call for other hunters. After about 10 years, I gained enough confidence in my turkey hunting to take a guest hunter. I found that I enjoyed the hunt just as much, or more, when I called up a gobbler for someone else, and watched their reactions with a gobbler so close you could see him blink his eyes!

I took a disabled man hunting in Comanche County who had a bad leg and walked with a cane, but he desperately wanted a gobbler. I went to a spot the day before and arranged some logs and brush for a makeshift blind. I knew we would be hunting from a fixed position, which was not my style of hunting. We were in the blind at dawn, and I heard a gobbler several hundred yards away.

I had mastered the mouth call, and I really put everything into some very seductive hen yelps. The gobbler answered a few times and went silent. We sat is the blind for about two hours without sight or sound of a turkey. I suspected a roaming hen had picked up our gobbler.

About 8 a.m., a hen came slowly by, looking at our blind at every step. We were well camouflaged from head to toe and the only movement

Chad Denman with his first spring Rio Grande gobbler, Kokernot Ranch in 1997.

we made was me pulling the mouth call in on my tongue. Even at 25 yards, she saw the movement and let out a loud "pert," which is an alarm call. She was soon gone, and I learned another lesson.

As a wildlife biologist, I knew a turkey could see about six times as good as a human, but it was hard to believe that she could catch the movement of my tongue at 25 yards! Remember that if you want to be a good turkey hunter.

We sat in the blind while I made three or four yelps every few minutes. Another 45 minutes went by; when suddenly a gobbler gave a loud GOB-BLE, GOBBLE, GOBBLE not 50 yards from us. I answered, and soon he was strutting in front of us at 30 yards. I whispered, "Shoot him in the head." The hunter, as many will do, lowered the boom on the gobbler right into the center of the body. The turkey fell and then got up and ran straight at us. As he passed, we both tried to get a shot, but the brush was too thick. I ran behind the turkey, trying to keep him in sight.

After the gobbler disappeared into the brush, I yelled to the hunter to keep his place while I looked for the turkey. After some searching, I saw the gobbler under a pile of brush. He was dead, but only after running at least 100 yards. I was lucky to find him.

When I returned with the gobbler, the hunter was beside himself with joy, and he had learned another lesson: Always shoot a turkey in the head and neck. A gobbler can carry a lot of lead shot if you shoot him in the body, and his wings can shed a lot of the shot before they get to his vitals.

I took a 14-year-old boy on a public hunt at the Kerr Wildlife Area. The kid had never seen a wild turkey. To help get him a gobbler, I used a dummy hen placed within shotgun range in front of our blind. I called, and four young gobblers came running up to the rubber hen. They all had about 3-inch beards. The kid whispered, "Which one should I shoot?" I replied, "Any one of them. Just kill one."

He aimed and shot at the one that was standing still — my dummy hen! The four gobblers flew off, and we inspected the hen. She had 13 holes in her head, neck and body—a good shot, but at the wrong turkey.

The last gobbler I called for a friend was on Al Brother's place in Goliad County. Brenda Landrum had killed a gobbler the year before with a deer rifle, but wanted to get a turkey with a shotgun. The first evening I put her in a ground blind, and I got into a deer stand a few yards away. My calling produced four jakes with 2-inch beards, and they came in behind Brenda, and she didn't see them.

The next morning before daylight, I put her in a ground-level deer blind with shooting windows. In the dark, I put out a decoy hen and positioned myself in the thick brush behind the blind. My call was sounding good, and we waited. We heard several gobblers at a distance, and a gobbler was courting several hens about 200 yards away, and Brenda had her attention on them.

At 7:30, a gobbler let out a gobble that nearly blew my cap off! He had come across a wide-open field to the decoy hen, and his arrival was undetected because the deer blind blocked my vision. Brenda hadn't seen him because she was still watching the gobbler and hens across the pasture.

At the gobblers loud gobble, I expected Brenda to shoot. He gobbled again right in front of the blind — but no shot. I whispered loudly for Brenda to shoot. He gobbled again, and she took a shot. At the loud boom, I saw the gobbler run off, untouched by the shotgun blast. Brenda was so excited, and I was so disappointed.

Then I realized the problem. In the dark, I had placed the decoy hen about 15 steps from the blind, much too close for a good shotgun shot. Brenda's shot missed the turkey's head completely. Another lesson learned.

When a "new" turkey hunter asks me for advice, I always have a few stock dos and don'ts for best results. What a hunter does with the gun and body while calling is more important than the calls they are making.

1. If you know that there are turkeys on the property, go there and learn the terrain and listen for gobblers the first hours of light and the last hour before dark. If there is a creek or other large timber, these are the best roosting places. Most turkeys roost on lowlands and go to the higher elevations for the day.

2. Don't hesitate to use a dummy hen, setting her up in a clear area about 25 yards from your spot. Camouflage yourself from head to toe, with facemask and gloves. If possible, always shoot a 12-gauge full choke shotgun with Magnum 4s or 6s, aiming for the head.

3. If a gobbler has come a good distance to you, don't get impatient. He will come all the way, so give him time. When he's getting close, pull up your knees and rest your gun on one knee, with the stock to the shoulder. You don't want to move anything much when you get ready to shoot. If the gobbler is strutting, don't shoot until you can see his head and then shoot him there.

4. Always try to sit on the ground against a large tree or in thick brush that will block your outline. Shoot from your knees while sitting. Never wear white socks or anything else white when hunting. No smoking or tobacco chewing or anything else that will cause you to move. Be patient. Give the turkey a chance to get to you. Some gobblers are fast, but others are slow. Young

> *"Why do people reach for that which is over their heads?"* — Goreism

gobblers may come to your call and never gobble, so keep your eyes peeled while you call.

5. One hunter makes half the noise and movement as two hunters, so it's best to hunt by yourself. If the property is large, you will do well to walk slowly, stopping every hundred yards to yelp four or five times and then wait a few minutes before moving on to the next stop. If you hear a gobbler, immediately find a good place to sit and then continue to make four to five yelps and wait for him to answer. With any luck, you'll find out how heavy a gobbler can get as you tote him to the truck.

If a hunter will follow these five simple rules of the hunt, he or she may get a turkey. Every hunt is different, which makes spring turkey hunting such a challenge. It is a lucky hunter who finds how heavy a gobbler can get while walking back to the truck!

CHAPTER 9

"What a Shot!"

When I was a teenager, I spent a couple of summers with my cousin in Sevier County, Arkansas, just north of Texarkana. We would hunt anything that didn't get away, and swim in the Cossatot River. We didn't own any guns, but we had a borrowed single shot .22, and we shot at everything. The old Winchester had no trigger guard, but it was accurate, and we brought home rabbits, squirrels, doves, and fish. We shot fish in the river.

During the summer of 1949, the mourning doves were big and fat, and there were several around my cousin's house. A big red oak tree nearby was a good place to find doves, and we went looking for some to eat. I'm not sure Arkansas had a dove season, and certainly not in July.

I had the .22 as we approached the tree, and I could see a dove on one of the lower limbs. I got a rest and pulled the trigger on that dove. It fell out, and I noticed something else falling on the other side of the tree. We found another freshly killed dove, and realized that I had shot a dove on one side of the tree and killed another one on the other side of the tree — a shot to remember.

Bud Woodley and I were hunting quail in 1953, near Avery, in Red River County. The dogs were on point on a grown-up fence row, when Bud and I walked up with our pump shotguns. A huge covey of bobwhites came out of the weeds, and they all tried to fly through a small opening between two trees. Bud and I got off one shot each at the close-flying birds and quail fell like rain. The dogs retrieved seven quail — from two shots!

A local rancher near Brownwood and I became good friends and hunted together a lot. Treldon Cutbirth ran the large family ranch south of town. We both shot .222s with scopes, and did a lot of riding and shooting. One day we jumped a jackrabbit while riding in the Jeep and Treldon jumped out and took a quick shot at the rabbit, which was

Treldon Cutbirth and Horace Gore, "Crack Shot" hunting compadres in 1963.

running full blast through the broom weeds at about 30 yards. At the shot, the rabbit tumbled about 15 feet, head over heels, and lay dead. It was a miraculous .222 shot.

On a deer hunt with Treldon in his Jeep, we were looking for a buck. It was a cold 20-degree morning in December, and I was holding my war relic .30-06 Enfield. As we rounded a curve, a big buck and doe were standing in the road at 60 yards. I quickly put the Weaver 4-power on the buck and pulled the trigger. Nothing. The cold firing pin didn't fire the cartridge.

I bolted a new round in just as the buck broke into a run. He turned off the road, and jumped a large brush pile just as I fired. The 150-grain Sierra caught him in mid-air over the brush pile and he hit the ground like a sack of feed. It was a running shot at a whitetail to remember, second only to a running mule deer in Wyoming.

In 1979, I was mule deer hunting south of Buffalo, Wyoming, with Ted Clark, Charlie Winkler, and Earl Thomas. I had been sitting on a big rock at daybreak, looking over a flat where we had seen some deer. About eight o'clock I got off the rock and started walking to warm up. As I passed through some huge boulders, I jumped two bucks that bounded toward the side of the mountain.

I took a quick shot at the biggest buck at about 50 yards. He kept running, and I bolted the .257 Roberts Improved and fired again. By this time, the two bucks were going up a trail. I followed them, and soon I came to a big blood spill. The buck lay dead in a deep ravine by the trail.

We got the deer out, gutted, and back to camp. I later skinned him and found two bullet holes behind his right shoulder that I could cover with my hand. That was good shooting at a running mule deer — my best running shots — ever!

The longest shot at a whitetail came in South Texas, when Ted Clark and I were parked in his Jeep, overlooking a big pear flat in Zapata County. We had the front of the jeep covered in a tarp, and were glassing the flat. A spike buck came out of the brush and started feeding. He was at least 400 yards downhill, so far that we could hardly see his long spikes through our binoculars.

Ted asked, "Can you hit that spike from here?" That was a challenge, and I got situated for a long shot. The rifle was sighted dead on at 300 yards, so I held just over the spike and pulled the trigger.

The rifle cracked and after a slight pause, the 117-grain Sierra hit the buck, and he flipped backward, motionless on the ground. We waited a few minutes, and Ted said, "Gore, that is the best shot you will ever make on a whitetail buck." We got the tarp back in the Jeep, and headed down a dim road to the deer.

When we were about 100 yards from the buck, he jumped up, looked around, and bounded off in the brush, his tail flying high. Ted and I were dumbfounded because we thought the buck was dead. After a lot of discussion and surmising, we decided that my bullet had grazed the buck's head or neck, knocking him out for a few minutes. He regained consciousness, got up and was gone, but it was a good shot, and I remember it well.

In 1984, I was going to a Brownwood deer blind about 3 p.m., when I saw six jake gobblers in the dim road about 70 yards toward my deer blind. I quickly got into the brush and slipped up on them. I could see

> "The truth — and nothing but the truth — is often boring." — Goreism

a lone turkey through the cedars and aimed for his head. The Winchester .243 roared, and the gobbler fell and began to flop around.

I put my foot on his head to stop the flopping, but I could still hear something flopping to my right toward the blind. I picked up the gobbler and went to the noise, and found a turkey hen flopping under the corn feeder. I could see that something had hit her in the head, and realized the bullet that had killed the jake gobbler had hit the ground and glanced sideways, hitting the hen in the head. I took both turkeys back to the truck, and went to the deer blind. The hen was illegal, but she tasted good, and no one believed me when I told the story.

My last "shot to remember" came while Jimmy Gallagher, Al Brothers, Tommy Kaye and I were "safari" deer hunting on Jimmy's ranch near Mirando City, in Webb County. We would sprinkle corn on several roads and come back later, hoping to see a good buck. It was on one of these annual hunts when I made my longest shot that killed the buck.

I always tried to kill a big eight-point on our hunts, and one morning Jimmy spotted a big eight with his binoculars. He said, "Gore, that is a good eight. Can you hit him from here?" I got out with my .224 TTH and took a rest on the pickup mirror. The flat-shooting rifle was on the money at 300 yards, so I screwed the Leupold up to 8-power and squeezed the trigger. The buck left the road and disappeared. Tommy said, "Gore, I think you hit him."

We drove the truck to the spot while Tommy counted the fence posts. The buck was dead across the fence, and Jimmy retrieved it. Tommy calculated the shot by the number of fence posts, and said, "Gore, you made a good shot." It was 275 yards, the longest shot I ever took at a buck, and killed it.

CHAPTER 10

Aoudads: Texas' Most Bizarre Trophy

Most hunters in Texas who have a "bucket list" have their eyes on the unique aoudad, an outstanding big-game trophy. In my long hunting career, I have killed only one male aoudad. It was a management proposition, because I had a friend in Webb County who was trying to get all exotics out of a 1,000-acre high fenced pasture that were competitive to whitetails.

The aoudad is erroneously called "Barbary sheep," but the aoudad is no more a sheep than a Big Bend jackass is a racehorse! It's not a sheep and not a goat. It is an aoudad!

Everything about an aoudad points to him being goat-like — the scientific name; the Arabic name "aoudad" (sand goat), his DNA, and his life characteristics and food habits. But aoudads are a species of their own, *Ammotragus lervia*, and their DNA shows them to be more goat than sheep. Needless to say, the aoudad is the most bizarre game animal in Texas!

Since the aoudad's scientific name and new DNA results put him closer to goats, I'll just put "ram" in quotes and get on with the story. Fact is, the aoudad is as strange as a $3 bill! It looks strange; it acts strange, it smells strange, and it's one of a kind. Aoudads will eat anything, including dirt, and can live almost anywhere. Like most of the goat family, the aoudad wants to be higher, even on top of your pickup!

A little history about the aoudad: In 1738, The Reverend Thomas Shaw saw the animal on the Barbary Coast of North Africa, and because of the sweeping horns, called it a sheep. In his published writings, he referred to the Barbary sheep on the African coast, and the name stuck, even though Greek taxonomists named it a goat 40 years later.

A Texas aoudad

No one cared what the aoudad was called until some notable Americans started hunting the animal in the 1940s. The old Texas Game and Fish Department stocked aoudads in the Palo Duro Canyon of the Panhandle in 1957, and noted hunters like Jack O'Connor and Elgin Gates hunted the aoudad in its home habitat — North Africa. O'Connor called it his strangest sheep hunt. No wonder. He was not hunting a sheep!

Early on, ranchers in Texas brought the aoudad to high-fenced pastures and charged for hunting. It seemed much more reasonable to advertise "sheep" hunting, than "goat" hunting. Today, aoudad hunts in the Panhandle and West Texas draw a pretty penny, and 30-inch horns make a good trophy. I've never eaten meat from an old male, but young female aoudads are tasty!

Any good, bigger-caliber deer rifle works well on aoudads, but leave the smaller .22-250, .243, 6mm, and 6.5 Creedmoor at home! Rifles like .270, .30-06, and most Magnums are good with heavier bullets. I've used a .257 Weatherby Mag. with 117-grain Nosler on a big male, and a .270 on females.

Al Brothers lived just south of Laredo, and was longtime ranch manager for two large ranches in Webb and Jim Hogg counties. The 4,000-

acre high-fenced Webb County ranch had a large herd of aoudads that stayed in the south end, where the habitat was hilly and rocky with a lot of thick brush. Al and I are old Aggie buddies from our days at Texas A&M, and have hunted together many times. I was living in Austin, working for Texas Parks and Wildlife as Whitetail Deer Program Leader, and I enjoyed going to Webb County to visit Al, especially during hunting seasons.

Al had decided to clean all exotics out of a big pasture that he had cut off from the rest of the ranch with a high fence. His intent was to use the 1,000-acre pasture for white-tailed deer management, where he would provide supplement feed. When he put up the high cross-fence, he caught several exotic animals inside, including some aoudads. He had managed to get most of the exotics out, but there were still a few aoudads that he planned to shoot on sight.

I visited Al on the ranch and planned to stay a couple of days and remove one of the better male aoudads from the management pasture — so I thought. After hunting three days, I wondered if there were any aoudads in the pasture. I sat morning and evening at a feeder, but no aoudad.

On the third evening, a few minutes before dark, I was about ready to quit the hunt, when a big aoudad suddenly appeared at the feeder. I didn't see him walk up — he was just there — like a brown ghost. I got the .257 Weatherby mag up and put the cross hairs on his shoulder at about 80 yards. The rifle rang out, and the 117-grain Nosler put the old "sand goat" down quickly.

The aoudad was big — probably close to 350 pounds, with horns that measured 30 inches. I was proud of the trophy, which turned out to be my only male aoudad in many years of hunting. I did kill two or three females on the same ranch for meat, and if you've never eaten bacon-wrapped aoudad, you're in for a treat!

The Texas aoudad is one of three trophy exotics that are really on the hot plate these days. The others are the nilgai antelope of South Texas and the axis deer of the Edwards Plateau. The axis has become rather common, even on open range, and it remains popular because of the long, high antlers and the beautiful white-spotted cape.

The nilgai is popular, but pricey. However, the upper echelon of the trophy-hunting world has discovered the "blue bull of the wild horse desert" that was first brought to the King Ranch in 1926, and again in

> "I'd rather have it and not want it, than to want it and not have it." — Goreism

1930. It is a large animal with small horns. Males weigh as much as 600 pounds and the meat is delicious. Hunters going after nilgai soon find that the large, tough animals are hard to bring down, and are usually taken with a large-caliber rifle on guided hunts.

The aoudad, which was once held on high fenced ranches, has spread over a large area of Texas. The Texas Game and Fish Department stocked aoudads in Palo Duro Canyon in 1957, and the exotic is flourishing in the Edwards Plateau, South Texas, and the mountains of West Texas. Like nilgai, aoudad hunting has gradually become pricey, because hunting is limited and sometimes difficult. A big male aoudad makes a great, unique trophy, but is not recognized by the Boone and Crockett Club because it is not native to North America.

The goat-like characteristics of aoudads make them hard to hold in a high-fenced pasture. I remember when a landowner near Magnolia, in Montgomery County north of Houston, high-fenced a large ranch and stocked it with about 25 aoudads. A year later, the ranch manager called me to report that several searches failed to find a single aoudad behind the high fence, and we suspected that the aoudads had escaped by some means.

Another incident occurred in the late 1960s, when a large male aoudad appeared on the high-fenced Kerr Wildlife Management Area near Hunt. No one could determine how he got inside the high fence, but several local ranches had aoudads.

The exotic aoudad is a fine Texas trophy, and one to be proud of. If you've been thinking aoudad, go for it, but don't call it a Barbary sheep! It is simply an aoudad, and its DNA spells goat, just as the Greeks said 223 years ago. Aoudads are unique, tough, and a hunt to remember, just like my hunt in Webb County 42 years ago.

SECTION 2

DOWN THE STRETCH

CHAPTER 11

The Quintessential Quail Hunter

Recollections of Quail Research, Hunting and Good Dogs

My first bird dog was an English setter named "Corky." Johnnie Smith gave — or should I say loaned — the young setter to me when I was 15, and I kept Corky until I went to the Army in 1954.

Van and Johnnie Smith lived in Hooks, and Van had a two-man portable sawmill. However, he and Johnnie made most of their money bootlegging whiskey from Texarkana, Arkansas, to Oklahoma City. The state of Oklahoma was "dry," and it was tempting to haul whiskey from the "wet" side of Texarkana to driving-distance places like Oklahoma, where booze would fetch a pretty penny!

Johnnie was the daughter of Nyta Barrow, who was also the mother of Jerry Barrow, my closest friend in high school. Jerry was a year older, and lived on a small farm north of Hooks, with his mother and his Uncle Jess. They owned about 100 acres of farm and pastureland, and Jess farmed some rented land in the Red River bottom.

The Barrows lived in a vintage log house with dog trot between two large rooms, and a fireplace on each end. It was typical of houses built in the late 1800s, and most had been remodeled to include a kitchen, and sometimes a bedroom or two on the back side — such was the Barrow house.

The house water came from a well near the back porch, and heat came from the kitchen stove and a wood-burning iron stove in the small "living room" next to the kitchen. That room had a desk, a couple of

Horace Gore and Ruff quail hunting.

chairs, and a double bed. Jerry's Uncle Jess used the desk, and I remember that he kept a loaded Model 10 S&W .38 Special laying on the desk at all times. I can't remember them ever using either of the fireplaces, because firewood was too hard to cut, and was high-priced.

Jerry and I started hunting together when I was 15, when his sister gave me Corky, a black and white English setter. I had a paper route in Hooks, with about 50 customers. I threw the papers from a bicycle most of the time, but when Jerry and I were hunting, he would meet me in town, and we would divide the route so that we could get through in time to go hunting soon after daylight.

I had Corky about a while, when Jerry's Uncle Jess bought him a trained English pointer and a 16-gauge Remington Model 11 shotgun for his 16th birthday. Both the dog and gun came from J.R. Guinn, who owned a general store in Hooks, and had been a long-time bobwhite quail hunter. J.R. was getting up in age, and decided to sell "Mike" and the shotgun to Jess, as a gift for Jerry. The dog sold for $50, and the shotgun for about half that much.

Mike was about two years old, but was fully trained and a super quail dog. Corky was a so-so quail dog, and didn't have the nose that Mike had. However, they made a good team, with Mike usually getting the covey "point," and Corky "honoring" him — they were beautiful when stretched out on a covey of bobwhites. They both did a good job on single birds, and that is when you put the quail in the bag!

When Jerry got his first shotgun and bird dog, I didn't have a shotgun. The Barrows had a Fox Sterlingworth 12-gauge with sawed-off barrels, and I used it on my first quail hunts with Jerry. A typical quail hunt for us would be six or eight quail in a day of hunting in and around the Barrow farm where Jerry and I were very familiar with the haunts of several coveys of quail. In the timber around McCutcheon Branch, a small creek that ran through the Barrow farm, we would usually find a woodcock or two to enhance our quail bag.

My First Shotgun

The next year after Jerry got his 16-gauge shotgun, I traded Eugene Ruff, a friend in Hooks, a cheap bicycle for a Winchester Model 1912 16-gauge pump. The shotgun had a cylinder-bore barrel (no choke) and

I struggled with it, trying to kill ducks and squirrels with a gun that shot a wide pattern of shot that was no good for anything but quail.

At the time, I was reading a lot from *Outdoor Life* magazine, especially every column that Jack O'Connor wrote. There was an ad in each magazine for a "Poly-Choke." It was a choke mechanism attached to the end of the shogun barrel that would allow the shooter to change chokes by hand from open bore to full choke — all with just twisting the choke. Since my shotgun was good for quail — and nothing else — I decided to send the barrel to Andy Anderson in Oklahoma City, and have a Poly-Choke installed, at a cost of $16.25 which included the return postage.

Quail To Ducks

The Poly-Choke gave me a shotgun that was good for quail at close range, and good for squirrels and ducks at long range. I kept the gun for about three years, and killed a lot of quail and ducks. I recall one time when I was quail hunting in the Red River bottom on some land that Jess Barrow rented. I had Corky, and as we hunted near a slough, I could hear the loud quacking of mallard ducks. I took off my belt and tied Corky to a bush, and crept up to where I could see what looked like 50 green-head drakes swimming in the slough. It was early February, and the male ducks were going back north.

When I quail hunted, I took the plug out of the shotgun, so that it would hold six shells. I also carried a few No. 4 heavy loads just in case I needed something for squirrels or ducks. I unloaded the No. 8 quail loads from the shotgun, and put in six heavy loads of No. 4, and slipped up to the edge of the slough.

The whole area in front of me was covered with green-head mallards, as I began to fire. The first shot got three of the birds on the water in front of me, and the rest of the six loads were at flying mallards as they left the water. When the smoke cleared there were about a half dozen ducks either dead or crippled.

I hurried back, turned Corky loose, and took him to the ducks. He immediately hit the water, and began bringing me ducks. I would take the duck and send him back. When it was all over, I had more mallards than I could carry — all pretty green-head drakes. It was a duck shoot with Corky that I will never forget, even though the duck season was closed. Back then, we didn't pay too much attention to seasons and bag limits.

The Quail Hunters

Jerry Barrow and I hunted bobwhite quail before, during, and after the season, as far as we could walk in a day. After a couple of years, we knew every covey within walking distance of his house, and several more in the Red River bottom. Quail need certain types of habitat, and each year there would be a covey of quail in the same area as the year before. Jerry and I would walk to the coveys close enough to home, and sometimes we would go farther in his army surplus Jeep that Nyta and Jess had bought him when he got a driver's license.

The "before" was in October, when we were getting Mike and Corky ready for the November season. The "after" was in January, after the regular season, when we knew of a few coveys that had a lot of birds that had gotten through the regular season.

On one occasion, we were hunting a big covey of bobwhite quail just behind the Barrow house. The season had been closed since January 16, and the weather was rain, sleet and snow. When we got back to the house in late evening, Mrs. Barrow informed us that we had nearly been caught hunting out of season by Johnny Shadick, the local game warden.

"I saw Johnny driving slowly down the road. He had the windows rolled down and could hear you boys shooting behind the house." Nyta recalled. "Just as Johnny got out of his car, and started to climb through the fence, it began to rain, and he got back in his car. He sat there for a while, and I could hear you all shooting quail. The rain persisted, and the warden drove on down the road. You boys were lucky."

That was the closest call that Jerry and I had quail hunting. We didn't let a little rain interfere with our hunting, and on that day, the rain saved us from embarrassment. We wouldn't have had to pay a fine, because Nyta and the Barrow family were too influential.

Bowie County had a scattered bobwhite quail population in the late 1940s and up through the 1950s. Most quail coveys were associated with old farmland that went to weeds during World War II, that ended in 1945. By the time Jerry and I were quail hunting around the community of Hooks, much of the old cotton and corn fields were in pastureland for cattle. They were weedy, and provided a good food supply for quail.

We knew where most of the quail coveys lived, and we simply went from one known covey area to the next. A good day of quail hunting would give us about six to eight quail and two to three woodcocks. We thought we were in quail heaven!

Jerry and I hunted quail and ducks through high school and a year or two after. He graduated in 1950, and after working at local jobs, joined the Navy. Mike, his pointer, was about 8 years old, and Jerry left him with Nyta on the farm. About six months after Jerry left home, I walked out the backdoor of my house in Hooks, and there stood old Mike.

It was strange — Mike had never been to my house in his life. The distance to Jerry's home was about two miles, through the woods, and how Mike got to me was a mystery. I took him home, and Nyta said he was nearly blind and would hardly eat. She wanted me to put him out of his misery, and so I did. He was a fine dog.

Corky was about eight years old when I went to the Army. I had him and another young setter, and I returned Corky to Johnie Smith, and gave my setter pup to Robert Green, a good friend and quail hunter who worked for the Hooks schools.

Years later, after I graduated from Texas A&M and was living in Brownwood, I was visiting in Hooks. I would get a dog that Mr. Pearson owned, that was sired by Robert Green's setter "Smokey" to a pointer bitch. The 3-year-old "drop" (cross between a setter and a pointer) had never been out of Mr. Pearson's backyard, or seen a quail when I bought him for $60 on credit in 1961. I hunted "Jack" a lot, and he would end up being the best bobwhite and scaled quail dog I ever owned.

Quail Hunting/Research

When I graduated from Texas A&M in the summer of 1960, I got two job offers. One was a waterfowl job with the Fish and Wildlife Service on an island off the coast of Louisiana. Travel to the island was by boat or air. The other job was with the Texas Game and Fish Commission, working in the Possum Kingdom Regulatory District, headquartered

> *"I hope that's his mother — if it's his wife, he made a bad choice." — Goreism*

in Decatur. Clyde Holt was the Project Leader, but I would be working with Charlie Winkler, a seasoned biologist, in Mineral Wells.

When I inquired about the state job, I found that it would be mostly bobwhite quail and deer work, with a five-year quail research project in the planning stage. My youthful quail hunting pulled me toward the state job, at a lower salary, to work with Clyde Holt and others on quail and deer. The decision to go to the Possum Kingdom Project was a big decision, but a wise one.

Frank Wood, a wildcat oil man, and a devout quail hunter was Chairman of the (then) Texas Game and Fish Commission. Frank, who lived in Wichita Falls, felt that quail season and bag limits should be extended, and asked Clyde Holt to do a research job to determine if a quail season could be longer, without affecting the quail population.

A Quail Biologist

Soon after I joined the Possum Kingdom Regulatory District, we started a long-term bobwhite quail research project involving quail habitats, age and weight, food habits by season, and turn-over in quail populations. It was a heavy workload, involving quail census on designated land, collection of quail-in-the-bag from known quail hunters, as well as hunting a lot of quail on my own. Sounds good to be a "professional quail hunter," but when you hunt day after day, quail hunting gets to be a hard job.

Each biologist on the project had a goal of about 100 quail per week—sex, age, weight, crop for food analysis, and location of kill. I drove long miles to meet with quail hunters and examine their freshly killed quail, usually after dark, and miles from home. I also hunted about three days a week during November, December and January. I had "Little Jack," the best quail dog I ever owned, and together, we bagged a lot of quail for the research project.

I also censused quail on two large properties twice per month with Jack, from September to March. During the five-year period, project biologists aged and weighed about 12,000 quail, and examined the contents of 1,200 quail craws.

We discovered the annual turnover (loss of birds from year to year) was just over 60%, and quail losing weight from 165 grams down to 140 grams were quickly removed from the population by varmints and accidents. Quail on good habitat weigh more, and are less vulnerable to predators or weather.

Quail on the north edge of the study, the Red River Basin, weighed up to 175 grams, while birds closer to the Edwards Plateau to the south, weighed closer to 165 grams. The annual turnover (mortality) in quail showed that an 18-month-old quail was "old."

We also learned that quail go from insects to weed seeds in October, that preferred seeds are eaten first, that quail have to "scratch" for a living in late January and February, and that they turn to greens in March. Regardless of the time period, every quail craw had at least one insect. Seldom, if ever, did a covey have more than 12 members, although the individual quail in a covey change regularly, usually before sunrise.

Clyde Holt: Quail Hunter And Leader

You know the axiom: "I thought I was a ____, until I met a real ____." Well, I thought I was a quail hunter until I met Clyde Holt, who was a quail hunter of the first order! Not only did Clyde have two of the best female English pointers that I have ever seen — he had access to some of the best quail country that I have ever hunted.

I let Clyde know I grew up quail hunting, and we talked a lot about good dogs. When the first quail season opened after I joined his wildlife crew, Clyde invited me up to Decatur for a quail hunt. I got there with my full choke Browning automatic 16-gauge, with white tape wrapped around the end of the barrel and some factory "scattershot" made specifically for quail hunting with a full choke barrel.

I had bought the shotgun while I lived in East Texas, and had a full choke barrel for doves, squirrels and ducks. Shortly thereafter, I went to the Army, and had no need at the time for a quail gun.

We went to Christelle Waggoner's ranch, just out of Decatur, and put his two pointers, June and Harriet, on the ground about 3 p.m. Sundown came about 5:30, and it was too dark to shoot by 6 p.m.

The Waggoner Ranch is 5,000 acres of rolling hills and wet-weather creek bottoms. It is excellent quail country with broom weed and ragweed being the choice early season seeds for quail. The daily routine for quail is to wake up in a covey roosting on the side of a hill, and feed for two or three hours as the covey moves toward the cover in the creek bottom for lounging during the day.

In late evening, the quail coveys comes out of the creek brush, and begin to feed along the hillsides. By dusk, all coveys are well up on the hillside, where they finally put their tails together, making a circle of quail for the night's roost. The circle has quail facing every direction, ready to fly, even in the dark, if a predator discovers their roost.

The next morning, long before the sun peeks over the horizon, each covey will wake and start moving about, sometimes giving the covey call that can be heard by other quail in the vicinity. Occasionally, a bird will leave the covey and fly to the call of a covey in the distance, or a bird will arrive at the covey from somewhere across the pasture. If a predator disturbs the covey during the night, they will call to each other at dawn, and get back together as a covey.

Quail Hunting With Clyde Holt

June and Harriet hit the ground running, and before Clyde and I could get our guns, shells, and hunting vests, they were stretched out on a covey of bobs. I soon learned that Clyde was a very good shot, but he was deliberate in his shooting, and I found out why.

Clyde wore yellow-colored glasses that reminded me of old type sunglasses, the kind Gen. MacArthur wore during the war. Clyde had an eye problem as a young man, and when he was grown, his right eye failed. He was a strong-willed quail hunter, and learned to shoot a shotgun left-handed. He was a very good shot on quail and dove, but he always took his time when bringing the gun to shoulder, and leading the bird before firing. On the other hand, I was a quick, point-and-shoot type of hunter, as I learned to shoot a shotgun while trying to beat Jerry Barrow to the quail. Jerry and I were very competitive, but he usually beat me on the first shot.

Clyde and I walked up to the dogs on point, and a big covey of bobs came up out of the grass. We got a bird each, and the dogs fetched them to Clyde, right into his hands. We looked for singles, and the dogs pointed two or three that we killed. "We don't want to take over five birds from a covey," Clyde noted. "As long as there are six to eight birds, they will stick together as a covey.

Quail were plentiful, and we had our limit of 24 birds well before sundown. Clyde told me to take off my belt, and he did the same. We caught the dogs and slid our belts under their collars, and went back to the truck. "Why did you call the dogs and take them back to the truck on our belts," I asked. Clyde grinned and replied. "The dogs would be pointing quail all evening, while we were trying to get back to the truck and go to Christelle's house to clean the birds." We loaded up and went to the ranch house, where Christelle met us at the front porch.

Clyde and Christelle Waggoner were old friends, as I could readily tell. She was about 60, an old maid, and the granddaughter of Dan Waggoner, the bigwig of the early Western cattlemen in the area between Fort Worth and Wichita Falls. The 5,000 acres was part of her inheritance, and she never married. Clyde kidded her about not finding a man that could keep up with her, but I noticed that good looks had failed to come her way. She had a black man who took care of her, and they were very friendly with each other.

Christelle offered Clyde and me a bourbon and water, and we cleaned the 24 birds and put them in her fridge. I learned on that first hunt with Clyde, why he had so many good places to hunt. He was not selfish with the quail. He told me to share the birds, or give all of them to the landowner. "Nearly everybody likes quail. And they like them better if they are clean, and in the ice box."

That was only one of the many pieces of advice Clyde gave to me, and I tried to remember all of them. I've always thought that the many days with Clyde made me a better person. I grew up without a father — I never knew what it was like to have a father —and Clyde was the only surrogate father I ever had.

Clyde Called, And I Answered

Each Federal Aid Job we did required an annual report, and when the job was finished, a final report of some depth was submitted to the Austin office, where it was reported to the Federal Agency in charge.

The Possum Kingdom Regulatory District was all under Federal Aid, W-73-R, so we had a lot of reports each year.

Clyde Holt was an excellent supervisor, but he did not like reporting. Working with him revealed his dislike for reports, and I saw that early on. When a report was due, whether it be annual or final, I would offer to do a "rough draft" for Clyde to approve. I was pretty good at writing reports, and after one or two, I could see that Clyde would probably ask me to write the final report on the quail study, W-73-R Job 9. I helped him with some of the annual reports, and when Charlie Winkler left the Possum Kingdom District, and moved to Pearsall as a Project Leader, Clyde depended on me even more.

Northern Bobwhite Quail

When the time came for the final report on Job 9, Clyde asked me if I wanted to write it. I agreed, and he turned the final report over to me. I did the best I could, and by doing so, I became even more acquainted with the results of the five-year study. I finished the report in a few weeks, and Clyde submitted it to Austin, where it was well received by all members of the Texas Parks and Wildlife Commission. Ex-Chairman Frank Wood of Wichita Falls was pleased with the results of the long quail project.

The Quail Study Gets Season And Bag Limit Changes

Frank Wood was a friend of Clyde, and wanted biological proof that the season and bag limit for quail season could be extended without harm to the quail population. The study that we submitted in the final report substantiated what the ex-chairman wanted, and the statewide quail season was extended by 30 days, and the bag limit was raised from 12 to 15 per day, and 45 in possession. In terms of state employment, Clyde and I came out smelling like a rose! The Commission commended us for our work, and so did the Austin office staff.

I wrote a couple of papers on the work we had completed, and presented them to the Southeastern Association of Fish and Wildlife Agencies at annual meetings in Mobile and Charleston. The hunting public in Texas was pleased with the changes in quail seasons and bag limits.

Not long thereafter, I got a call from Gene Walker, director of the Wildlife Division in Austin. He offered me a vacant job as Wildlife Supervisor in the Region 2 office in Waco. I was not the first choice for the job, but I was the first to accept it, and work with the Regional Director, Capt. Allie Lewis. Capt. Lewis was known for being hard-nosed, but I knew that I could work with him, because I hunted quail with him, Clyde Holt, and a few of our friends every year!

Waco, And On To Austin, By Way Of Oklahoma

My six years in Waco were ones to remember. Capt. Lewis and I were good friends, although he was always the "boss," except when we were quail hunting. I had the dogs, and I was in charge when it came to quail. The office staff were all close friends, and we all enjoyed working together.

This story is not about Waco or Oklahoma, so I will make it brief. In 1971, things were not going well in the Austin office. There was internal strife, and I had asked for a promotion that didn't happen. My Federal Aid Supervisor, Pierce Uzzell was as frustrated as I was, and I was ready for a move. I was contemplating the situation when I got a phone call from Oklahoma.

The call came from Farrel Copeland, the Executive Director of the Oklahoma Game and Fish Department, and he wanted to know if I was interested in the Game Chief job that was vacant. I had met the Oklahoma folks several times at the Southeastern Association of Fish and Wildlife Agencies annual meeting. As a rule, I would not have been interested in a move to another state, but things were so hectic in Texas that I took the job.

To make a long story short, we sold the house in Woodway, and moved to Edmond, Oklahoma, where most of the people lived that I would work with. My experience in Texas was hardly enough to get me by, working with a new state agency in Oklahoma, but I managed. After about six months, I got accustomed to the job, and things were going smooth.

We had settled down in Edmond, which was a short 20-mile drive from the city, and I had put down money to buy a nice house. Things were going fine until the phone call.

One Saturday night in December, just before Christmas, the phone rang and to my surprise, it was Pierce Uzzell calling from Austin. After we talked awhile, he told me that the Texas Parks and Wildlife Department had gone through a reorganization, and that retired Gen. James U. Cross, from Bergstrom AFB, had been appointed as executive director.

"I am in charge of fish and wildlife," Pierce said, "and I want you to come back and take over the wildlife division." The offer came as a shock, and I hardly knew what to say. I was not exactly happy with Oklahoma, but I was in deep, and buying a house.

"Let me think it over for a few days," I said, and Pierce agreed. "I'll call you back in a few days. There's no hurry," he replied.

I was definitely interested in the wildlife chief job in Austin, and I immediately began a process to get most of my escrow money from the house deal. Then we quietly made plans to move back to Texas, and take the job in Austin. I resigned from Oklahoma, and by mid-January of 1972, we were back in Austin. After renting for three months, we bought a nice two-story house in the community of Manchaca, in South Austin.

My position changed two or three times while I was in the Austin office. There was another reorganization, and I had several jobs with Texas Parks and Wildlife—statewide projects, upland game, white-tailed deer, and special projects—until my retirement in 1993.

When I moved back to Austin, I built a nice chain link dog pen, where I kept a couple of good bird dogs. Most of my hunting was done in a rural area east of Lockhart, where there were a lot of quail and the landowners would let me hunt. I had a good pointer named Ruff, and a Brittany spaniel named Zeke. They were a good pair, and I enjoyed many quail hunts while in Austin—many of them with my close friend, Al Springs.

Horace Gore's quail-hunting truck.

I hunted with Herbert Purtle, a helicopter pilot for the Texas National Guard. Herbert was from Bowie County, like me, and he had some good English pointers. On one hunt near Dale, east of Lockhart, we hunted all day. The morning hunt was extra good, and we didn't miss many shots. After a barbecue lunch in Lockhart, we went back for the evening hunt. About sundown, we came back to the truck, put the dogs up, and counted our birds. I won't say how many quail we killed that day, but it was a big sack full! The Dale area had a lot of quail and some big rattlesnakes.

While in Austin, I quail hunted mostly between Austin and the Rio Grande. South Texas has some good quail habitat, and I enjoyed many good quail hunts while watching for rattlesnakes and javelinas. However, it is my opinion that the best quail country in Texas is north of Cisco to the Red River, and east-west from Breckenridge to Sweetwater. Quail are plentiful; few snakes; water for the dogs; and ranches large enough to get lost in. I'll take North Texas quail hunts every time.

Retirement And A Life Change

When I retired from Texas Parks and Wildlife in 1993, I had two good English setters, two good pointers, and was doing a lot of quail hunting in North Texas, as well as a few places in South Texas. Roy Wilson was running a hunting camp on the Clear Fork of the Brazos above Albany, and he wanted me to come to his Crocked River Camp and bring my dogs and be a quail hunting guide. I worked for Roy for two winters, and helped Roy with guiding, cooking, and anything else that I could do to help. Quail hunter's tips kept my pockets full of money.

I got in a lot of quail hunting between work and time off, but my job with Roy at Crooked River was interrupted by a visit to Gonzales and an invitation from Dr. Brian Denman to move to Gonzales County and live on the Kokernot Ranch. I took the offer, and spent the next 22 years enjoying the 2,200-acre ranch and working for Texas Trophy Hunters Association as editor of *The Journal of the Texas Trophy Hunters* magazine.

When I moved from Austin to the Kokernot Ranch in East Gonzales County, my quail hunting slowed down, but I still managed a few hunts on the Clear Fork of the Brazos near Albany. On occasion, I reminisce about my days as a quail hunter. I've had some good dogs: Corky, Jack, Molly, Lucy Belle, Ruff, Zeke, Sue, Patches, and Chief. Jack, the half-breed pointer/setter was the best dog I ever had, but Lucy Belle, Zeke, Molly, and Patches came in a close second.

I had several good quail guns through the years. My favorites were my first Winchester Model 1912 16 gauge, and my Winchester Model 12 20-gauge Skeet Grade. Both were pump guns, and my favorite over/under 20 gauge was a Browning Grade VI, with engraving and gold quail, ducks, and pheasant. Another favorite was a Winchester 21 double in 20 gauge, a real high-dollar shotgun that fit like a glove! Ernie Davis wanted it, and I took his check for $10,000 for the 21 and a couple more guns.

By the turn of the century, my quail dogs were all gone, and I hardly ever quail hunted any more. I did have a good black Lab that was excellent at retrieving ducks and doves, and was also good at trailing wounded deer and hogs. So, my quail hunting days were over, but I had a retriever named "Belle" that changed my wing-shooting from quail to doves and ducks, and my big-game hunting to deer and hogs, on the Kokernot Ranch in Gonzales County that was a wildlife haven.

CHAPTER 12

Little Jack

The best bird dog I ever owned was half pointer, and half setter. "Jack" was small, black and white speckled, with short hair and ears. He didn't look like a bird dog, He didn't stand regal when pointing quail like an English pointer or English setter, but when Jack did point, you could bet that he had quail.

Jack was the only pup left from a litter sired by Smoky, a small English setter owned by a good friend, Robert Green. The dam was an English pointer, and the breeding was accidental. Robert gave all the pups away, but kept one — Jack — to suckle the female for a few weeks. After that, Robert gave Little Jack to Mr. Pearson, who worked for the Hooks High School, where his wife taught. The Pearsons lived in the old superintendent house on the school grounds, which had a wooden fence where Little Jack lived for three years.

I had been out of Texas A&M for about 18 months, working for the Texas Game and Fish Department, and living in Brownwood. A big part of my job was a long-term quail research project involving everything about bobwhite quail — food habits, weight and age, covey size and distribution, and annual gain and loss in quail numbers. I needed a good quail dog!

I had quail hunted in Bowie and adjacent counties from the time I was 15 years old. I had a good English setter, "Corky," and my friend, Jerry Barrow had a good English pointer, "Mike." We hunted quail before, during high school. I shot a 16-gauge Winchester pump, and Jerry shot a Remington "humpback" 16-gauge automatic. We were both good shots on quail!

After high school and working for a while, I joined the Army in 1954 and gave Corky back to Johnnie Smith, and my other dog to Robert Green. My quail hunting was over for two years during my time in the Army, but I got Corky back and hunted quail for two seasons while at Texarka-

I was told "His name is Jack, and he is a good dog." They were right.

na College. I didn't have a quail dog at Texas A&M, but I started looking for a dog soon after I graduated in 1960.

In summer of 1961, I was visiting back at Hooks (Bowie County) when someone told me that Mr. Pearson had a dog that he might sell. I went by to see him, and he showed me the dog. "His name is Jack, and he is a good dog," Pearson said. I looked at Jack, and he didn't look like a bird dog to me. "Have you hunted him much?" I asked. "No, he's never been out of the yard," Pearson said.

When I heard that I walked toward the car, when Pearson yelled, "He's only three, and he'll make a good bird dog. Let me show you what he will do." I turned back as Pearson called Jack and got a wash tub from the garage. "Jack, why don't you come and get in this tub," Pearson said to the dog. Jack came over and got in the tub and laid himself down. "Ain't he something?" Pearson joked. I wasn't impressed, but I watched.

Mr. Pearson went into the house and brought back a hen egg. He told the dog to sit, and Jack sat quietly. Pearson went around the house and hid the egg in the flower bed. He came back and said, "Jack, go get that egg." Jack immediately went around the house and in a few minutes, brought the egg back in his mouth. Pearson took the egg from Jack and remarked, "Ain't he a good retriever?"

I liked what I saw, but I said, "Mr. Pearson, I'm not interested in dog tricks. I need a good bird dog that will find and point quail, and Jack has never seen a quail." Pearson petted Jack as he replied, "Tell you what I'll do. Take Jack on credit for $60, and if he don't pan out, keep the money and the dog."

I thought about the deal and figured I couldn't lose. The dog was 3 years old, hadn't been out of the yard, but could do tricks, and responded to commands. "I'll take Jack, and if he does good on quail I'll send you a check. I put Jack in the back of the station wagon and went back to Brownwood.

As soon as the weather got cool in September and October, I took Jack out to a shooting resort north of Bangs, where a friend had quail to release for hunters. There were a lot of quail out in the pasture, left over from prior quail hunts, and I got Jack into his first quail. He pointed good, but when the quail flew, he chased them.

I broke Jack from chasing quail, but he also liked to chase rabbits. I broke him from chasing rabbits, and by November, the opening of quail season, Jack and I knew what to expect of each other. In the last days of the season, Jack was pointing quail, and I was shooting good. I found he was an excellent retriever and fetched quail just as he had brought Pearson the hen egg. I sent Pearson a check for $60, with a Thank You note.

The next three years were good for quail, and I hunted Jack about three days a week. My quota for weighing, aging, and taking the crops was 100 quail per week. I chased down quail hunters to get the data and crops from their birds, and I hunted several ranches to finish my weekly quota. Any quail hunter knows if you hunt a dog two or three times a week, and kill 25-30 birds each week, you will soon make a good bird dog. Well, I did just that, and Jack became the best dog I ever had — and I had quite a few!

The quail research project was over in 1964, and I wrote the final report. Our quail work paid off when the (then) Parks and Wildlife Commission added to the season and bag limit, which pleased quail hunters across the state. I was selected to fill a supervisor position in Waco, and moved there in late August 1965. In a short time, we bought a house in Woodway, a new housing addition near Waco, and I build a dog pen for Jack and Molly, a young pointer that I had traded from Clyde Holt. Jack and Molly were excellent quail dogs, and I was doing a lot of hunting in the Waco area.

During my time at Brownwood, I had bought and sold several quail dogs to hunters I knew near Breckenridge and Albany. Quail hunting was good, and I would buy a dog for $100 and sell it for $200. In that day, the profit was good, and I had hunters calling me for quail dogs.

On one occasion, when I lived in Woodway I got a call from a Breckenridge banker who was looking for a good dog. I had sold him a couple of dogs while I was in Brownwood, and he was calling again. Quail were numerous in the Breckenridge area, and he asked If I would bring Jack and Molly up for a hunt.

I accepted, and he and I took Jack and Molly hunting one morning. He had a young man working for him, and the man took a single barrel 20-gauge along, but never fired it. We killed 36 birds (three limits) by mid-morning, and the banker was very interested in my dogs. We haggled over the price of Molly, and I told him Jack was not for sale.

We three went hunting on another evening, and by sundown we had three more limits of quail. I told the banker I would take $450 for Molly, but no sale on Jack. He pulled a roll of $100 bills out of his pocket, and I could tell that I had priced Molly too cheap. I took the money and used it to buy a Chevrolet pickup.

One of my shortest quail hunts was on the Lambshead Ranch north of Albany in 1969. A group of us were hunting in a bumper year for bobwhites, and I paired up with Morris Stallcup, a game warden friend from Wichita Falls. Morris had a very good pointer, and I had Jack. Morris was shooting his Browning over/under 20-gauge and I had a 28-gauge Charles Daley over/under. We left the truck about 8 a.m.

Morris and I never got out of sight of the pickup, and the dogs were on point most of the next hour. We killed two birds each on every covey rise, and I can remember Morris yelling, "Dead, a pair." We didn't miss a shot, but I crippled my last bird on the covey rise. The dogs caught and retrieved it, so we had a perfect morning of shooting. Our hunt was 24 quail in one hour and 20 minutes—the shortest quail hunt of my long career.

I kept Jack at Woodway, and hunted him in the Waco area for two more years before he died of old age. In the last year, Jack had arthritis in his front legs, and I asked my veterinarian friend for advice. "Give him four aspirins before you leave for the hunt." During that quail season, I killed a sack full of quail with Jack, but I always gave him the aspirins in a piece of bread before we left the house. He hunted and pointed quail just fine for about two to three hours.

Jack was a fine dog — a half-breed, but a great dog. My eight years following him in quail country are memorable times that I will never forget.

CHAPTER 13

Guns: 75 Years of Buying, Selling, Trading and Collecting

I started buying, selling and trading early in life. When I was 13 years old, I traded a Schwinn bicycle for a Winchester Model 1912 16-gauge shotgun. The next year when I was 14, I traded an older friend a Sears Roebuck single shot .22 (and boot) for a Marlin Model 39 .22 lever rifle. These two trades were the beginning of a long life of buying, selling, trading and collecting firearms. I kept the shotgun for several years for quail, doves and squirrels in Bowie County. The Marlin .22 was used for about two years for everything that you shoot with a .22 rifle.

I traded the .22 to a cousin for another bicycle for my paper route, and I sold the Winchester shotgun for about $50 to a friend, and bought a new Browning "Sweet 16" automatic with a full choke barrel for $129. I shot ducks, squirrels and doves with the full-choke barrel, and I put a band of white tape around the end of the long barrel, and used "scattered loads" on quail. The scatter loads were designed for use in choked shotguns, and were good for quail up to about 25 yards. I shot that Browning shotgun during my time in the Army, and while I was in college. While going to Texarkana College, I found an improved cylinder barrel for the Browning, and bought it to shoot quail.

During my army days at Fort Hood, I bought a war-relic Enfield .30-06 from a captain for $40, and after I got out of the Army for college in 1956, I put a Bishop stock on the Enfield and converted it to a deer rifle. I killed my first deer with it at College Station while at Texas A&M. One reason for buying the .30-06 was the gift of 500 rounds of Ball-2 military ammo with 150-grain solid bullets. The ammo was confiscated by a military EOD unit, and one of the guys in the unit gave all of the .30-06 ammo to me. I had shells for my .30-06 Enfield for several years.

When I graduated from Texas A&M, I went to work for the Texas Game and Fish Department, living in Mineral Wells, and then moved to Brownwood in the spring of 1962. I made friends with Marvin Reid, who had a gun shop on the Coleman Highway, on the west side of town. Through the next three years, I traded several guns with Marvin, including a trade for a Remington 721 in .270 for my Enfield .30-06. I also traded Marvin out of a High Standard H-D Military .22 pistol with custom walnut target grips. That pistol was deadly on squirrels on Pecan Bayou and Jack rabbits in the pastures.

While in Brownwood, I shot my first round of sheet with my Browning 16-gauge. I found that 16-gauge wasn't part of skeet shooting, and

Browning Grade VI 20-gauge shotgun.

I was doing a lot of quail and dove hunting. An old friend from Texas A&M wanted a full-choke gun for game in East Texas, and I traded him my 16-gauge Browning with two barrels for a new Browning auto 20-gauge with vent rib barrel with a Cutts compensator and three choke tubes.

I loved that gun for skeet, doves and quail, and kept it for three years. A good friend wanted it to trade with a doctor in Llano for a Browning Superposed over/under. I sold the Browning auto to him, and bought a new Charles Daly over/under 20-gauge for $209. I did some more trading with Marvin Reid, and when I moved to Waco in the fall of 1965, I had five or six shotguns and rifles, and my High Standard pistol.

During my four years in the Brownwood area, I was doing a lot of quail research and hunting. I found there was a good market for bird dogs, and I bought and sold several dogs to hunters in the Albany-Breckenridge area. Quail were plentiful during those years, and buying a dog for $100 and selling it for $200 was easy, if I could find a dog to buy! I had only one bad experience during that four years. I sold a dog for $250 to a hunter in Breckenridge, and it got rattlesnake bit and died before I collected my money. However, the hunter did send me the dog's collar!

The Waco move from Brownwood (Bangs) was the result of a promotion to Wildlife Supervisor, Region 2. I would be working out of the Waco Regional Office, and under Capt. Allie Lewis, Regional Director. After I got settled down, and got the kids in school, I visited Leo Bradshaw at Cogdell's, where Leo had a big gun shop. During the next seven years, Leo and I did a lot of gun trading, and I also got acquainted with Joe McBride in Austin, and did a lot of business with Joe.

Colt Peacemaker .45 single action; ivory grips and engraving by Tommy Kaye.

One of the biggest single trades I ever made was with Leo Bradshaw for a Browning "Pointer Grade" over/under. It was a high-dollar, elaborately engraved gun with extra good French walnut wood. Leo had it priced at $600, which was about what I made each month on my job. I wanted the shotgun, and worked out a trade with Leo, whereas I gave him four rifles and shotguns for the Browning Pointer grade over/under 20-gauge — a 4-for-1 trade! I kept the Pointer Grade 20-gauge for about 30 years, and sold it for $8,000 to a Houston oil man.

Texas Sesquicentennial 20-gauge, 1 of 100

Through the seven years I lived in Waco, I bought and swapped several guns with Leo, and we became very good friends. Two guns that I prize highly are a pre-war Model 70 in .257 Improved, and a Winchester Model 97 hammer gun that I used to kill about 30 spring turkeys. I also did some trading during the '60s with Earnie Davis for some Winchester Model 70s and 63 .22 rifles. Through the years, Earnie and I did a lot of gun trading.

I left Waco in 1972, and went to work for the Oklahoma Game and Fish Department. That job didn't last long, because I got a good offer from Texas Parks and Wildlife to come back to Austin as Director of the Wildlife Division, after the department had been reorganized. That job lasted about one year, and when the department was reorganized again, I ended up as Program Leader of White-tailed Deer.

I spent the rest of my 33-year career in Austin, and during those 23 years, I bought and traded many guns from Joe McBride. I had a very good collection of rifles, shotguns and pistols when I retired from TPWD in 1993, and later moved to the Kokernot Ranch in Gonzales County in 1995.

The Sesquicentennial year of 1986 was big in Austin. The world-renowned author James A. Michener was in town to celebrate his new novel, "Texas" and a big shindig was held on the lawn of the University Chancellor. I had spent a lot of time with Michener as an aide for

Single-action pistol with longhorn grips and engraving.

wildlife, and we were all invited.

As a part of the 150th year of Texas, Joe McBride got 100 white barreled actions from Winchester in the 101 Winchester over/under 20-gauge. He sent the actions off for elaborate gold and engraving, and made a deal for the best walnut and high-dollar checkering. The end result was one of the finest shotguns you will ever see. The 100 guns sold fast, and I have one in my collection. The gold scrolling in front of the trigger guard reads, "One of One Hundred for Texas."

During my 22 years on the Kokernot Ranch, I continued to hunt, work for Texas Trophy Hunters Association, and do a few gun deals. The biggest deal I recall on the Kokernot was selling eight high-dollar shotguns and rifles to four hunters from Cotulla and Houston for nearly enough to buy the Taj Mahal. Three gun models — Winchester 12 and 42, and 70 — and any Browning Superposed are premier models for buying and selling. I bought and sold a lot of Winchesters and Browning Superposed over a 40-year period, and built up a pretty good savings account!

There is a certain amount of satisfaction in buying, trading and selling. Some folks trade in automobiles, some in fancy rugs and blankets, some in real estate, some in farm implements, and some in jewelry. Whatever the choice, nearly everyone I know who buys and sells gets

a lot of joy in making a good deal. It's a real challenge to buy cheap and sell high, and I've had many years of experience in buying and selling guns. I still have a good collection — some one-of-a-kind engraved by master engraver, and my old friend, Tommy Kaye.

CHAPTER 14

An Aggie Discovers Country Skeet

The year was 1961. I had moved from Mineral Wells to Brownwood as a wildlife biologist. I was an Aggie graduate and my monthly check from the Game and Fish Department was $315. I drove a state pickup — a 1960 International with a heater.

John F. Kennedy was president, and I was as happy as a hog in a mudhole! It was also the year I discovered the shooting sport of skeet, and for the next 50 years I would shoot country skeet as a pastime, in Bangs, Waco, Austin, and Gonzales, with a few places in between. I enjoyed every minute of skeet shooting, and recommend it.

I'm not going to try to describe a skeet range here, but I will say that eight shooting stations are set in a half-circle, and every station has a different angle at the clay birds coming from each end of the half-circle. The clay birds come from a high house on the left side and a low house on the right side. The shooter sometimes shoots a single clay coming from a particular station — sometimes two birds, called doubles, are the targets.

Historically, the eight station, which is in the center of the half-circle, is the hardest to hit because of the short distance to the target house. But once the shooter gets the angle and the quickness of the shot figured out, the high and low eight station becomes two shots that are fast, but doable!

Skeet shooting is methodical, because all of the clays come at the same angle and speed every time. However, some stations, like low house seven, have a speed and angle for right-handed shooters that has fooled a lot of skeet shooters, including me! Many were the times when I shot a "24" and the missed clay was the low-house seven.

When I discovered skeet, I was fresh out of Texas A&M as a new wildlife biologist in the Brownwood area, with white-tailed deer and bobwhite quail as my prime workload. Bill Harris had a shooting resort (quail, pheasant, chukar) north of Bangs, and he had put in a home-made country skeet range. He had laid out the range on the ground, built a high house and a low house, and put square concrete slabs to stand on at each of the eight shooting stations.

Horace Gore at a country skeet shoot in Bangs, Texas

The high and low house traps that threw the clays were hand-operated, usually by two school kids, and the shooters would yell "Pull" when they were ready to shoot. A full round of skeet requires 25 shots, and by today's standards, the skeet range was crude, and my first.

When I moved to Brownwood, I had two guns: a war relic .30-06 and a 16-gauge Browning auto with two barrels — full choke for ducks and doves, and improved cylinder for quail. I soon found skeet requires four gauges: 12, 20, 28 and .410. Sixteen-gauge is not included, but if you shoot a 16, you compete with the 12-gauge shooters. So, I was at a disadvantage with my 16-gauge.

Not long after I moved to Brownwood, I got a phone call from a friend in East Texas who knew I had the 16-gauge with two barrels.

He wanted to know if I would trade him my 16 for a new Browning 20-gauge with ventilated rib and a Cutts compensator. The Cutts was a gas-dispelling tube on the end of the barrel that contained an extended choke tube.

I had shot guns with Cutts compensators before, and of all the choke devices, I liked the Cutts. The 20-gauge had four choke tubes: full, modified, improved cylinder, and skeet. Had it not been for skeet, I wouldn't have traded the 16 gauge, but I needed a skeet-and-quail gun that I could also use on doves and ducks.

We made a deal on the phone, and set a date and place where we would meet and trade guns. I told Clyde Holt, my boss, that I needed to talk quail with a fellow biologist in Tyler. I drove the state pickup about 250 miles to our meeting spot, an old church on the outskirts of Tyler. I got to the church after dark, and slept in the truck. The next morning, my biologist buddy showed up, and we visited and traded guns. I was back home with my new Browning 20-gauge with a skeet-tubed barrel by sundown.

I was doing a lot of quail work, which included census and hunting. I needed to weigh, age, and get the crop from about 100 quail each week, and this took all the quail I could kill, plus all that I could get from my quail-hunting friends. The 20-gauge with improved cylinder tube in the Cutts and No. 7½ shot was perfect for quail. With No. 9 shot, the skeet choke was good for skeet. I started reloading 20-gauge shells, because I was shooting a lot at quail and skeet.

A small group of us would shoot skeet on the weekends, and I remember one time when Bill Harris set up a BIG shoot at the skeet range. Several shooters from far away came to shoot for money. I recall one from Abilene, one from Bryan, and others. I didn't get in on the shoot because I wasn't a match for those shooters, and I didn't have the money for an entry fee. But there was a lot of food and drink, and I was there.

John Guitar was there from Abilene, and he shot the first .410-gauge Winchester 21 double — and the only one — I ever saw. His family was in oil and cattle, and that shotgun was worth thousands. He shot short shells in .410 competition, and 3-inch shells in the 28-gauge competition. And he was good!

The shooter that I remember most at that skeet shoot was a rather rotund guy with carpenter bib overalls and a J.C. Higgins (Sears) 12-gauge with a power pack. The power pack was a gas-dispelling tube on the barrel with reverse tubes that screwed into the ventilated tube. At the time, that gun cost about $80. The guy had his pant legs turned up above his brogan ankle-high shoes, and was either chewing tobacco or dipping snuff. I couldn't tell which. But when the smoke cleared, we all knew he could shoot a shotgun. He cleaned out everyone in the 12-gauge event, and was smiling when he left with the prizes and money!

Skeet Host Joe McBride, McBride Guns, Austin

Those were my first days on the skeet range, and since then I have shot more shotgun shells at skeet than you could carry in a small pickup! I shot 12-gauge only when I had too, and most of my skeet was 20 and .410 for many years.

I have a Model 12 Winchester 20-gauge skeet gun I shot skeet and quail with, which was customized with a 2-ounce ball of lead in the end of the shell magazine beneath the barrel. That piece of lead compensated for the high-grade walnut butt stock that had a feather pattern in the dense walnut that was a little heavy on the rear end. The lead in the front of the magazine made the balance perfect, and I shot the gun well.

> *"One night in jail teaches you more than four years at Texas A&M."* — Goreism

My favorite .410 for 25 years was a Winchester Model 42 skeet with ventilated rib and a Cutts compensator on the end of a 26-inch barrel. I used the modified tube in the Cutts, which gave me a little more range that I needed with my swing on clay birds. I shot the gun so much that, sometime around 2000, I broke the bolt.

Finding another bolt for a Winchester 42 pump was like looking for a needle in a haystack, but after about a year, Robert Bueltel found a bolt, and put it in the gun. I shot it several more years, and traded it to a guy from Brownwood who offered me two over unders, 20 and 28 SKB for the .410. I couldn't refuse. I suppose he thought he could shoot the .410 like I could.

I soon had another Winchester 42 skeet gun, but none of the .410s that I later shot were comparable to the old skeet with the Cutts compensator. That gun fit me like a glove, and I could never find a replacement. However, I continued to break 22 to 24 clay birds with the Winchester .410, and it continued to be my favorite gun on a country skeet range.

CHAPTER 15

Make the First Shot Count

Second shots seldom happen in a successful hunt

My hunting partners, Al Brothers, Jimmy Gallagher, the late Tommy Kaye, and I have spent many days and nights chasing whitetail bucks, talking guns and bullets, and expounding on the virtues of our favorite loads for deer, pronghorns and hogs. We all had our favorite rifles and bullets, but the one thing that we all agreed on: Bullet placement is the most important element of the shot.

Big bullets, little bullets, no matter. Standard loads, Magnum loads, no matter. What is important is where you hit the animal with whatever bullet at whatever velocity with the first shot. You can shoot a Winchester sporter that holds five rounds, or a single shot Ruger. Maybe you like a lot of firepower, and shoot a "black gun" with a 30-round clip. Just remember that the first shot in a vital area is the one that counts.

Al Brothers is a crack shot! For most big game, his favorite caliber is the .264 with Nosler partition bullets. He can't praise it enough, and for good reason. When he pulls the trigger on an animal, it soon meets its demise! This Magnum rig has tolerable recoil, and with a good 7-power Leupold scope, Al seldom misses. His philosophy: Shoot the biggest caliber you can handle well, and put the bullet exactly where you want it.

Jimmy Gallagher has hunted in a lot of far-away places, and for some big animals. He is fond of his .375 Ultra Mag. and his 7 Mag. with heavy bullets for the big stuff, but on his ranch, he usually totes a .224 TTH with 75-grain Scirocco bullets hand loaded to 3,650 fps in a 26-inch barrel. This load kills a buck or a coyote like a bolt of lightning.

The .224 TTH is a "wildcat" cartridge that has to be hand loaded, and comes from a 6mm case necked down to .224 with 46.5 grains of RL22 and a Magnum primer. It is a typical example of a small, well-designed bullet that can be shot with extreme accuracy, and Jimmy is deadly with it. The key to his success with the fast, small bullet is exact bullet placement and extreme hydrostatic shock.

The late Tommy Kaye didn't shoot rifles in the off-season as much as the rest of us. But he loved good rifles, and was a world-class engraver of firearms. He had all kinds of fine rifles, mostly Model 70 Winchesters, custom engraved, and stocked with the finest walnut. But he hunted with a factory Winchester Model 70 featherweight in .270 with 130-grain bullets.

Jimmy Gallagher and Horace Gore with a King Ranch "Blue Bull" nilgai.

Tommy killed some good bucks with that rifle, but he used more ammo to get his deer than we did! I remember one hunt when the four of us were cruising a ranch road and jumped a trophy buck close to the truck. Tommy jumped out and took a quick shot at about 25 yards. He missed the buck because he had his 3-9x Leupold on 9 power, and all he could see was hair at 25 yards. Al yelled, "You missed him, Tommy. Kill him again!"

The buck stopped in some thick brush about 75 yards away, and Tommy adjusted the scope to 4 power and put him on the ground with a shot just where the neck and shoulders met. This well-placed shot did a quick job on the buck, which turned out to be a 10-point with a 5-inch drop tine. The moral of this story is to keep your variable scope on low power until you need more, and you seldom get a second chance at a missed buck.

My hunts with our foursome have involved several rifles. I killed both bucks and does with my .224 TTH, but I also used a custom .300 Weatherby, a favorite .270 Model 70 custom engraved by Tommy, a custom .284 Winchester on a short Mauser action made by P.O. Ackley, and a Ruger single shot in .22-250 engraved and stocked by the master, Tommy Kaye.

I wasn't as hard to please as Al and Tommy, and Jimmy seldom killed a buck on our hunts unless it was a Muy Grande! I liked big eight points, which are easier to find than big 10s or Grandes, so I usually scored on a good buck, even when they couldn't salve their childish egos!

I've already commented on the .224 TTH and its ability to kill animals up to 300 pounds with instant fury. On occasion, a bull elk or an aoudad ram has bit the dust from the .224 and the 75-grain Scirocco bullet at 3,650 fps.

My opinion, after several years and many deer, hogs, pronghorns and exotics, is that the small, fast bullet sheds a tremendous amount of hydrostatic shock, which downs the animal instantly. Quite often, an animal that is not hit in a vital area (heart or lungs) will lay on the ground for a time, not able to get up, and will eventually expire.

Whitetails and mule deer are not hard to kill. They are small, with a thin skin and usually react favorably to a well-placed bullet in the front third of the body. Head shots should be avoided because they present a small target that can be hit without putting the animal down. The same is true with neck shots because a bullet can penetrate the meat of the neck and not bring the animal down unless the neck vertebrae are hit.

A good area for a fatal shot is the base of the neck where it comes to the shoulder. The target is large, and the animal will go down quickly. However, this is a shot that should be restricted to less than 150 yards.

The best shot on an animal (except the nilgai antelope) is directly behind the shoulder midway between the backbone and brisket. This is the lung area, with a radius of about six inches. It is a deadly shot, but the animal may travel a few yards while the lungs fill with blood. The blood trail is usually easy to follow, and the animal will be dead.

Nilgai lungs are between the shoulders, rather than behind the shoulders like a deer. A good lung shot on nilgai requires a direct shoulder shot with a heavy bullet that will break bone, such as 180 grains bullets in a .30 caliber Magnum.

The only time a shot should be taken through the ribs is when an animal is standing at a slant away from you. An angling shot from the back rib up through the lungs to the off-shoulder will be good. The same is true if an animal is facing you at an angle. A shot through the shoulder angling back through the lungs and out through the last rib on the offside will be a good shot.

Where you shoot is more important than what you shoot. You're better off with a .243 than a 7mm Magnum if you can't accurately shoot the magnum. ALWAYS SHOOT THE RIFLE THAT YOU SHOOT BEST. A 100-grain bullet in the lungs is better than a 300-grain bullet in the belly!

Years ago, back between the "great wars," a rifleman and shooting author named Edward C. Crossman established a theory on what it takes to kill a whitetail that is as true today as it was in 1935. He argued that a fast expanding 100-grain bullet that maintains 1,000 foot-pounds of energy upon impact was adequate to kill a deer. During the last 60 years, I've shot a lot of deer with different bullets at velocities that delivered up to 3,000 foot-pounds of energy at 100 yards, and 1,000 foot-pounds up to 300 yards.

Since most deer in Texas are killed at less than 100 yards, many of the milder calibers such as .243, .250-3000 Savage, .257 Roberts, 7mm-08, and all of the new 6.5mm medium velocity cartridges, may be better choices than the hard-kicking Magnums. At 100 yards, the milder cartridges seem to kill a 200-pound animal as quick as a .300 Magnum, with half the recoil.

Do I have to tell you every time?" — *Goreism*

Almost anyone can accurately shoot a rifle with recoil ranging from the .243, 6.5 Creedmoor, 7mm-08, .25-06, to the.270 or .30-06, and they are excellent for deer-sized animals. The idea is to put the bul-let where you want it to hit with the first shot, and you won't need an elephant rifle that rattles your teeth every time you close your eyes and jerk the trigger! Practice makes perfect, and most hunters who enjoy shooting their rifles will practice more, and be better at making the first shot count!

CHAPTER 16

My Days with James A. Michener

I learned a lot from America's greatest novelist

The City of Austin, Texas, was buzzing with excitement in the summer of 1983 because James A. Michener, one of the world's most famous authors, was in town. To my knowledge, Michener was one the most famous persons to ever walk the streets of modern-day Austin.

James Michener had come to town to set up shop at the University of Texas to begin writing a novel about the state to commemorate the Texas Sesquicentennial. Gov. Bill Clements had promised Michener the use of all state archives and other history of Texas, with full cooperation from the university.

I was working for Texas Parks and Wildlife, in the Wildlife Division, as program leader of white-tailed deer. My previous work in wildlife was with wild turkey and bobwhite quail, but I prided myself that I knew quite a bit about all of the wildlife of Texas. I also was a hunter, and had spent time chasing pronghorn in New Mexico with a good friend, Nelson Franklin. Nelson was a retired naval officer, and worked as a financial advisor in one of the big Austin banks.

Sometime in July of 1983, my phone rang about 10 a.m., and it was Nelson calling from his office at the bank. "I'm sitting here talking to James Michener," he said. "Do you know who Michener is?" Of course an Aggie would know who James Michener was. I had read some of his long, historic, fictional novels, but that was about all. My favorite had been "Centennial" because it was a novel about the settling of Colorado and the West.

Michener had inquired about someone to help him with his writing about wildlife, because the history of Texas involves so much about hunting and the use of wildlife in everyday life. Nelson knew that I could fit Michener's need for a wildlife biologist, and so he called me.

"I want you to meet Mr. Michener, and he wants to meet you." Nelson said. "Can you come to my office about 2 p.m. I didn't know what to expect of Michener because I had never seen his picture anywhere. I was pleased to meet a tall, slender, clean-shaven gentleman in his mid-70s, dressed in khaki pants and plaid shirt, open collar and bolo, covered by an African bush jacket with a belt.

Nelson introduced us, and Michener got straight to the point. "Do you know anything about Texas wildlife?" he asked. I could see a glint in his eye, and realized that he was putting me on, and that Nelson had told him that I knew Texas wildlife.

"I'm going to be covering a big part of Texas from here to Brownwood, to Beaumont, and south to the King Ranch with you. Can you answer any question I have about deer, turkey, quail, and snakes," he asked. I didn't hesitate to say yes, and the rest of the conversation was about the state, its wildlife, and some of the places we would go to, and talk about. For me, it was a good day.

Since it was evident that I would spend some time with Michener, I immediately went to the Austin library and checked out everything I could find about the man. Considering my surprise about getting to meet him, I was even more surprised when I read a biography written by one of his longtime friends.

James Michener was an orphan, and was born in the early days of February 1907. Some say New York City; some say Doylestown, Pennsylvania. That is probably the only bits of truth that you will come by when reading biographies on his early life.

There is speculation that 34-year-old Mable Michener, the widow of Edwin J. Michener, was the baby's real mother, becoming pregnant out of wedlock, but there is no proof of this. However, Mable spent several months in New York, about the time she became James Michener's adoptive mother, and Young James became a resident of Doylestown. The poor widow made a living taking in laundry and sewing buttonholes in shirts.

Michener would never admit who he thought his real parents were. There were insinuations that his father was a local banker, but this was never proven. There's reason for this birth secrecy — neither woeful widow Michener, nor the father, would have gained from revealing the truth in that Pennsylvania community, and the truth is still unknown today.

The plot thickens: To hold face in the strait-laced Amish/Quaker town of Doylestown, and knowing that the police would call her, Mable may have left the baby at the station. If you read biographers who got all their information from Michener, it is obvious he told a story that salved his ego. I like the biography by an author who knew the early story about James Michener, and the Michener family. It sounded more reasonable and truthful, although it was fraught with mystery.

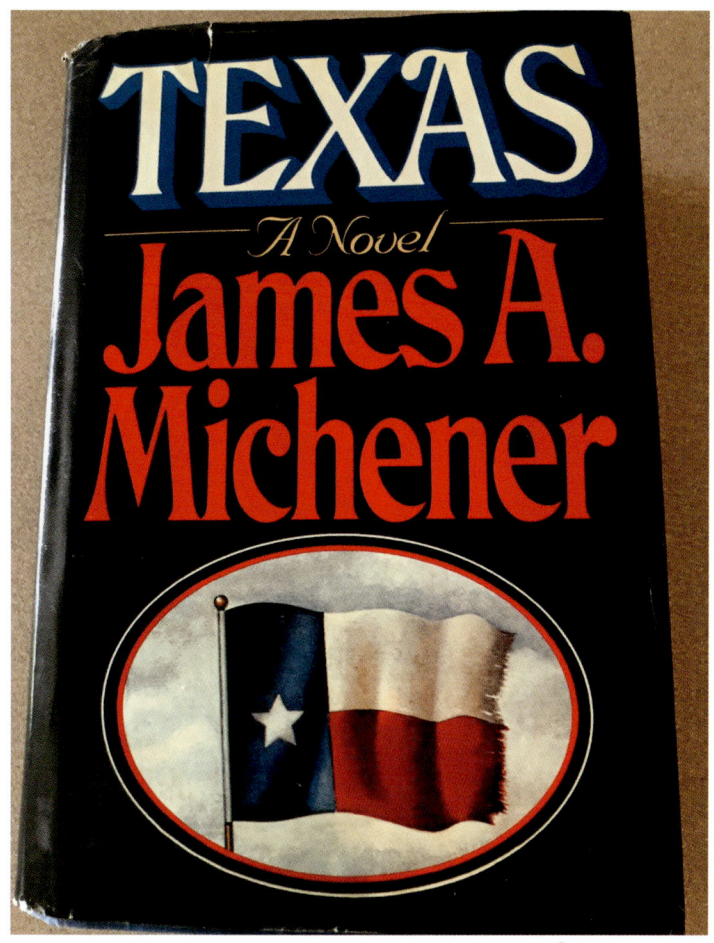

James A. Michener's 1,076-page "Texas," was published to coincide with The Sesquicentennial of Texas in 1986.

One morning in February 1907 a police sergeant almost stepped on a baby boy in a pasteboard box as he walked out the door of the station. He took the baby inside, and called Mrs. Michener, who he knew well. "Mrs. Michener, I hate to call you again, but I've got a baby here that someone left on our step. Can you take one more baby?"

Horace Gore with James A. Michener who was in Austin while writing his novel "Texas"

Mable Michener answered, "Sergeant, I don't know. I've already taken six, and I just don't know. Is it a boy or girl?" The sergeant replied that it was a boy, and Mrs. Michener agreed to take the baby, because all of the other six babies that she had taken in at her home were girls.

"I'll take him if you promise that you will never call me again with an orphan." The sergeant agreed, and she named the baby after her deceased uncle, James Albert Michener. The boy grew up in destitute poverty in Doylestown, Pennsylvania, graduated as a basketball star from Swarthmore College and became a world-renowned author and novelist.

All of his life, Jim Michener despised the way his mother was treated by the Michener family and the town of Doylestown. He never had a birth certificate. This caused Mable Michener some problems when James was drafted into the Navy during World War II, since there was no evidence of who he was. To get him into the Navy, Mable signed a sworn statement that James was her son, and that his father was Edwin Michener (who died five years before James was born).

On a trip to look at the Brazos River that his book character would have to cross in the 1820s, I was sitting in the back seat, while the student driver and Michener sat in the front. Michener insisted that I call him "Jim", and he called me "Horace" with a Pennsylvania twang.

On the road, we were killing time talking, and Jim leaned over from the front and asked, "Horace, how long have you worked for Parks and Wild-

> *"There is no excuse for ignorance."* — Goreism

life?" I told him, and he immediately asked, "Where were you born, and when's your birthday. I hear that you are a Texas Aggie?" I answered him, and after a few minutes, I asked, "Jim, when's your birthday?"

Michener was silent, and finally looked over at me and replied, "You've been doing your homework, haven't you? You know I don't know my birthday. History says February 3, 1907, but I don't know." I replied with a grin, "I thought I needed to know more about you, and I do."

At various times during the next 12 months, I either traveled around East, Central, or South Texas with Michener, or was on the phone or in correspondence with his chief assistant named King. We talked wildlife, plant vegetation, making jelly from mustang grapes, and if a cottonmouth moccasin bite was fatal! I remember King calling about a sentence Michener had used about wild turkey. "Turkey don't roost on the ground, do they?" he queried. I replied, "No. As soon as her poults can fly, the hen takes them to the tallest trees." King was satisfied.

I tried to get advice out of Michener about writing. He was pleased to make suggestions. "Always write to tell a good story, but try to educate your reader on the subject. Don't worry about grammar, spelling, or facts. Get your thoughts on paper. You can clean them up later. Use everyday language; don't make your reader carry a dictionary. If you're good at humor, use it, but not to excess. And go to great length to spell names correctly." I asked him about the length of his novels. "If you keep your readers interested, they will finish any length book."

Michener finished "Texas," his 1,076-page novel on the history of the state, on schedule, even though it contained some clerical and surname errors. The University of Texas threw a big "*pachanga*" in the chancellor's back yard, and hundreds of invited people attended the party celebrating "Texas" and the Sesquicentennial. We were there, and James Michener was all smiles with the many friends he had made since his arrival in Austin. I will always remember my days with James Albert Michener, one of the greatest writers of our time.

CHAPTER 17

The Unique American Pronghorn

The American pronghorn is one of the most unique ungulates in North America. Seventeen western states, including Texas, along with parts of Canada and Mexico have the world's pronghorn population. Ten states, Canada, and Mexico have seasons on the little "antelope" that is not an antelope at all. But hunters and landowners have referred to *Antelocarpra americana* as a pronghorn antelope, and the name has stuck.

Actually, the pronghorn is the only species of its kind, and its closest relative is the giraffe! They are physically made to run, and unlike a lot of animals that depend on camouflage for protection, the pronghorn stands out like a sore thumb, and depends on fleetness of foot to escape danger.

The American pronghorn is in a battle with habitat loss and predation. The Sonoran and Peninsular pronghorns of Mexico are on the endangered species list. However, the United States and Canadian populations are holding their own against farming, urban development, and predation from eagles and coyotes. Wyoming alone has some 400,000, and the total U.S. population is probably close to one million.

Pronghorn bucks are a prized trophy, high on the list of animals recognized by the Boone and Crockett Club. Minimum net score for a "book" trophy is 82 inches, and this score is not easy to come by. Of the 10-12 bucks that I have killed, only one came close — 80. Others scored around 77-78, which is a good pronghorn for most hunters.

The pronghorn is the only one of its species, and is unique because his horns develop from a glue-like substance mixed with long hairs, that form into bony sheaths with a forward prong. These sheaths drop off after breeding season is August and September, leaving a blade-like

A Texas Pronghorn

base on which new horns (sheaths) grow back each year, with the distinct prong.

Pronghorns have split hoofs, but no dewclaws, and they do not jump. Their stiff, brittle hair is hollow, and unlike deer, they have a gall bladder and chew their cud. Their color is quaint, with a white rump patch that can be readily seen at some distance. They are tawny in color, with white throat bands and a white belly. Bucks with 14- to 17-inch horns are considered fine trophies.

Texas has two pronghorn herds — West Texas and the Panhandle. The better pronghorns are taken from Hudspeth, Brewster, and adjoining counties in West Texas, and the counties nearest the New Mexico line in the Panhandle. The largest population of pronghorns east of the Pecos is on a large ranch in Irion County west of San Angelo. Predation takes a heavy toll on Texas pronghorns, and Hard Yellow disease from sheep is detrimental to growth and horn development.

Any good deer rifle works fine for pronghorns. Most shots are made between 200 and 400 yards, depending on the terrain. My closest buck was

40 yards as I crawled out of a long gully. My longest was probably close to 350 yards on the Rocker b Ranch in Irion County. Running shots at the swift pronghorn are difficult, to say the least!

Any rifle scope of 4-power is OK, but a variable on 6-8 power is better. Rifles like .243, 6mm, .270, .30-06 and the smaller Magnum calibers will take a pronghorn, post haste. I killed a wide-horned buck at about 300 yards with a .22-250 and 55-grain bullet on the Rocker b Ranch.

I recall a hunt on the Rocker b with a hunting *compadre* named Matt Martinez, Jr. Matt was a great hunter, and the son of Matt Sr. and Janie Martinez who founded Matt's El Rancho restaurant in Austin in 1952. As expected, Matt Jr. was a celebrated chef of Mexican cuisine, and his cooking and shooting a pronghorn with a pistol were memorable events of the hunt.

Matt and I were old dove-hunting buddies, and we got to the massive Rocker b Ranch west of San Angelo at sundown on a Friday. We camped at a windmill, and before dark, Matt had a pot of something delicious with flour tortillas. He put a lid on the pot, and the next three or four meals were out of that same pot, with other things added. For Sunday brunch, Matt pulled out two of the finest pre-cooked game hens I have ever eaten. It is nice to hunt with a prize-winning chef!

On the hunt, Matt carried a Colt Python .357 with 6-inch barrel and a small scope. I laughed when he pulled it out, because I had killed a few pronghorn with my rifles, and I figured he would go home empty handed. On Sunday morning, we spotted a lone buck near a hillside, and Matt decided to make a stalk. He ended the stalk by crawling on his belly to within 100 yards of the buck — a skittish 14-inch with good prongs that had probably been run off from the herd by another buck.

I watched through the binoculars as Matt lay prone on the ground. The buck was facing away as Matt took aim with the scoped pistol in both hands, and I heard the BOOM of the shot. The bullet grazed the pronghorn's rump and back, sending stiff, hollow hair 15 feet in the air. The bullet went on to hit the buck in the neck, dispatching him instantly. Everyone on the 172,000-acre ranch could hear us hooping and hollering over the shot. That was a hunt to remember!

I got my first pronghorn north of Roswell, New Mexico, in 1975. A nephew of the rancher gave me a landowner permit, and I went alone to the Martin Ranch and took a fine 14-inch heart-shaped trophy.

That hunt was the first of several with Charlie Martin, who grew up on the ranch and knew everything about pronghorns. I have also taken pronghorns in West Texas and in Wyoming while mule-deer hunting.

On my last hunt with Charlie Martin in New Mexico, we were in his pickup driving and glassing the open plains of the ranch, looking for a good trophy. Shortly after lunch, about 2 p.m., we were glassing the outlying terrain, when Charlie pointed in the direction of some far-away pronghorns. I aimed the binoculars in that direction, and picked up six white rear ends: a buck and five does.

"How far are they — a half-mile?" I asked Charlie. "Close to that; 600 to 800 yards," Charlie replied. "Do you want to go get that buck? He looks pretty good; the best I can tell." Charlie looked at me and my clothes. I wore nothing bright to spook the curious animals. Our hats could be discarded, as well as anything else we didn't need.

New Mexico game laws prohibit driving the open plains chasing pronghorns, which meant we would have to leave the truck and walk the long distance for a shot at the buck. "You mean, leave the truck and walk in the open close enough to get a shot?" I asked. I couldn't imagine covering all the open ground and getting that close to six pronghorn antelope! That would be 12 sharp eyes looking at us before we got close enough to shoot. I kept looking at the faraway buck — and he looked good.

Charlie smiled, "We can walk fast for about 400 yards, stop and sit for 3-4 minutes, then walk another 200-250 yards bent over, and sit some more. The last 100-150 yards will be duck-walking with no hats. Pronghorn antelope have a security zone of about 200 yards before they decide to run, and we are coyotes! Let's try it, and I'll show you how to stalk a pronghorn."

When we left the truck, I didn't have much faith in Charlie's plan. A pronghorn can count the buttons on your shirt at 300 yards, and I had no confidence we could get close enough for a shot with my .270 and 4-power Weaver. After about 400 yards of fast walking, we stopped and sat on the ground for a few minutes. Charlie glassed the animals, and we slowly crouch-walked for about 250 yards, and sat down again.

Charlie glassed the pronghorns again to detect if they were getting nervous. I glassed the group, which looked to be about 300 yards. "Take off your hat and leave your binoculars," Charlie said. "Swing your rifle around to your chest. We will crawl another 50 to 100 yards. Don't you look. I will tell you when to shoot."

Charlie and I left our binocs in our hats, I got to my hands and knees — good thing I had gloves — with the rifle slung under my chest, as I followed behind Charlie for a short distance. We stopped, and while we laid on the ground, Charlie glanced at the buck. "He's getting nervous," Charlie whispered.

The buck looked to be about 200 yards, and when I took aim with the .270 the tall grama grass covered my scope. "I can't get a shot for the grass," I whispered, and Charlie turned around on the ground so I could take a rest from his back, but it wasn't good. "Come up on my butt," Charlie whispered. The scope was now clear enough, with the crosshairs behind the buck's shoulder, as I squeezed the trigger. The .270 roared, and I could see the does running.

"Where is the buck? "I was still on the ground, but Charlie was standing. "He's down." I stood up, and Charlie said "Go take a look. I'll get our hats and things."

I walked up to a good 15-inch pronghorn, admiring the horns and prongs. By that time, Charlie was back, and asked, "Where did you hit him?" I was looking for the bullet hole when Charlie remarked, "No wonder he fell so quick. You hit him in the head!"

"In the head? I aimed behind the shoulder." Charlie grinned and replied, "Well, you didn't do bad — you just missed your mark by about 20 inches." I was thinking, "Dang grama grass!" We left my rifle with the buck and walked the long distance back to the truck. When we got there, I looked at my watch — 5 p.m.

Charlie drove the truck to the pronghorn, and when we got back to camp, the ranch hands ribbed me about shooting the buck in the head. After they had salved their amusement, I said, "Well fellows, I have  just been on the longest pronghorn stalk in New Mexico history." They laughed and we bragged on Charlie for his guiding ability. Charlie pushed back his Stetson and smiled. "It was nothing. You just need to know your antelope." And Charlie Martin knows his pronghorn antelope!

CHAPTER 18

From Wyoming to Argentina: Hunting Two Americas

My grandmother bought me a single-shot .22 rifle from our Sears-Roebuck catalogue in 1945, and I killed my first cottontail when I was 12 years old. The "flat woods" of Bowie County in northeast Texas had only a few species of small game, but I stayed in the woods a lot. Through my teen years, I hunted quail, doves, ducks, squirrels, bull frogs and varmints. Later on, I hunted from the Rocky Mountains of Wyoming and Utah, to Argentina's Patagonia, including Texas, New Mexico, Utah, Oklahoma, Louisiana, Colorado, Florida and Mexico.

My first white-tailed buck came in 1958, while attending Texas A&M, majoring in wildlife science. I drove a county school bus, and one of the school kids was a boy whose grandmother owned 10 acres near the Navasota River. He invited me to go deer hunting with him if I would loan him a deer rifle. I hunted with a war-relic .30-06, and killed a yearling buck with antlers that would fit snuggly into a feed store cap, but it was the first of many whitetails.

Upon graduation from Texas A&M, I worked for the Game and Fish Commission, later known as the Texas Parks and Wildlife Department, with principal species of deer, quail and doves. Over a 30-year period, I was fortunate to be able to hunt some of the best bobwhite quail country in Texas, and also the very best in mourning dove hunting, all between Laredo and the Red River.

Out of about 40 or 50 whitetails from Texas and Mexico, I consider at least 10 to be good trophies. Two stand out in my mind: a "perfect" 10-point from Brown County, and a 30-inch eight-point from San

Patricio County. Two of the bucks had a long drop tine, and a majority were big eight-points because I like a good, clean eight-point. Four of the biggest eight pointers (150-plus B&C) were taken with Marty Berry of Corpus Christi.

One hunt in Mexico was memorable because the deer was a Carmen Mountain whitetail. This diminutive life-zone subspecies occurs in mountain ranges in far Southwest Texas, into the Sierra Del Carmen of Coahuila, Mexico. Most are seen at elevations of 4,000 to 7,000 feet, and readily mix with mule deer. They characteristically are small (bucks 100 pounds), with gray pelt, big ears and long tail. Their antlers are small (100 to 120 B&C) and are mostly eight typical points.

Through the years, I was fortunate to get to hunt mule deer in Colorado, Utah, Wyoming, and Texas. Five bucks were taken in the Bighorn Mountains Northwest of Kaycee. Wyoming. I took one good buck in Utah while on an invite hunt with Al Brothers and the Zachry boys, Bartel and Jimmy. Another good 13-point muley came from a hunt

Horace Gore and a landowner with Texas Panhandle mule deer.

Horace Gore with a big Colorado bull elk.

with the same friends in Colorado, near Eagle. My widest mule deer came from the sand hills between Lubbock and Littlefield on an irrigated potato farm, while filming a TTHA television show with Brian Hawkins.

I'm not an elk hunter, per se, but I have killed two bulls and that many cows on hunts in Wyoming, Utah and Colorado. I killed a young bull with a .270 while mule-deer hunting in the Bighorn Mountains south of Buffalo, Wyoming. The other bull, a monster 340 B&C was taken in the Black Canyon of the Gunnison near Crawford, Colorado. The cows were killed for meat in Utah on the J-B Ranch while hunting with Al Brothers and the Zachry brothers, Jimmy and Bartel.

I have always loved the wide open, spot and stalk hunting style of chasing pronghorns. Some 17 states in the American West have all the pronghorns in the world. I've hunted them in Texas, New Mexico, and Wyoming, taking my best near Marfa, Texas and my smallest north of Kaycee, Wyoming while on a mule deer hunt.

There is a lot of talk about long shots at pronghorns, but of my 11, the longest shot was 300 yards and the shortest was 50 yards. My best pronghorn was spotted on the Bar-lite Ranch near Marfa, but Al Brothers and I passed him up the first day because he was high, but narrow. The next day the weather got bad, so we went back and found him again — a good pronghorn at 80 B&C.

Texas is famous for its exotic game animals. Such species as blackbuck antelope, axis deer, aoudad, and nilgai are sporting exotics. I have hunted aoudad, nilgai, and axis deer. My aoudad came from Zachry's Rancho Blanca South of Laredo. The axis does were killed for meat in the Hill Country. The nilgai came from the Norias Division of the King Ranch.

The spotted axis is a fine trophy, and so is a 30-inch aoudad. Nilgai are big and sporting to hunt, but as a trophy, they are not much. For eating, I would rate nilgai, axis, blackbuck (back straps), whitetail, aoudad ewe, mule deer and elk, in that order.

This is a good place to talk about South America, and my experiences with dove and red-stag hunting. I was invited (expenses paid) to Argentina in 1997 to recommend management and hunting practices for eared dove on the Pampas and red deer in Patagonia.

A rutting red stag in the Patagonia of Argentina

The excursion lasted one month, and I was a part of both dove hunting in the North, and red-stag hunting in the South. If you're interested, Pampas means "brushy, treeless plain." Patagonia means "Big Foot," from the brush sandals worn by the native Indians in the 16th century, when the country was first settled by the Jesuits.

Both hunts were extraordinary — flight corridors of 1,000 eared doves per minute on the Pampas brush, and red deer as thick as fleas on a hound in the rangelands of Patagonia, near San Martin. At that time, Argentina was just getting into dove hunting, which has developed into big business for ranchers on the Pampas. Red-stag hunting in Argentina was already famous in Europe, and the trophy stags are equal to those in New Zealand.

A morning of dove hunting might consume 8-12 boxes of shells per hunter, and include a fancy steak lunch with wine, in the brush. There was no bag limit, and two hunters might kill 400-600 birds per day, along with several wild pigeons. The eared doves, similar to mourning doves, but with a square tail, came over in flights that never ended, between the thick brush north of Cordoba and the grain fields about 60 miles to the east.

Most of the Pampas was "open range" for yoked hogs, and some older sows were smart to dove hunting. If a dove fell anywhere close to a hog, the bird boys had to beat the hogs to the dove. I watched hogs eat doves — they pushed the dove on its back, and took the whole breast in one bite.

Red deer in Patagonia were stocked in the late 1800s, with no natural controls. Hunting from the European countries has become popular, but red deer compete directly with cattle, and are a serious problem to ranchers near San Martin. Patagonia has large hunting and fishing camps that serve a brisk European market.

I spent the last two weeks of my trip on a 30,000-acre ranch in Patagonia, evaluating the needs for red-deer management. The landowner insisted that I kill a stag, and furnished a .300 Weatherby and shells, along with a German guide that spoke no English. The guide was hired annually by the ranch to kill as many hinds (females) as he could in a two-month period. The meat was saved and the ears of each hind were turned in to authorities.

We hunted on foot one frosty morning in April, seeing two top-dollar stags, but they were too good for a visitor. The guide finally pointed out an old stag on a high ridge at about 250 yards. The 350-pound stag was no match for the .300 Weatherby, and we took the meat and the ears to turn in. The stag had good antlers, and the rancher said that he would ship them to me at Gonzales, but ...

The Americas have a variety of game birds and animals, and you can see that I had a full plate hunting both in North and South America.

CHAPTER 19

Texotics

Texas has a variety of exotic game animals

Texas has the most exotic ungulate animals of any state. Ranch size, climate, and in some cases game-proof fences have attributed to the success of vast numbers of animals from foreign places. The trend started back in the '30s when the Schreiners brought exotic animals to the Y.O. Ranch in Kerr County. The large ranch was high fenced, and a variety of exotic ungulates were stocked on the arid, rugged terrain for hunting purposes. The most popular were the axis deer, blackbuck antelope, and aoudad, although there were numerous other exotics to be hunted for a price.

The King Ranch in South Texas brought nilgai antelope by rail from the San Diego Zoo in 1926 and turned about 30 loose on the Norias Division. The first animals simply vanished when released, but a second group of animals was held in a pen for several days before a quiet release, and they succeeded in establishing a large herd of nilgai on the ranch. It is estimated that some 15,000-20,000 nilgai roam the King Ranch and adjacent ranches north of Raymondville.

Many ranches have exotics for aesthetic values. Some are the scimitar oryx, Japanese sika, red stag, mouflon and barbado sheep, and gemsbok, to name a few. If you look close you may even see zebra, giraffe, water buffalo, rhino, or an occasional ostrich.

Exotic hunting became very popular in the '60s when several ranches in the Hill Country advertised hunts — especially the Y.O. and adjacent ranches. At first, axis, sika, and blackbuck were the most popular, but through the years, aoudad and axis have ruled. Nilgai hunting became popular on the King Ranch, and continues to provide good "blue bull" hunting today. Other ranches in the Wild Horse Desert obtained nilgai, and now a large number of ranches hunt the Indian exotic.

Although I have friends who have hunted several species of exotics, my hunting has been limited to nilgai, aoudad, sika, axis doe, and eland cow. I have never hunted axis bucks or blackbucks, but I have been on many hunts to kill a variety of exotics — some for trophies, and some for meat. Axis and nilgai are exceptionally good eating, as is the eland.

Most exotics can be taken with a good deer rifle, with exception of nilgai and eland. The "blue bulls" take a lot of lead because of their size, and the lungs are between the shoulders. A good lung shot must go through the shoulder bones, and this requires a big, fast bullet from a .300 Win. Mag, .300 Weatherby, or even a .375 H&H Rifles like the .270, .30-06, and smaller are not recommended for nilgai bulls.

I've been with Jimmy Gallagher, Tommy Kaye and Mick Hellickson on the King Ranch, as we chased some big nilgai antelope. Jimmy got a good bull at a water hole, and Tommy killed a young bull out of a group of four that were in a hard run. Tommy aimed at the lead bull, and killed the last bull in the chase, causing a cloud of dust as the bull tumbled to the ground. Jimmy and Tommy were both shooting .375s, and got clean kills on both bulls. I was along for the ride!

King Ranch "Blue Bull" nilgai

Jason Shipman's axis buck.

Jimmy's bull had 8-inch horns, rather standard for King Ranch. Tommy's young bull had shorter horns and ended up in Tommy's freezer. Although Jimmy had killed three or four blue bulls, this was Tommy's only nilgai. The "blue bulls" make good mounts, but the short horns are not impressive.

My lone nilgai bull was taken with a .30-06 Model 70 Super Grade, with handloaded 165-grain Nosler partition bullets. We had been stalking nilgai on King Ranch, and found one hiding in the brush about 75 yards away that fell quickly from a neck/shoulder shot. I didn't anticipate hunting nilgai on the trip, or I would probably have taken a bigger rifle.

I was hunting nilgai with a local game warden, and we were looking for a cow for meat. The old bull had a broken horn, and didn't qualify as a trophy, but the meat was good. On two other occasions I managed to get a nilgai cow for the freezer.

My eland antelope hunting is as thin as nilgai. I was invited to hunt a cow eland on the Comanche Ranch near Eagle Pass some years ago. I was visiting the ranch on other business when the owner, Dan Friedkin, handed me a .300 Rem. Mag. rifle and sent me out with a guide.

We found a big cow eland across a wide viaduct that carried water through the ranch. I shot across the waterway and killed the cow, but we couldn't get to her with the pickup. We returned to ranch headquarters and borrowed a ranch helicopter and pilot to lift the eland out of the brush and to a waiting truck. The cow probably weighed 600 pounds, and had 30-inch horns. There is a lot of meat on an eland, and it is delicious.

My aoudad hunting has involved one big ram and two or three ewes. All were killed on Zachry's Rancho Blanca south of Laredo. Al Brothers managed the ranch, and was cleaning a thousand-acre pasture of exotics to improve the whitetail herd. He invited me down to shoot whatever exotics I could find, and I took my .257 Weatherby for the hunt.

Al and I found a sika buck walking the high fence, and I gave him the *coup de grace*. The old buck was rutting, and I smelled him before we got to him. I took the antlers and some backstrap, along with a hindquarter. I later cooked some hindquarter as a roast, and I couldn't eat it. I gave it to my black Lab, but she wouldn't eat it. An old rutting sika won't pass the smell test. However, the backstrap was tolerable, and I put the antlers on a plaque.

While on the ranch, I hunted three days for an old aoudad. Al put me in a spot near an old wooden feeder, and I sat morning and evening waiting for a chance at the old "ram." Late on the third evening, I was sitting on the ground against some brush, when he finally showed. Like a ghost, he simply stood by the feeder — coming in from nowhere. I carefully put the crosshairs on him at about 80 yards, and squeezed the trigger of the Weatherby. The 117-grain Hornady hit him behind the shoulder, and he collapsed. I went to the trashing aoudad, as he kicked up a cloud of dust. I pulled my knife and stuck him — it was over. Aoudads are tough and hard to kill, as I found out!

The old aoudad had 30-inch horns, which were considered to be trophy size. I took the horns and gave the meat to the ranch hands for tamales. Later, I killed a yearling ewe for meat, and I was surprised how good a female aoudad can be as bacon wraps and fried backstrap. Like all ungulates, the females are always the best for eating, and I never turned down a hunt for an aoudad ewe.

Horace Gore, Charles Schreiner III, and John Jefferson talk exotics on the YO Ranch in 1999.

In my wildlife biologist days, we often had a project going in the Hill Country, and we would sometimes find a place to kill an axis doe. We would cook the meat in a variety of ways — bacon wrapped, fried, BBQ, or even a roast. The only exotics better than axis are nilgai and eland, and all are delicious!

I always planned to hunt a 30-plus-inch axis buck, but never did. And, for some reason I never cared to take a blackbuck, although the little antelope makes a good trophy. The old aoudad's horns decorated my trophy table at the Kokernot Ranch for many years, along with a big bull elk, the stinky sika buck, an 80-inch pronghorn, and about 20 or more trophy whitetail and mule deer bucks that gave me some good hunting thrills through the years.

CHAPTER 20

Dogs and Doves

Good dogs make good hunts

Dove and duck seasons are an exciting time! It's time to get out the shotguns, check the ammo and equipment, and get ready for the first hunts of the fall season. Most good retrieving dogs can tell when you start to get ready for the hunt, and they keep a close eye on you.

Dove hunting is a major sport in Texas, and on the first day of September, by U.S., Mexico and Canada Treaty, about 250,000 nimrods hit the fields and water holes in the North Zone to shoot one of the fastest flying targets in the hunting world. They are joined by the hordes of dove hunters in the South Zone in mid-September to make up a total Texas dove-hunting fraternity estimated at 400,000.

Come rain or shine, dove hunters hit the fields in September and October to test their skills at one of the fastest and hard to hit game birds between Amarillo and Brownsville. Anyone who can take home a limit of doves won't have any problem with Texas' other game birds. After the first few days of shooting, doves get tricky and hard to hit. The most ardent hunters may use a little .410, but the average hunter will be toting a 20-gauge.

These hunters will burn 2 million gallons of gas, fire 20 million or more shotgun shells, drink thousands of Lone Star longnecks, and bring home about 5-6 million doves. They will fry, broil, stew, bake and BBQ doves to the delight of their guests, and when it's over, the world of dove hunters and their dogs will simply wait for next year.

I began dove hunting in Bowie County when I was about 14 years old. I hunted at 12 with my .22, but I didn't get into shotguns until I got a bird dog. East Texas is not the best for doves — not enough crops or wild-seed items that doves like, but we had a few come to the weeds at the Hooks City Dump, just 2 miles North of Hooks. Jerry Barrow and I hunted the dump for doves, crows, and whatever else was there. I saw my first ever jackrabbit at the dump in about 1947.

Guadalupe Belle, Horace Gore's black Lab retriever.

After my days in high school, I worked around Hooks until the army in 1954, and later, Texarkana Junior College and Texas A&M. I got into dove hunting in a big way while attending A&M because the College Station area had a lot of doves. My college buddies — Al Brothers, Don Frels, George Litton, Bill Tutor and I got in some good pass shooting on mourning doves. I was shooting my Browning "Sweet 16" gauge auto with full choke barrel.

After graduation and a new job at Mineral Wells and later at Brownwood, dove hunting really got to be a big deal. I hunted water holes on local ranches near Brownwood, and the sheep country of Mills County. Some of the best dove hunting in the state was in Mills as a result of the close grazing of sheep that produced vast pastures of dove weed (croton) and sunflower. I had switched to a 20-gauge over/under with improve and modified barrels.

When I was younger, my dogs were all pointers or setters for quail. I didn't use a retriever for doves or ducks until I moved to the Kokernot Ranch in Gonzales County in 1995. My friend, Dean Davis, who was ag teacher in Gonzales, gave me a black female Lab pup. I named her

"Guadalupe Belle" and trained her to retrieve birds and trail wounded deer and hogs.

Belle turned out to be one of the best dogs I ever owned! She spoiled me, and today, I wouldn't hunt doves or ducks or hogs without a good dog. After Belle, I had another black lab female named Lucy, and she was also an excellent retriever. I seldom got off my dove-hunting stool — the dogs brought the doves and put them in my hand.

I recall an occasion when a high-dollar outfit near Hondo invited me out for a weekend of dove hunting and after-hour frolic. I told them I would bring Belle, and they told me that dogs were not allowed. I sent them word back that I would not attend. By that time, I had discovered that a dove hunt was not a hunt without my dog.

Both Belle and Lucy were excellent retrievers, but Belle had something extra in the way she could follow a crippled dove or duck for quite a distance and bring it back. On many hunts, she would watch a crippled bird as it flew away on the wind, and follow it until it fell. I'm sure she was watching the bird better than I was, and her nose took her to the bird. Whatever. She was fantastic at retrieving crippled birds.

Doc Denman of Gonzales and I hunted doves and waterfowl quite a bit. We were hunting geese near Eagle Lake, with our two dogs. A gaggle of snow geese came over, and we knocked out three, but one crippled bird continued to fly about a quarter mile before it fell. The area had an open visibility, and Belle was watching the goose all the way, as she went to the bird. A while later, she came back carrying the

Bobby Schmidt's dove hunt, Creedmoor, Texas

Bobby Schmidt and Horace Gore chat at the annual dove hunt, Creedmoor, Texas

goose by the neck. Doc remarked, "You've got a pretty good dog." I just smiled.

Dogs learn to watch fallen birds if they are trained to do so. I always kept my young dogs on a 10-foot nylon cord, tied to my leg as I sat on the dove stool. I didn't want the dog to go after the bird until it hit the ground. When the bird was retrieved, I could bring the dog to me with the cord. As time goes by, the dog will learn to watch the bird and keep an eye on it. That makes a better retriever that can follow a bird that falls some distance away.

Dogs are not only good for retrieving, but some make good deer- and hog-trailing dogs. Belle was very good at trailing wounded game, but Lucy was strictly a bird retriever. I became quite popular on the Kokernot Ranch when I used Belle to find several wounded deer and hogs for the Denman family!

When looking for wounded game, I would put a small, but loud bell on Belle's collar, which helped me find her when she found the deer or hog. If there was any life left in the animal, Belle would bark to high heaven, but if dead, she just chewed on the flank. The bell always brought me to the dog — and the wounded or dead animal.

> *"A young man looks for a good wife, when he should be looking for a good dog."* — *Goreism*

All good retrievers are not retrieving breeds. I've seen a Doberman that was a good dove dog. I had a friend in Gonzales that had a toy terrier that brought him doves. I suppose that any dog can be trained to retrieve birds, but no dog is so staunch at retrieving as a Labrador retriever. If you hunt doves and want a good dog, I recommend a Lab. Your hunts will be much more memorable, and you will lose less birds, I guarantee!

PS: Take these tips about training your dog:

1. Never hit your dog. If you want to get its attention, scold it, or pinch its ear.
2. Don't interfere with fighting dogs. Excited dogs will bite YOU!
3. Leave the kids at home when you are training a dog.
4. The more good relationships you have with a dog, the more they respond to your training.
5. Remember, training is repetition and excitement for the dog — quit while the dog is still excited.
6. Don't interfere or do harm to a dog while it is retrieving or trailing wounded game. Let the dog do its work without interruption. Interference will confuse the dog.

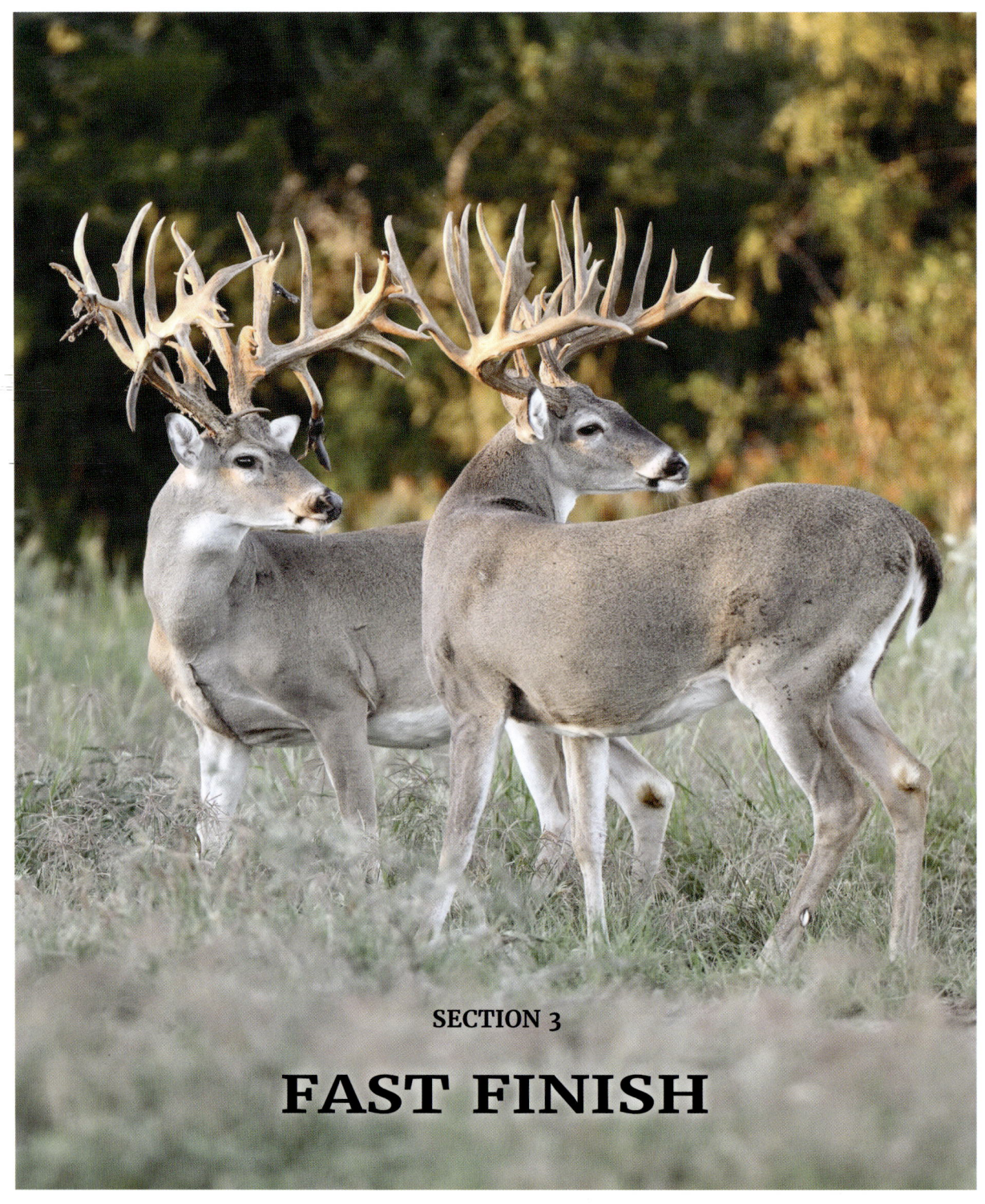

SECTION 3

FAST FINISH

CHAPTER 21

22 Years On the Kokernot

Leaving Austin

In September 1993, I retired from Texas Parks and Wildlife after 33 years in the Wildlife Division. I had been in the Austin office since 1972, and lived on the south side of town near the headquarters office when I retired.

Roy Wilson, who had a hunting camp on the Hendrick Ranch, a 30,000-acre spread along the Clear Fork of the Brazos in Shackelford and Throckmorton counties, had contacted me about guiding quail hunters and working at the camp after I retired. I had some good bird dogs and plenty of time, so I went to Roy's Crooked River hunting camp for two winters.

The Kokernot Ranch Deal

Sometime in July 1995, I got a phone call from my good friend and hunting partner, Al Brothers. He wanted to know if I could come down to Gonzales County and visit with him and Dr. Brian "Doc" Denman on the Kokernot Ranch. Doc was planning to lease the 2,200-acre ranch to deer hunters, and wanted some professional advice. I agreed to come, and the next week I was on the ranch.

I was familiar with the Kokernot because my close friends Al and Dorothy Springs had a nice ranch just up the road from the Kokernot, and I had been to Al's place and hunted quail and squirrels many times. I had also met Dr. Denman a few years before when I sold him a good bird dog.

Kokernot ranch house, 1997

I left the pavement of East Highway 90 about 9 a.m., and took the gravel road four miles to the Kokernot ranch house, where the road ended. Dr. Denman and Al were waiting, and we immediately went toward the Guadalupe River bottom and toured the ranch as we talked about Doc's intentions to lease the ranch for hunting. The two hunters from Austin planned to bring a double-wide to a camp site in the Hog Pasture on the river, and lease the ranch for deer, turkey and hogs.

Doc was interested in getting doe deer permits for the hunters, and he knew that I could handle the paperwork and do the deer census. We ate barbecue on the tailgate, and started out of the bottom and back to the ranch house, which was on the highest point of the ranch west of Peach Creek. The creek was a spring-fed water source that began near Bastrop and traversed the countryside down to Gonzales County, through the Kokernot and into the Guadalupe River that was the southern boundary.

"Are you going to let the hunters use the ranch house?" I asked Doc. "Oh, no," Doc said. "Baby (Mrs. Denman) wouldn't allow it. She has too many antiques and furniture in her father's house."

Ruth "Baby" Kokernot Denman was the daughter of Fred Kokernot, who had owned the ranch until his death, and had willed the place to Ruth and her brother, Fred, Jr. Although Doc ran the ranch, Baby was the boss when it came to the big decisions. Her brother had sold his partnership to his sister and moved to Cuero many years before.

"Well, it's a shame to let the house just sit there, not being used," I said, and immediately knew that I had said the wrong thing. Doc stopped the truck and looked hard at me. "If you're so concerned about the house being vacant, why don't you move in yourself."

"You mean, me move in and live here?" I questioned. Doc replied, "If you want to, move in. I know Baby will approve, and we need someone like you on the ranch." I didn't know what to say — I hadn't even thought of leaving Austin.

As we pulled up at the house, I asked Doc if I could have a drink of water. This was important, because I was well aware of the poor water quality in that area of Gonzales County. It had so much sulphur and iron that you couldn't drink it or take a shower without holding your breath.

Doc took me to the kitchen where I got a glass of water from the sink faucet. At first, I sipped a little and waited for the taste. It was good. I drank the glass of water, and suggested to Doc that he let me think about the move for a few days.

I needed to tell Roy Wilson I would not be coming to Crooked River, and give my landlord notice of my move. Doc agreed, and I left the ranch with the intent of moving in on September 1.

Al Brothers and I left the ranch about 4 p.m., and while we were on the gravel road, he honked his horn and I knew that he wanted to talk. I pulled over and went back to see what he wanted. "Gore, you must be living right," Al remarked as I leaned on his truck door. "Why do you say that?" I asked. "Well, Doc just asked you to move into the ranch house, and you'd be a fool not to move to the ranch."

Al knew the Denmans very well, because he was a distant relative. He claimed Doc was a great uncle by marriage (whatever marriage that is). As a child, and on through high school, Al and his twin brother David had lived just a stone throw from the Kokernot ranch house, on the adjacent ranch with their aunt and uncle. Al and I were close friends from our A&M days, and often hunted together.

I assured Al I was planning to move, and I went on back to Austin and informed every one of my intentions. There were a lot of things that I would have to do. I had some bird dogs, and I would need a good dog pen at the ranch. I also had two or three trailer loads of furniture that would have to be moved. The only utility I had to change to my name at Gonzales was electricity, because everything at the ranch was electric.

The Ranch House

I moved everything to the Kokernot ranch house on September 5, 1995. In a couple of weeks, I had a good chain-link dog pen. Doc gave me two nice doghouses for the pens, so I was set. A huge barn was near the house, and a big set of cattle pens with a joining barn were near the big barn. The pump house for the well water was just a few feet from the yard fence, and a small 10x10 "smoke house" was right behind the main house, where I kept a deep freeze and a lot of yard tools.

The ranch house was large, and had once had two porches. Through the years, the porches were converted to rooms. The house originally had two fireplaces, but during a renovation during the '50s, a third fireplace was built in the living room. I used it regularly in the winter, and often built a fire in another room that I called the "sunroom" because it had a lot of windows and faced the east.

The kitchen had a back door, and the side door entered the sunroom, which was the main door leading into the house. Although the house was large, it had only two bedrooms.

Moving In

Within a couple of months I had all the furniture arranged, and a TV antenna attached to one of the fireplace chimneys on the roof. The house was cozy for a hermit, but I doubt that a woman would have lived in it — no air conditioning and poor heat. I used the fireplaces all through the winter, and in summer I was in and out so much that I didn't need air conditioning.

I grew to love the old ranch house that was close to 100 years old, and had been used by the Kokernot family when on the ranch. They all lived in Gonzales, which was about 10 miles from the ranch. Fred Kokernot and the hired hands would stay on the ranch several days when they were working cattle or doing some farming. Some small houses that housed working families long ago were gone. The ranch had about two miles of Guadalupe River on the south end, and Peach Creek traversed the ranch and ran into the river.

The first Christmas after I moved in, I threw a big Christmas party and invited a large group, including the Denmans, my friends, and all the neighbors on the gravel road. It was my way of getting acquainted, and we all had a good time.

Hello, Gonzales County: The First Shot Of The Texas Revolution

Gonzales County is one of the most historic counties in Texas in that the townsfolk of the town of Gonzales fired the first shot of the Texas Revolution. On October 2, 1835, a company of Mexican dragoons came from San Antonio de Bexar to the Guadalupe river near Gonzales and sent a messenger to the town demanding the return of a 6-pound saddle cannon that had been loaned to the people in 1831 for protection against Indian raids. The people refused, and put the cannon on wheels and rolled it to the river.

The ladies of Gonzales had made a flag to drape over the cannon, which said in bold letters "Come and Take It." The citizens fired at the Mexican soldiers, severely wounding one. The soldiers fled back to San Antonio de Bexar, and the first shot of the revolution had been fired.

County History

Green DeWitt founded the town of Gonzales as the capital of his colony in 1825. Immediately after the Republic of Texas was formed, Gonzales County was the first county of the Republic, and the city of Gonzales had been named after Rafael Gonzales, Governor of Coahuila y Tejas, one of the constituent states of the newly established United Mexican States under its 1824 Constitution.

Gonzales is the County Seat of Gonzales County. The county population when I moved there in 1995 was about 18,000, with 65 percent being white and 35 percent Black and Hispanic. The county has always been heavily involved in the cattle industry, and in the days of the trail herds going north to the railroads in Kansas and Missouri, large herds of longhorn cattle were gathered in the river bottoms of the Guadalupe and San Marcos rivers in Gonzales County.

Large herds of longhorns were then trailed north on the Chisholm Trail. In a 15-year period, thousands of longhorns were trailed from Gonzales County, and several cattlemen in the county became rich. In fact, there are more colonial mansions in the town of Gonzales than any town of its size in Texas.

At one time, Gonzales County had more cattle than any other county in Texas. The county is also famous for its broiler chicken industry, and when I moved there in 1995, turkeys were also an important industry.

Gonzales, Texas

The town of Gonzales has some 8,000 residents who are cognizant of their Texas history, and celebrate "Come and Take It" each year on the Saturday nearest Oct 2. The city has a youth stock show each fall and in general, the town is "cowboy-ish" and very friendly.

Of course, I knew several people in the county from previous hunting and fishing trips to Peach Creek and the two rivers. I quail and dove hunted near Gonzales several times with Al Springs, a close Parks and Wildlife Department associate. His wife, Dorothy, inherited 800 acres that joins CR 345, a gravel road that ends at the Kokernot Ranch.

My close friend, Al Brothers, grew up in and around Gonzales, and I knew Wayne Spahn, the Denmans, and several others in the county through Brothers. It was a good place to live, even though I was 10 miles from Gonzales and 11 miles from Shiner.

Party Time in Gonzales

I always liked to party, and there were a lot of party times in Gonzales. The "'50s Rock and Roll" party each February was a blast. The "Come and Take It" celebration each October lasted through the weekend.

> *"Good judgment is cheap — so use it."* — Goreism

Occasionally, somebody would throw a party somewhere, and invite everyone.

I sponsored a fish fry each spring that brought 70-80 friends to the ranch. The first fish fry was for Jerry Johnston's birthday on May 25. I called it my $600 fish fry, because after buying the catfish, shrimp and oysters, renting the tables and chairs, and getting two toilets delivered, it probably cost more than $600. We were rained out one time, and had to move everything under the big hay barn that was near the river camp house.

Through the years, we had some good New Year's Eve parties. A big one occurred in 2000 at Jackie Williamson's (City Attorney) house. Practically everyone was there, and we had a happy time. Jackie had a hot tub on the porch, and several of us got in it at midnight. Rhonda Farrar was singing country songs, and Dean Davis was sparking a young lady from town. When a highway patrolman who was kin to Jackie left about 12:30, we all "let our hair down" and got a little rowdy!

Everyone was asked to bring something to eat or drink, and I took some high-dollar champagne. It was expensive because I bought three big bottles of $2.98 Sparkle, and changed the price tag to $29.98. They all drank it until it was gone, and said it was better than the cheap stuff. What could I say?

Gerald and Debbie Fougerat threw a New Year's Eve party in 2001, and we were all out in the yard at midnight, watching fireworks. Debbie is cute and quiet — she would hold a fart forever, if she thought someone would hear it.

Well, I was enjoying the New Year, and Debbie and Bubba Schmidt were standing close to me, and I blurted out, "I'd give $100 to see Debbie give Bubba a big Texas kiss — I mean a real lip lock." The words were hardly out of my mouth, when Debbie grabbed Bubba and pulled him to the ground, kissing him BIG all the way down. The fracas cost me a $100 bill, right out of my pocket! Debbie took the $100 bill and just smiled.

A problem with partying and drinking is that when you do it away from home, you have to get back home. I didn't have anyone to drive me back to the ranch, and on a couple of occasions, I was apprehended by the law before I could get back to CR 345. It was embarrassing, but I lived through it.

Jail Time in Gonzales

I'd like to say that I'm perfect, but that's not true. I challenged society a couple of times in Gonzales County, and lost. The first happened shortly after I moved to the Kokernot. Dean Davis and some of his friends threw a birthday party for one of the schoolteachers about two miles west of town. The party lasted until about 2 a.m., and I was driving back through town and to the ranch, when a city cop pulled me over. Of course, the law knew about the party, and was just waiting for us.

The city cop put me through the routine. He clamped the cuffs on me, and put me in his patrol car and hauled me to jail. Luckily, Jackie Williamson, the city attorney who knew me, and had been to the party, saw me being taken away, and followed the cop to the jail. She soon had me out of jail, before they could put me in a cell.

About 10 years later, I was planning to attend a wildlife meeting at Bubba Schmidt's house north of Little New York, just off the Moulton Road. I was going hog hunting after the meeting, and had on my old cut-offs (it was hot summer) and rubber boots. It was a big shindig, and about 9 p.m., I drove back to the Moulton Road. I had Belle in the truck bed, and was happy as a lark, headed for the hogs.

As I pulled out on the Moulton Road, a red light flashed, and a Highway Patrolman pulled me over. I suspect that he knew we were having a meeting (party) at Bubba's house, and was waiting for someone like me to leave. I was a little tight, but after eating barbecue and beans, I was feeling fine.

The officer got me out of the truck, and asked me to "blow," and I refused (Jackie Williamson told me never to blow for the law). Refusing to blow automatically puts you in jail in Gonzales, so I left the truck with Belle, and the patrolman took me to the new Jail. I called Bubba and told him to go get my truck and Belle.

I spent the night in the hoosegow, and the next morning Bubba brought my truck and dog to the jail. I was embarrassed, to say the least. I didn't care about society, but I was worried that the Denmans, who were pretty strait-laced, might run me off the Kokernot Ranch. I knew that they knew, but they never brought up the unlawful incident!

A few days later, my good Aggie friend, County Judge David Bird and I were eating lunch in the Taco Hut, when he looked at me and said, "Gore, you've got to be more careful with your partying. The law is watching every move you make."

"Every patrolman knows about all the parties and dances, and they know that you are usually alone driving your pickup, and they just wait for you." I assured David I would take his advice about driving from a party, and with the help of my friends, my days in jail were over. I didn't quit partying, but I was more careful about getting to CR 345, and home.

Donna Athey with big Kokernot Ranch whitetail

A Skeet Shooter

For 50 years, I was a skeet shooter. I shot my first skeet at a country skeet range near Bangs (west of Brownwood), where I lived for three years, before moving to Waco in the fall of 1965.

Waco and Austin both had good skeet ranges, and I reveled in shooting my Winchester model 42 pump .410. The skeet range in Waco, out toward the lake, was popular, and I shot regularly with Leo Bradshaw Sr., Leo Jr., Allie Lewis, Harley Berg, Texas Ranger Gaines de Graffenried, and a few others.

When I moved to Austin, I hooked up with some friends who shot skeet at the new club near Decker Lake, and each Wednesday and weekends were skeet shooting days. I shot my Winchester Model 42 .410 most of the time, but on occasion I would switch to a Model 12 skeet gun in 12-gauge, if I was challenged.

I shot the .410 pump gun so much that I broke the bolt, and searched for a year for a replacement. I finally found one, and Robert Bueltel installed it. Robert, in my opinion, is the best gunsmith in Texas!

On one of our Wednesday skeet shoots, hosted by Joe McBride, I was told that one of our deep-pocketed friends had just returned from England with a new Purdy double 12-gauge, one of the most expensive shotguns in the world.

I wanted to shoot the gun, and we arranged for a prestigious outing where I would wear a cowboy tux, alligator boots, and Stetson hat while shooting a round of skeet with the Purdy. The gun owner was my shell barer. The shoot was a hoot, and we all had a grand time. I broke 23 of 25 clay birds, and the light, expensive shotgun was very nice. However, I just couldn't see $65,000 worth of gun in the Purdy!

When I moved to Gonzales in 1995, I found that there were two places to shoot skeet. James Cowey had a private skeet range at his ranch near Smiley, and Wayne Spahn had built a skeet range on John Barfield's ranch just up from Gonzales on Highway 183. We had a large group of shooters who used both ranges, and Doc Denman and I shot quite often.

The Kokernot Ranch

The Kokernot Ranch in Gonzales County is all that is left of a large parcel of ranch land bought by David Lee Kokernot and his family around the Big Hill District of Gonzales County. He sold all of his property in Colorado county in 1853, and began buying land near Big hill (now called Kokernot Hill) in early 1854. Later, his relatives sold much of that land to Czech farmers in small parcels. The rest was divided by relatives through the years, and Ruth "Baby" Kokernot and her brother Fred Kokernot, Jr. inherited the 2,200-acre Kokernot Ranch.

Fred, Jr. deeded his half of the Kokernot to Ruth for money and moved to Cuero. When I moved to the ranch in 1995, it was leased for cattle, with about 225 head of mixed breed in a cow-calf operation. Before the oil boom in 2010, the Kokernot was one of the finest unspoiled ranches in that part of Texas.

A Shooting Bench

One of my first projects (other than a dog pen) was to set up a shooting bench. I had several rifles; I was a reloader, and I liked to shoot. I had said something about it to Wayne Spahn, who had a shooting bench at his house, and he said that he would help me put up a good, solid bench in the back yard. It was a good place to shoot and a bench in the yard would be handy.

Wayne came out to the ranch with a large, square concrete top for a bench, with concrete construction blocks to hold it up. I bought a tall stool to sit on, and it turned out to be a fine bench that lasted 20 years.

One of my favorite past times in the summer months was target shooting from the bench in the back yard. I reloaded ammunition for all of my rifles, and I was always experimenting with new loads, or powder, or bullets. After 20 years of shooting, the small deep freeze is used for targets had a hole big as a Stetson hat!

When Ralph Lermayer and I developed the wildcat .224 TTH in 2000, as a 25th Anniversary cartridge for Texas Trophy Hunters, I spent a lot of time and ammo finding out what bullets were best for game such as deer, hogs, and coyotes. I used my chronograph to check a lot of loads, and enjoyed shooting. Actually, I shot more shells in a year than most hunters shoot in a lifetime, and I must say — it made me a pretty good shot with a rifle!

Figs for Preserves; Grapes for Jelly and Wine

The next spring after I moved to the Kokernot, Doc Denman gave me four fig plants, and I planted them on each corner of the yard. Two were on poor soil and died. Another was girdled by rabbits, and died. The fourth, on the east side of the front yard, lived for 20 years, and produced a good crop of figs every year, except the nine-year drought from 2006 to 2015, when it died.

A large cedar elm in the yard also died and fell over. Records showed that 2011 was the driest year ever in Texas! Peach Creek quit running, age-old bur oaks in the upper bottom died and fell over. It was the driest time of my stay on the Kokernot.

When the fig bush would have an extra good crop, I would pick the fruit and make fig preserves. I had a good recipe, and made a lot of ½ pints of fig preserves.

The ranch had a lot of mustang grape vines, both in the uplands the edges of the river bottom. I picked a lot of grapes in the wet years and made half-pint jars of mustang grape jelly. Grapes, like figs, made good in wetter years, and you could hardly find any during drought. I gave a lot of grape and fig jelly and preserves to Donna and many friends.

Texas Trophy Hunters — Jerry calls

I had been on the Kokernot Ranch only a few weeks, when I got a phone call from Jerry Johnston, founder and president of Texas Trophy Hunters Association (TTHA). I had known Jerry a long time, and was in the group when he announced that he was going to start Texas Trophy Hunters in 1975.

Jerry knew that I had retired from Texas Parks and Wildlife, and he asked what I was doing. I told him that I had just moved to Gonzales County, and was living on the Kokernot Ranch. Then, he asked if I wanted to edit *The Journal* —the official magazine of Texas Trophy Hunters. I told Jerry that there was no way that I would move to San Antonio. He explained that I could edit *The Journal* from the ranch, and come to San Antonio as often as needed.

I thought it over a few days, and met with Jerry to figure out the details. I would be the editor of *The Journal*; help with the TV show, and run the deer contest at three Extravaganzas. I would live on the Kokernot, and go to San Antonio once or twice a week — all for a tidy sum.

That was 1995, and now, in 2024, under the umbrella of Safari Club International (SCI), I'm still editor of *The Journal*. I continue to do other things for TTHA, such as help with the three Extravaganzas in Fort Worth, Houston and San Antonio, and write for *The Journal* for a nice half-time salary. My time with Texas Trophy Hunters has turned out to be a second career.

Doc and Doves

I had been on the Kokernot for about a year when dove season opened in 1996. I soon found that Doc Denman liked to dove hunt, but the

> *"A farting mule never tires."* — Goreism

ranch had very few doves because it was mostly in the flood plain of the Guadalupe River, with little dove habitat or food sources. Both Doc and I wanted to hunt, and I suggested letting some water troughs run over and buying some milo or wheat "to feed the chickens." Doc agreed on the project to bring more doves around the house.

I went to E-bar Feed and bought a sack of wheat and began to "feed the chickens" at the front gate where a group of mesquite trees made a good place for doves. I also caused one of the water troughs to run over to provide water for the doves. Wheat is excellent for doves (and chickens) and is not noticeable on the ground like milo or corn chops.

On one hunt, we had a good bunch of doves, and Doc wanted to cook them. He invited me and a couple of his friends to our dove meal in his private kitchen at the rear of the palatial Denman residence in Gonzales. It was the first of many meals that Doc would cook in his kitchen, using game that we killed on our many hunts.

Ranch Vegetation

The 2,200-acre Kokernot Ranch is situated on the East side of Gonzales County, between S.H.90-A and the Guadalupe River. Peach Creek, which has its beginning near Bastrop, comes down through the countryside — through the center of the Kokernot, and empties into the Guadalupe River on the ranch. The spring-fed creek is important to the deer and turkey habitat, and is full of channel catfish and bass that have never seen a fishhook!

The creek banks are also home to a large oak, *Quercus sinuate*, which I called the "mystery oak" when I moved to the ranch, because I felt that it was a shin oak, but it was much too big and tall to be a shin oak. With the help of a good botany book and some friends, we found that it truly was a shin oak, and that it was tall because of the deep, rich soils along the creek bank.

I know a little bit about vegetation in Texas, and I soon learned that the Kokernot Ranch had trees, shrubs, and other vegetation that were mixed between East, South and Central Texas. The ranch had upland

and river bottom habitats, with the creek in between, and there were species of trees and understory that were native to Tyler, San Antonio, and Brownwood, Texas.

For example, there were four eastern red oak trees on the creek. The uplands had mesquite, Texas persimmon, live oak, post oak, red buckeye, Mexican buckeye, American elm, cedar elm, winged elm, eastern red cedar, mustang grape, blackjack oak, and a few pecan trees.

The creek had most of the trees and brush species that were on the uplands, plus red oak, Durand shin oak, pecan, saw briar, box elder, and red mulberry.

Ruth "Baby" Kokernot Denman and Horace Gore at ranch fish fry

The Guadalupe River bottom is dominated by pecan and hackberry trees. Along the riverbanks are cypress, cottonwood, sycamore, and pecan, and off into the bottom are scattered bur oak, hackberry, pecan, cedar elm, and some box elder, dogwood, and mulberry.

Many trees in the river bottom are draped with Spanish moss, and some have poison ivy, and Virginia creeper. Where cattle are absent, giant ragweed can grow to ten feet in wet years. The edges of the bottom have Osage orange, huisache, and honey locust (thorn tree), and small anaqua trees that have a summer fruit that draws squirrels from everywhere!

Vertebrates that show both east, south and western communities are the eastern swamp rabbit, cottontail rabbit, fox squirrel, eastern gray squirrel, cottonmouth moccasin, eastern flying squirrel, coyote, bobcat, sandhill crane, bald eagle, golden eagle, cattle egret, pileated woodpecker, wood ducks, Rio Grande turkey, peccary, canebrake rattlesnake, diamondback rattlesnake, broad banded copperhead and coral snake.

Russian (Eurasian) hogs had been introduced along the river by a neighbor, and the Kokernot Ranch had several hundred hogs, quite different from the spotted feral (domestic gone wild) hogs in other areas of the county. These black hogs could be vicious when hunted with dogs, and big boars were hard to stop in the chase.

Peach Creek

An all-weather spring fed creek runs the full north-south length of the Kokernot Ranch. The creek is navigable in wet weather from the Guadalupe River up to the only low-water crossing that is concrete headed by a 4-foot concrete dam.

Water flows over the dam and down onto the concrete driveway across the creek. Above the dam, the water is held back to a deep waterway, and below the dam the creek has shallows and deep holes in summer, and is a full navigable stream during the winter.

The creek banks are a natural travel lane for wildlife (deer, turkey, bobcats, coyotes and hogs) from the river bottom to the upper reaches of Peach Creek. All manner of fish use the creek, including channel catfish, bass, gar, humpback blue catfish, and numerous sunfish (to name a few).

Doc Denman and a friend set a trotline above the dam in a big hole of water in the 1970s and caught an alligator gar that weighed 98 pounds. During floods, fish can come all the way up the creek, so there can be fish of any kind and size.

During my 22 years on the ranch, I saw one small alligator sunning on the concrete dam in 1998. I killed two nutria on the creek in 2000, the only nutria I saw in all the years, and I saw one beaver at the confluence of the creek and the river. At that same spot, I saw an alligator gar that was about 6 feet long.

Fun Time on the Creek

The low-water crossing on Peach Creek was a good spot for fishing and fun time on a moon-lit summer night. When Donna or the kids wanted to fish, they went to the crossing. The fish bait was usually worms or grasshoppers, and the fish were bass, perch, an occasional long-nosed gar or drum, and small channel cats. We usually threw the fish over the dam to the deeper water, or took them to a large pond in the Mesquite Pasture.

Another fun activity on the crossing was watching the moon come up big on a full moon night, while sitting on the dam in cutoffs, listening to good music, and sipping Jack Daniels. Dean Davis had some female friends in town who occasionally joined us. Before Dean and Allyson married, he and I had good times carousing, squirrel hunting, going to dances and other county functions. It didn't take a lot of effort to find good times in Gonzales County!

On a few occasions in the hot summer, a group of us would cut a watermelon on the crossing, listening to Conway, George, Mel, Loretta, and other good music discs that Dean had in his truck. Sometimes we got rather loud, but there was no one to hear us for miles.

The Guadalupe River

The Guadalupe River begins with two forks (north and south) west of Kerrville, coming off the east side of the divide. The two forks converge west of Kerrville and the river flows southeast through (or near) Comfort, New Braunfels, Seguin, Gonzales, Cuero, and Victoria on its way to San Antonio Bay in the Gulf of Mexico. The river passes the Kokernot Ranch at about the 140-mile marker, and is a waterway used by canoeists on the Texas Water Safari.

The Kokernot Ranch has about two miles of river front. Several gravel shoals provide good swimming areas, and the entire stretch is good fishing. Peach Creek empties into the river on the Kokernot side, about 20 river-miles from Gonzales. The ranch has a camp house on the river, which was used by hunters, and also by family members for outdoor parties such as fish fries. The camp also had a washer and dryer for ranch laundry.

Fun Time on the River

We all had good times on the Guadalupe. The camp house was on a high bank close to the river, where we had fish fries, hamburger cookouts, and hunting camp parties. I spent a lot of time at the camp house washing clothes, catching mice, and shooting turtles from the high riverbank.

On occasion in the summer, Al and Claudia Brothers would bring up some grandkids, and Donna would come down with Ross, and we would watch the kids swim along the gravel shoals. Sometimes we would bring enough .22 rifles for all the kids, and they would shoot 400 to 500 .22 shells in an hour or two — anything that floated down the river, or things we threw in. They would sometimes fish the river, but they had rather fish at the low-water crossing on the creek.

Kokernot Ranch Wildlife

The Kokernot Ranch, with its versatile habitats, was a mecca for wildlife. The uplands, along with Peach Creek provided a mesquite-dominant habitat for white-tailed deer, nesting wild turkey and mourning doves. Quail habitat was scarce, and I saw only one covey of bobwhites during my 22 years. Coyotes and bobcats used the uplands for both shelter and food. Whitetails and hogs also used the creek in their movements from the river to the uplands and back.

Peach Creek was a haven for deer, wood ducks, squirrels and turkey. Hogs used the creek regularly for farrowing, but the hogs on the ranch were Russian-type hogs brought in and released by a neighbor. Russian hogs are much wilder in nature than "feral" hogs (domestic hogs gone wild), and they hide their farrowing places. In 22 years, I never found a spot where the sows prepared a place to farrow. In fact, they may not have used a particular place, but may have birthed the piglets wherever they were at time of parturition.

On the far east part of the ranch, a natural wash provided water for a long, narrow lake. At some time, someone had put in a vertical 6-inch pipe to form an artesian well, and I'm sure it flowed in earlier days.

When I moved to the ranch, the well pipe was visible, but it did not flow. The bank of the long lake was a roosting place for hundreds of sandhill cranes and white ibis. Several hundred cranes also roosted on a slough a few hundred yards away on the Bouldin Ranch, which joined the Kokernot on the east side.

The cranes arrived about October 15th each year and stayed all winter, feeding out every day in all directions. About sundown, you could see and hear cranes coming back to the roosts from everywhere. In the spring, cranes could be seen feeding in most of the large pastures, and about March 10, they all went north.

The river bottom is a forested haven for both fox and gray squirrel, along with hundreds of hogs. Clyde Hinton brought the Russian-type hogs several years ago and they have done well along the Guadalupe River and Peach Creek.

The Russian strain of hogs are different from feral hogs — big at the shoulder and little at the rump; long snouts; thick shoulder pads on males; long split hair along the back from head to tail, and a long, straight tail that they wag when feeding. Their color is solid black, with an occasional red or gray hog — no spots. In 22 years, I never saw a spotted hog on the Kokernot.

Pure Russian sows can weigh 175 pounds, but most weigh less. Boars can get up to 250 pounds, but most will weigh less than 200. The piglets will be about eight per litter, with two litters per year. All piglets are orange-striped length ways until they are about eight weeks old.

Deer tended to stay out on the fringes of the river bottom, and there was a herd of 25-30 bucks and does that emerged to the timber's edge each evening. All told, I figured that 125 to 140 whitetails lived on the Kokernot year-round. The river herd was supplemented by another herd of 25-30 south of the camp house, and another 30 roamed the length of Peach Creek. About 25 deer stayed just north of the ranch house; another 20 or more stayed near a water hole in the north Mesquite pasture, and about 20-25 used the uplands near the East fence.

The deer on Kokernot Ranch are Avery Island whitetails, a sub-species that originated on Avery Island in Western Louisiana. The subspecies covers an area roughly from Avery Island, Louisiana down the Gulf Coast to Corpus Christi, then up through DeWitt and Gonzales Counties, East through Lavaca county and on to Jasper County and down to Avery Island.

The Avery Island whitetail is smaller than the Virginia subspecies, and has a noticeable amount of white on its face, ears, front legs, belly, hind legs and tail. The ears are short, as is the skull length. Mature males weigh about 115 pounds field dressed, and a dressed doe weighs about 65 pounds. Mature male antlers are predominantly eight points, with an inside spread of 16-17 inches. Non-typical antlers are rare.

Fishing

I would prefer to smell gunpowder than fish, but the Kokernot offered good fishing, both in the creek and the river. A favorite place for kids to fish was the low-water crossing on the creek, which had a deep hole of water just below the concrete. This was the place where Donna and the kids did most of their fishing. When we wanted bait for trotlines, we caught our bait at the crossing.

A favorite place to fish the river was just below the camp house. The riverbank had a sandy ledge where people could stand or sit, and fish. Most of the fish were bass, catfish, and an occasional drum. The biggest catfish that I saw caught there in the river was a 26-pound humpback blue that Joey Gore caught with rod and reel, using shad for bait.

In the 22 years that I lived on the ranch, I went fishing in Peach Creek one time. A good friend, Don Bunojch, who lived in Seguin, called one day and asked if I ever fished the creek. His mother lived across the creek toward Shiner, and he had fished for catfish many times. Don suggested that he bring the punch-bait and show me how to catch channel cats in the creek.

One morning we fished a long stretch of creek below the low-water crossing for about two hours. We used chicken blood punch bait, and caught about 12 catfish that weighed 2-3 pounds each. The creek was low, and we caught the fish in the holes just below shallow ripples.

We took the fish to the house, and Don cleaned them while I watched. I didn't want any, so he took all the fish to his mother. It was the only time we ever fished, and I don't know why we didn't fish more. The creek is full of channel cats.

The Floods

When I moved to the Kokernot, I knew that the ranch was in the flood plain of the Guadalupe River. Doc Denman had told me about some flooding, but I soon found out, firsthand, about the high water caused by the confluence of Peach Creek and the Guadalupe.

I moved in during September, and shortly after, we got a good rain across the state, including the area between Austin and Gonzales — the flood plain of Peach Creek. I got up one morning and went to the kitchen to make coffee. As I stood at the sink, looking out the window to the north, I suddenly realized that I was looking at water — a whole ocean of water! The 50-acre hayfield north of the house was solid water, which came to within 50 yards of the house. I went to the back door and looked out at water below the barn to Peach Creek.

I was surprised at all the water, and went to the front sunroom and peered out the window — solid water toward the river, as far as I could see. I was witnessing my first flood since moving to the Kokernot.

The high water between the creek and the river was the first of many floods that I would see in the coming years. The house was on a hill, and the creek water would come close to the house, but never to the house, and would get close to the barn and my dog pens.

The creek would flood to the south side of the house and meet the flood water that came across the Turk Ranch from the west. The flooding water would reach the cattle guard just south of the house (about 50 yards), but never higher.

At 29 feet, the river would come out of its banks about 1½ miles up on the Turk property, and come down across the pastures to an historic flood ditch just south of the house, and go on to Peach Creek. The entire scenario of floodwater meant that during a flood, water was everywhere except where the house and barns stood, and was a lake of water all the way to the river, about a mile to the south. A good flood on the Kokernot was a sight to see!

The Dogs

When I moved to the Kokernot in 1995, I was still doing a lot of quail hunting, mostly north of Albany, on the Clear Fork of the Brazos. I had spent some time there with Roy Wilson on the Crooked River hunting

Horace and Bill Gore on the Kokernot Ranch

camp, and I knew a lot of places where I could hunt. I would take the dogs and go north for several days at a time, and quail hunt with my friends.

I had three bird dogs when I moved to the Kokernot. Two of the dogs, Lucy and Patches, were English setters, and Champ was a big English pointer. They were all good dogs, and on occasion I would get a handsome fee for taking them to a private hunt, mostly with pen-raised birds that were put out for the hunters.

The Kokernot did not have any quail, but when we needed to work the dogs, Doc Denman and I would buy 30-40 quail and put them out in 3s in the front pasture by the house, and take the dogs on a "quail hunt."

Gore's Guadalupe Belle

The year after I moved to the Kokernot, my friend Dean Davis, who was the ag teacher in Gonzales asked me if I wanted a lab pup. I had three bird dogs, and I wasn't interested in a retriever. I knew that Dean's lab, Claire was going to have a litter from a male lab that I knew very well. "Buddy," was Bill Archer's dog, and a good retriever that I had hunted doves with many times.

Sometime in late summer of 1996, Dean came by with a cute little female lab pup, and I couldn't refuse. She was about eight weeks old, and solid black. I kept her in the house, and when she got older, she slept on a pallet in the living room all her life. She was registered under the name Gore's Guadalupe Belle, and I called her "Belle."

Belle had good bloodlines from Archer's Buddy and King Ranch, and turned out to be one of the best dogs I've ever owned. Not only was she an excellent retriever for doves and ducks; she was very good at trailing wounded deer and hogs.

I killed a lot of Russian hogs on the ranch, and Belle learned to pick up the blood trail and find every hog. I put a bell on her collar so that I could keep up and find her with a hog. If the hog was dead, she would bark a little and chew on its flank. But if the hog made any moves, Belle would bark to high heaven!

When Belle got about two years old, I put her on a wounded deer trail and she found the dead deer and did the same thing as with hogs — chewed the flank until I arrived, or barked at the deer as long as it had a breath. Most of the time, I would get her direction from her barks, and she was easy to find with the bell on her neck. Belle was the best dove and duck retriever, and also the best hog and deer trailing dog that a hunter would want.

Gore's Apollo Lucy

When Belle died in the summer of 2006, I immediately started looking for another retriever. I had had a good retriever for many years, and I didn't want to hunt without a dog. But, at my age, I didn't want to start a young pup — I wanted a dog ready to hunt — a female about a year old or older.

After a month of searching, I found a dog trainer near Cuero who had three young dogs — one female. I went and watched him work the 15-month-old dogs, and they looked good. I wanted the female, but he wanted to keep her. The male dogs were priced at $1,200 each, and I told him that I would give $1,500 for the female, and he took her collar off!

Lucy was an excellent retriever, but she would have nothing to do with anything with hair. She was a bird retriever, plain and simple — and she was good with doves and ducks. I kept her in the house, just as I had kept Belle, and Lucy also became a constant companion.

The Deer Hunters

Doc Denman leased the ranch in 1995 to two hunters from Austin. They had all the hunting for deer, turkey and they could also hunt hogs. Doc reserved deer for his immediate family, and he reserved some hog and squirrel hunting for me and my friends.

The Austin hunters moved a new double-wide trailer into the camp site on the high riverbank in the Hog Pasture, and set it up with electricity, sewer and water. The water source for trailer use was a 1,200-gallon water tank for city water to be brought in as needed. All other water came from a well near the camp site that was usable for everything except drinking and cooking.

Doc had a deer/hog skinning rack constructed on a concrete slab where game could be hung, skinned and washed. The camp was very nice, and the house could sleep five people and one on the couch. I had an extra couch that I gave for the camp house, and Doc gave them an 8-foot folding table and chairs for dining. Three small bedrooms had single beds, and the master bedroom had a queen-size bed. The camp was ready for the 1995 deer season, shortly after I moved to the ranch in September.

Through the years, four groups leased the Kokernot for hunting. The first two hunters lasted three seasons, when the big flood ran them off. After that, a company from North Houston had it for about three years. They went broke, and Phil Lamey from Katy leased it for about seven years.

Phil fed year-round and built up a good deer herd with some good bucks. He bought a ranch in South Texas, and the Denmans sold the ranch to Russell Gordy, an oil man in Houston, who leased the ranch to his employees. They kept the lease until Gordy sold the ranch to Fletcher Johnson of Gonzales, who kept it two years and died. The widow Johnson sold the ranch to Marvin Boedeker of Shiner, who has it today.

When Phil Lamey bought his ranch near Fowlerton in La Salle County, the ranch had several 300-pound feeders with legs and battery powered spinners. He didn't need all the feeders, and I bought five and brought them to the Kokernot Ranch. I already had three 55-gallon feeders, so with the five additional feeders, the ranch was covered with corn feeders for hunting blinds. Most of the feeders ran all year, which tended to keep the deer and turkey on the ranch.

Beginning with Phil Lamey, who was a good friend, all of the leasers let Donna kill a buck each year, so she enjoyed deer hunting for about seven or eight years. All of her bucks were eight pointers, by arrangement, but she killed two or three that were real dandies. In all, she took seven bucks, and the best one is on her office wall in Lorena. Her favorite rifles were two Winchester Model 70 bolt actions, in .243 and 7mm-08, and she was a crack shot with both.

A Doe for Doc

I killed one deer — a doe — during my 22 years on the ranch. I got doe permits each year for the lease hunters, and one year Doc invited about six of his close friends to the camp house for hamburgers and a doe hunt.

The hunters showed up about noon, and Doe and I cooked the meat, and made a nice lunch for his guests. Then, about mid-evening, Doc and I took the hunters out to their deer blinds for the evening, and Doc instructed each hunter to kill only adult does. When we got all of the hunters out, Doc surprised me by saying he wanted to sit in a blind.

There was one small ground blind about 300 yards from the camp house that was not big enough for both of us — Doc was pretty hefty — but he insisted that we go get into it, and he wanted me to shoot him a doe. We went to the blind about 4 p.m., and finally got into the blind with me on the right side. It was a tight fit, but we made it.

About sundown, a single doe came wandering through the brush, not over 60 yards away, and I pointed to her and motioned to Doc. He nodded yes, and I pulled the .224 TTH up and out of the blind window. I didn't want to shoot her in the head — too messy, but I also didn't want to waste any meat.

I aimed at where the neck meets the shoulder, and pulled the trigger. It was a solid hit, but the doe bolted out of sight in the brush. I went to the camp house and got Belle, and we soon had a fat doe. Doc tagged the deer, and we dragged it out. It was the only deer that I killed in my many years on the ranch. I hunted deer every season, but not on the Kokernot.

Dixie's three does

One year when we were short on the number of does that had been taken, I asked Doc if Tommy and Dixie Kaye could come over from Yoakum for a hog/doe hunt. He agreed, and the Kayes came over for an evening hunt. I put Dixie in a river blind, and Tommy closer up in a blind near the camp house. It was their hunt, and I kept busy on the ranch while they hunted.

About dark, I picked Tommy up with no doe. He had seen several bucks, but no does that were close enough to shoot. We went on to the river blind, and found Dixie waiting for us, as she stood over a doe. Tommy complemented his wife on her fat deer.

"There's two more," Dixie said, as Tommy and I looked at each other. "One is over there in the trees, and the other one is down by the river," Dixie said as she pointed out the locations. We all went and gathered up the deer, and as they left the ranch house, Tommy said, "I won't bring Dixie back this season. We've got deer meat to give away." I didn't tell Doc that Dixie had killed three does — I just reported that they had a good hunt!

The Turkey Hunters

The Kokernot had two large flocks of wild turkey that roosted in the bottom near the river, and on Peach Creek up behind the ranch house. The deer hunters were allowed to take gobblers during deer season, and I think they killed less than a half dozen with their rifles through the years.

The hunters were not proficient at calling gobblers, and the only turkey killed in the spring season was taken when I called up a gobbler for Chad Denman, Doc's grandson, who had just graduated from A&M, and was living in Austin.

In the spring of 1997, Chad called me and asked if I could call up turkeys. I didn't brag about the 30-40 gobblers that I had called for myself and others through the years, but I convinced him that I could get him a turkey if he wanted to come hunting.

We arranged an evening hunt, and he got to the ranch about 5 p.m. I had told him to have necessary camo clothing, face mask, cap and 3-inch No. 4 copper coated shells for his full choke 12-gauge shotgun. He was fully prepared, and we got to the creek about 6 p.m., near a spot where I knew a gobbler had been roosting.

I put Chad against an oak tree about 25 yards from where I would

Brian "Doc" Denman at ranch fish fry

be sitting against a tree, and after we let things quieten down, I gave three loud yelps on my slate turkey call. After about 5 minutes, I gave out three more yelps on the call. We heard a distant gobble up the creek, and I motioned to Chad to get ready, with his shotgun balanced on his knee.

I continued to call with three yelps, and we could hear the gobbler getting closer with every gobble. When the turkey got to about a hundred yards from us, I quit calling because I knew that he would be strutting up soon.

I was right — in a few minutes the gobbler let out a big gobble right near me. I didn't move and I was hoping that Chad would shoot the turkey. The old bird gobbled again, and he sounded like he was about

10 feet away! In a minute or two, Chad's 12-gauge roared, and the old gobbler began to thrash around on the ground from a good 25-yard head shot.

We had gotten Chad a turkey less than 30 minutes after we sat down on the creek. When he came to me I said, "Chad, why did it take so long for you to shoot this turkey?" Chad replied, "He was so close to you that I had to wait for him to move so that I wouldn't shoot you!" That made sense!

Chad was excited about the hunt, and wanted to take it home to show it off before he skinned it, so we gutted the bird, washed it out, and I sent him on his way — a happy hunter! That was the only turkey I called up on the Kokernot during my 22 years on the ranch.

A Gobbler for Dean

I was in Gonzales one morning in April, about five years after I had moved to the ranch, and ran into Bill Booth, one of the oldtimers of Gonzales County. He invited me over to his office, and we talked about turkey hunting. "Do you hunt turkey in the spring?" he asked. I told him that I had killed a lot of turkey in the spring, "Would you want to hunt on one of my places on the Guadalupe? I told him I didn't know the country. "Dean Davis knows it well. He could go with you."

When I approached Dean about hunting on Bill Booth west of town, he was all for it, and we planned a hunt. The idea was to call Dean up a gobbler because he had never killed one. We scouted out the place where we would hunt, and one morning we were there before daylight. Turkeys were gobbling at dawn, and I began talking to them. It wasn't long until we had a gobbler coming our way.

Dean was carrying my Winchester 97 hammer gun when the old Tom came strutting up close, and he quickly put a load of No. 4s in the old gobble's head. The turkey was big and heavy, with a 10-inch beard. Dean was so thrilled, and I gave him a good pat on the back for his first gobbler.

That was the first hunt on Bill Booth. Before the season was over, Bill wanted me to take one of his friends hunting who was visiting from out-of-state. The guy wanted to hunt by himself, so I put him in a good spot and I went farther down toward the river.

> *"Men are made equal, but not for long!"* — Goreism

At daybreak, several turkeys were gobbling, and I was talking to them. About eight o'clock, I could hear a gobbler getting closer. He was an old bird, and didn't come in quickly, so I waited. Finally, he came out strutting, but the shot was long.

I shot at the turkey's head anyway, and the gobbler flew toward me and over my head. At about 25 yards, I rolled him up like a snowball, as he crashed through the mesquites behind me. I had killed my first and last Gonzales County gobbler. My hunting partner didn't get a turkey, so I gave him mine. He gladly took the gobbler, and gave me the long beard for my collection, which was a cigar box full of long beards. That hunt was my last for spring turkey, and it was a hunt to remember.

The Squirrel Hunters

I grew up squirrel hunting in Northeast Texas, and when I moved to the Kokernot, I couldn't wait to go hunting in the river bottom. There were plenty of fox squirrels in the big pecan trees loaded with pecans. During the times when the deer hunters weren't there, I spent a lot of time squirrel hunting with Dean Davis and Al Brothers.

When two or three of us would go hunting, we often set a four-squirrel limit so that we would have only eight to 12 squirrels to skin and clean. We ate every squirrel we killed, and we killed a lot of squirrels!

Al Brothers shot an Anschütz .22 bolt action with a 5-shot clip, fitted with a 7-power scope. He was a crack shot, and hit most of his squirrels in the head. I had several .22s, but two of my favorites for squirrels was a Ruger automatic with a 10-shot rotary clip, fitted with a 2½ power Weaver scope, and a Winchester 63 auto with a 2½ power Lyman Alaskan. Dean used a lever action Winchester .22 with a 4-power scope. We always got our share of fox squirrels, and even some gray (cat) squirrels close to the river.

We hunted squirrels in the fall, when pecans were ripe, but June hunting was very good when the anaqua trees were loaded with berries that drew squirrels from everywhere. The hunting could be hard when squirrels got up into the thick branches where they could fill up on berries without moving, and most squirrels were killed going or coming from the berry-laden trees.

When we hunted close to the river, we sometimes killed one or two gray (cat) squirrels, but they were difficult to hit with a .22 rifle. They were very active, and hunters had to take quick shots when the squirrel were still. I recall one hunt when I walked up to a big pecan tree right next to the river. The tree was tall, and I could see three gray squirrels cutting pecans.

I watched one of the squirrels get a pecan and began eating it on a big tree limb. He stopped long enough for me to take a rest and roll him out. At the shot, another squirrel came around the trunk of the tree and stopped. I put the cross hairs on his head, and killed him. The third squirrel was high in the tree, and finally stopped long enough to grab a pecan. I shot him and he fell from the very top of the tree. For the first and only time on the ranch, I had killed three "cat" squirrels in one tree — a rare incident.

The Hog Hunters

Some of the most thrilling hunts on the Kokernot were hog hunts. When I first moved to the ranch, there must have been 500 or more Russian hogs, and they were reproducing every day. Before the big flood of '98, Doc Denman contracted with a local hog trapper to trap hogs during the summer. Doc would get 20 percent of the income from live-trapped hogs sold to local buyers.

The trapper set up his traps in the spring, and caught 352 hogs the first summer. The next spring, he set up his traps and caught another 100 hogs, but the trapping got difficult and the trapper lost interest in running his traps.

In the hot summer weather, hogs began to die in the traps, and the trapper caught a few young deer. Doc told me that the trapper had not given him his 20-percent share of the money, and he ran the trapper off. The hog population began to increase again, but was interrupted by the great flood of October 1998.

I ate a lot of hog meat when I lived on the Kokernot. Belle was a good trailing dog, and I seldom lost a wounded hog. I processed all of the sows, and all of the boar hogs less than 100 pounds. I gave good eating hogs away, and cooked pork every way possible.

Through the years, I killed about 50 hogs on a straight stretch of road in the Mesquite Pasture. We videoed Kokernot Ranch hog hunts for the Trophy Hunters TV show. Donna would kill a hog any time I needed one, such as the time Bubba Schmidt, John Parr and I cooked a 100-pound sow on a fire spit, as part of a hog cooking contest at "Come and Take It." The big weekend celebration was an annual affair on the first Saturday of October, marking the first shot of the Texas Revolution.

The old Russian boars make good trophies when you boil out the skulls. Through the years, I killed about 15-18 old boars with 3-inch tusks, and boiled out most of them. I gave a few away, but the trophy room had 10 or 12 good boar skulls.

I told Donna about a big red boar that was coming to the River Blind feeder. She and Bubba got in the blind, and when the boar showed up, Donna put a 139-grain Hornady from her 7mm-08 right through him. He took the shot and ran into the brush, and on the ground behind him was a dead sow that weighed about 60 pounds. The boar died in the woods, but we didn't have a trailing dog and we had a fine eating hog to gut and skin.

Two or three of the hog hunts were exciting. I went hunting on several moonlit nights, and on one hunt, I lost a $15 Timex watch chasing a wounded boar on Peach Creek. Belle was in hot pursuit and I was yelling, "Git 'em," and she was barking. When we finally got the big boar, I looked at my watch, because I knew it was close to midnight. The watch was gone. I had lost a Timex for a trophy hog.

I killed a lot of big hogs in 22 years on the Kokernot, and these are just a few of many hunts. Belle and I made a good hog-hunting team, and it wouldn't have been the same without her.

Coyotes and Other Varmints

I don't have anything against coyotes, but I did kill one on occasion. There were probably six or eight bobcats on the ranch, and a dozen or more coyotes. I liked to see coyotes and bobcats, but they catch and eat fawns and young turkey, and I didn't want too many of them, especially coyotes. I always carried a rifle, and if I got a good shot at a coyote, I took it. Bobcats were "off limits" to everyone by rule of Dr. Denman!

Belle would trail a wounded coyote, just as she would a hog or deer. On one occasion, I had her and the .224 TTH in the Rhino when I flushed a coyote out of the brush. I hardly ever hit a coyote running, but that time I clipped him pretty good as he disappeared into the Creek Pasture, with Belle on his trail. I sat in the Rhino, listening for her bark, and when it came, I jumped out, leaving the rifle and went to the loud barking in the distance.

When I got to Belle, she had the wounded coyote bayed under a thick persimmon bush. The young coyote was backed up, and they were fighting back and forth. I didn't have anything to finish off the coyote except a mesquite club about two feet long. When I got a chance, I clubbed the coyote on the head and Belle finished him off. The moral to the story: Don't chase after a wounded coyote without a gun.

Two other times I killed a coyote from the house. I looked out the kitchen window one morning, and two coyotes were pulling on an old deer hide, each trying to take it away from the other. I went to the safe and grabbed the first gun I saw, which was a .300 Weatherby. It was a little big for coyotes, but I grabbed a couple of shells and went to the back door. The two coyotes were about 200 yards away, in grass almost as tall as they were. I put the cross hairs on one and squeezed the trigger.

The shot was difficult through the long grass, but I saw only one coyote run away. I didn't know if I hit the other one, but later that morning I got my answer. Two buzzards were sitting on fence posts, and I could see a third in the grass where I shot the coyote.

On another morning, I looked out and saw 4 coyotes trotting across the Front Pasture, headed for the Turk hayfield — they would cross the entrance road. I had the .224 TTH loaded and handy, and I grabbed it and ran out the front door and took a rest on the walnut tree in the front yard.

I pulled the trigger just as one of the coyotes stopped in the gravel road, and it wheeled around, and followed the other coyotes out of sight. It was a 150-yard shot, but not much for the .224. Later on, I drove up the road, and saw a big spot of blood on the gravel. Three buzzards were sitting on separate fence posts a few yards away, and I knew.

During my 22 years on the Kokernot, I probably killed fewer than 10 coyotes, and the deer hunters killed two or three. We didn't put a dent in the coyote population on the ranch, and I always loved the sound of three or four coyotes (that sounded like 20) yelping near the house in the still of summer nights.

The Buzzard Shoot

In the winter of 1999, turkey vultures began to gather in the river bottom, and before long there were close to 500 buzzards roosting between the outer tree line and the river. The cows were calving and Doc was concerned about all the buzzards, and what they might do to some of the newborn calves.

"We need to stir those buzzards up," Doc told me one day. "It's illegal to hunt buzzards, isn't it?" I queried. "Not when they are roosting by the hundreds on a cattle ranch. We won't be hunting buzzards; we will be shooting them," replied Doc. "I'll talk to Glen (the game warden), and let him know that we are going to 'relieve' some birds from the buzzard roost. He may come and help us."

In a few days, Doc and I went down to the roost, carrying both rifles and shotguns. "We'll shoot as many as we can in the trees, and finish up with the shotguns when they are flying around," Doc instructed. We set up right near the roost and waited for the birds to come in. I had my .222 Winchester and my 12-gauge duck gun. Doc had a Browning lever gun in .223, and his 12-gauge duck gun — we were loaded for bear!

About sundown, buzzards began to come into the roost from every direction. While it was light enough to see good, Doc and I began to shoot buzzards that were close to us. Doc got four or five, and I got about that many before the birds left the trees, and began to swirl around above us.

The sailing buzzards through the trees was tough shooting, but we emptied our shotguns (six shots) and reloaded a couple of times. When the smoke cleared (no pun) we had killed or crippled about 20 buzzards, and the rest had left for quieter places.

Barry Gore with Bradley (7) and Mitchel (9) at Peach Creek crossing

"Will coyotes or coons eat buzzards," Doc asked as we finished off the cripples and started back to the truck. "I don't think so," I replied. "I think it will be like the emu you shot on the ranch a while back that lay in the pasture for days. The coyotes didn't eat the emu and I don't think they will eat these dead buzzards."

We left the roost area, and Doc told me to watch for a few days to see if the buzzards returned. I spent two or three evenings watching, and saw only 20 or 30. Our one-and-only buzzard shoot had paid off.

Deaths on the Kokernot

We had one death on the ranch that was attributed to hog hunting. Two young men from Yoakum were hog hunting with dogs on a neighbor ranch late at night in January of 2004. They got after a big hog that the dogs couldn't stop, and the hog crossed Peach Creek and came toward the camp house on the river. One of the hunters stayed with the chase, while the other came around and crossed the low-water crossing on the creek, driving an ATV.

The hunter following the dogs came to the river at the camp house to find that the hog and dogs had crossed the river into the Turk Ranch. He decided to swim the river, and in the process, drowned. The search party found him in the river when they saw the light from his flashlight, still in his hand, in the deep water. The young man had a wife and kids back in Yoakum, and I suspect that he was drinking — at least, doing something that caused him to use poor judgment.

Another death, that had nothing to do with hunting, was a Black man who committed suicide just across the river from the camp house. He had been in Gonzales with his wife when they had a domestic quarrel. In the fracas, he killed her; then came to the Turk Ranch where he had been working, and shot himself in the head.

A third death occurred on the ranch in about 2007, when the cowboys were working cattle. One of the workers in his 70s died in the camp house in his sleep, after a long day of working cattle. When I went down to see what all the commotion was about, the cowboys were burning the mattress where the fellow had died.

The Duck Hunters

When winters were wet, the Kokernot had good duck hunting in the sloughs and natural water ponds on the pasture flats. The first 10 years of my tenure on the ranch were wet, and Belle and I hunted ducks off and on all winter.

Dean Davis would come out on occasion, and we would hunt some of the bigger water courses on the front pasture. Some of the hunting was illegal after sundown, when we would shoot ducks coming to roost and fire would flare out of our shotgun barrels.

We didn't kill a lot of ducks — just enough to keep us and the dog interested. Most of the ducks were gadwalls and blue-winged teal, but on one occasion I killed two mallards, and on another I got a young male wood duck. In 22 years, I killed one sandhill crane, and that was enough. The lone crane came over low enough for me to break one wing, and the bird fell, and fell, and fell, and...

When the crane hit the ground across the pond, it stood up and started walking. Belle swam the pond and started chasing the crane. I was afraid it would peck her in the eye, and I took a long shot with the No.

4s when Belle was clear of the bird. I hit the crane in the head with a pellet or two and Belle dragged him by the neck, and swam the pond — bringing the crane to me in my makeshift blind.

I was anxious to cook the bird, and I put all the spices I had on it and baked it in the oven. I couldn't eat it — it tasted terrible. I threw it in the backyard, thinking that Belle might eat it. It lay there on the ground for two days, when something (I suspected a 'coon) carried it away.

One evening in the winter of 2005, Mike Turk on the neighboring ranch called me and invited me up for supper. I accepted and when I got to the house, he and his brother David had cooked a delicious supper of fried sandhill crane, gravy, biscuits and French cut green beans. Mike had sliced the breast and chicken fried it. After a couple of bourbons and water, the fried crane was tasty. If I ever eat another sandhill crane, it will be chicken fried, with bourbon and water!

Doc Denman liked to hunt ducks on the coast, and we went hunting on Mustang Island two or three times each winter. We would go down and spend the night eating a lot of seafood and drinking good whisky.

The next morning, long before daylight, we would be on our way to the guide's trailer on the beach. He would take us out in the air boat to a blind with lots of decoys for a morning of shooting redheads and pintails, and watching Doc's lab retrieve the birds. We sometimes got teal and widgeons, but they were rare.

After a morning hunt, we would come back to the motel, lay around and eat or go sightseeing during the day. In the evening, Doc would drink his scotch, and I my bourbon. The next morning, we would repeat the duck hunt, eat a seafood lunch, and go home.

Doc always took the ducks — I didn't cook them, but he would broil the breasts on open fire in his kitchen and invite me to town for drinks and duck. I figure that the six ducks we killed on each hunt (four redheads and two pintails) cost us $50 each, or more!

The Big Flood

I mentioned before that there were many floods on the Kokernot during my 22 years. Some were bigger and deeper than others, and I can remember deer hunters trying to walk out of the bottom in waist-deep water. On one occasion, Sam and Jimmy Turk picked up two hunters in their motorboat and took them to high ground where their wives had come from Austin to take them home.

On another occasion, three hunters were trying to walk out in waist-deep water, but it got so deep that they went back to the camp house (the camp house was on the highest spot in the river bottom, and was dry when all else was under water). Most of the floods were tolerable, and did little damage, but a big flood in the fall of 1998 was a disaster.

Historically, the flood months for the Guadalupe River are June and October. These are rainy months, and through the years, most floods occurred in these two months. The riverbanks could hold a lot of water, and flood stage was usually more than 29 feet. But, on October 18, 1998, a steady rain for two or three days pushed the flood water of the river to 53 feet, which flooded the countryside on both sides of the river, and caused a tremendous flood where Peach Creek and the Guadalupe River merged — the Kokernot Ranch.

The Biggest Flood Ever

The '98 flood was thought to be the biggest flood ever for the Guadalupe River. Heavy rain in the Edwards Plateau caused the Canyon Dam relief gates to fail, causing a great flood of water to come down the Guadalupe toward Gonzales; the Kokernot Ranch, and on to the Gulf.

One of the towns on the river to get the brunt of the flood was Gonzales. The next town to catch the flood waters of both the river and Peach Creek was Cuero. The river also caused major flooding as far east as Victoria.

The high waters of the Guadalupe and Peach Creek came from about 15 inches of rain in two days on the watersheds of both streams. Both flooded, and the water from both sources merged on the Kokernot Ranch.

Flood water was a mile wide, from the Brown's Oak Valley Ranch to the east to the high hills of the Turk Ranch to the West. The highest point on the Kokernot — the hill where the ranch house stood — was six feet deep in water. This meant that the ranch house, which had underpinning of two feet, had four feet of water in the house.

> *"A good writer can stretch the truth without lying."* — Goreism

Practically everything in the ranch house was destroyed by flood water, which was 48 inches deep. I had put everything of value up on tables and beds before I left with the dogs about 5 p.m. on October 18. It would be a week or more before the water got down below the house, and was still deep on the lower elevations.

Ross Chanberlain was visiting with me on that weekend, and we watched the hard rain all day on Saturday. That night, it was still raining, when Ross and I decided to go to town and eat pizza.

We went to town in my Ford Explorer, but when we got to town, everything was closed, and water was deep everywhere in Gonzales. We started back home, and hit something in the road that caused a blowout on the car. I pulled into the nearest driveway, and called Doc on my new cellphone. He drove out and picked up Ross and me, and took us back to the ranch. I left the car in the driveway, not knowing who lived there.

When Doc left us at the ranch house, he told me to watch the water on the driveway to the house. "If the water runs over the drive from the gravel road, you get out of here. If the water gets two feet high over that drive, you can't get out."

Sunday morning came, and it was still raining. I watched as the creek flood water came closer to the house, and a tractor on the Turk side of the fence went under water. The Turk hay field next to our hayfield was full of round bales, and they began to float across the Turk fence and hang up in our hay field fence — 40 or 50 bales. By noon, I knew that Ross and I would have to leave the house.

I put on a raincoat and rubber boots, and went outside to see what needed to be tied down before we left with the dogs. Luckily, my Ford Explorer was in town, but I had to chain down my four-wheeler, the riding lawnmower, and the John Deere tractor.

I chained all of the equipment with wheels to the iron cattle pens. Back in the house I put everything of value as high as I could—my gun

Jimmy Gallagher, Al Brothers, Horace Gore, Tommy Kaye — hunting aficionados

collection on the bed, and other things on tables. I didn't think that water would get into the house, but I didn't know for sure.

Leave Before It's Too Late

About 3 p.m. on Sunday, Ross and I put the dogs in the truck; I got some dog chains and feed; we took everything we thought we would need, and left the ranch through a foot of water over the drive to the gravel road.

I had called Al Springs and asked if Ross and I could go to his deer camp about a mile up the road. He told me where the key was, and Ross and I went to the camp, not knowing when we would be back.

On Monday morning, the rain stopped, and Ross and I went back down the road toward the ranch house. Water was very high when we got about 400 yards from our front gate, and we had to stop a long way from the house. As we watched the sea of water for over a mile to the camp house on the river, Jimmy Turk came up in his Boston Whaler 16-foot boat, and we walked down to the edge of the water.

"Bad news," Jimmy said from the boat. "I came by your house last night about midnight, and the water was up to the windows. It's higher than that, now." While we were talking, Dean Davis drove up with Allison, and we looked at the high water. After a while, Ross and I drove back to the Springs camp, and called Donna and Jeff to come get him for school. I stayed at the Springs camp for several days, waiting for the water to recede so that I could see what damage had been done.

Gun Collection Soaking Wet

On Tuesday, after the flood had peaked on Sunday night, I got Jimmy Turk and Dean Davis in Jimmy's boat, and we went to the back door of the ranch house and crossed the 4-foot fence in the boat to the back door. We stepped right out of the boat into the house.

The muddy floor was as slick as glass, and we barely made it to my bedroom where all the guns were on the bed. Water had risen well over the bed and all of the rifles and shotguns were full of silt and water. I was afraid that they would rust, and I called Joe McBride at McBride's Guns in Austin and ask him what to do.

"Bring the guns to me as soon as possible, and don't let them get dry, or they will rust." I had four or five old sleeping bags, and we wet the bags and filled them with guns, and I went to Austin. Joe had a crew waiting for me, and we unloaded all the guns and took them upstairs to the gun shop.

Joe was taking the guns out of the bags when I left the store. I picked all the rifles and shotguns up later, and my cleaning bill was $790. Every piece looked good, and I was glad to have the help of McBride Guns, and Joe McBride.

Evaluating the Losses

Back at the ranch, there was not much we could do, so we left the house for several more days until the water went down, and things began to dry out. I stayed at Al Springs camp another week with the dogs, and then went back to the house during the day, taking everything out of the house and stacking it in the yard. It was a terrible mess.

The Kokernot Ranch was only one of the places flooded by the high water. The south end of Gonzales, next to the river, suffered big losses in housing and yards. After the flood, there was a pile of wet furniture and other things as big as a two-story house on a vacant lot next to the football field.

Livestock losses in Gonzales County were high. The Kokernot Ranch lost 146 head of cattle, and other ranch losses were enormous. I saw dead cows up in trees 15 feet high, and a lot of cattle drowned against fences. The round hay bales that were once on the Turk hay field, were now scattered for miles toward Yoakum and Victoria.

A 7-foot picnic table that once was in my back yard at the ranch house was found down on Peach Creek about 12 feet high in a tree. I had just bought a cord of split oak for the fireplace, and it was scattered all over the ranch. The deep freeze floated in the little storage house, and the 4-wheeler and riding lawnmower were upside down, but still attached to the chains.

After the floodwater subsided, I went to the big barn to see how things fared there. In a side room, facing the floodwater, was a Red Devil upright vacuum cleaner. The cord was loose and running toward a side door that had been opened by the flood water. Where the vacuum came from, we never knew. I took it to a repair shop in Austin, and got it cleaned and running. We used it in the ranch house for 10 years.

A nice deer blind came from somewhere and was in the trees just inside the Kokernot north fence line. I was checking he fences after the flood, and found it. Doc and I went up with the tractor and bucket, and took the blind to the river camp house. It was in good shape, and we set it up and used it for years.

Doc Denman got some help, and we took everything out of the house and put things to dry in the sun. Jeff Chamberlain came down from Austin and power-washed the house, cleaning out all the mud. The wood floors buckled for two weeks, but finally went back to normal.

Most of the antique furniture in the house was ruined and had to be thrown away or sent to the cleaner. The wooden antiques were refinished. The French piano in the living room was mostly under water, and when it dried out we never did look inside.

Things were back to normal about a month after the flood, and what furniture was left was in use. The bathroom floor was replaced, and shortly afterward, Doc had a contractor from Shiner come and put metal siding on the house, and a new metal roof.

I put a Direct TV dish in the yard, after Belle had found the wire going under the house and pulled all of it out into the yard. The only thing in the house that showed the flooding was the paneling on the walls, which was basically destroyed about two feet above the floor. We never repaired it — just lived with it.

The wildlife managed to survive the flood. Ground dwellers went out ahead of the high water, and the birds — eagles, buzzards, hawks and turkey flew to higher ground after daylight. It took about two years for

> *"Diplomacy is the art of saying 'Good Doggie' while you are looking for a rock."* — Goreism

wild things to get back to normal, but by the new century in 2000, everything was back in order and deer hunters were back in the camp house.

Hunting Vehicles Under Water

When the big flood hit, the deer hunters were in the camp house. As the water came up, they decided to try to get out, but too late. They had two vehicles — a new Suburban, and a new pickup. I watched from the ranch house as they came out of the bottom, and onto the road that came up to the ranch house. They got about 200 yards from the Hog Pasture gate, when the lead vehicle ran off the narrow road and down into the side ditch. It was nearly submerged in water.

When the Suburban slid into the ditch, the pickup couldn't get by, so the hunter got out, and both of them walked back to the camp house, leaving the Suburban two-thirds under water and the pickup about halfway under. One of the Turks was down on their property in a boat, and the hunters hollered them in and got a boat ride out to high ground, where their wives picked them up for the trip back to Austin. Their vehicles were fully submerged in flood water for weeks.

The Flooded Camp House

At the peak of the flood, the camp house in the river bottom was submerged to the ceiling. Everything that wasn't tied down washed away, including the 1200-gallon water tank. After the flood, the hunters gave the camp house to Doc, and returned, only to get the Suburban and pickup that had been completely under water for two weeks. After the wreckers got their vehicles, the Austin hunters never returned.

Doc spent some money getting the camp house cleaned and back in shape, but it was used by hunters and the family for another 18 years. When the Denmans sold the ranch to Russel Gordy of Houston, Gordy's lease hunters used the camp until he sold to Fletcher Johnson, and all lease hunting ended.

The Canebrake Rattlers

After the flood, a hired hand that Doc used quite a bit came to him and asked if he could have the outhouse that he had built for Doc when the camp site was a fishing camp. The toilet had washed away in the flood, but they found it down in the timber about a quarter mile from the camp house.

One Saturday morning, Doc and the hired hand went down to the toilet with a trailer, planning to take it to town. When they pushed the outhouse upright, a large canebrake rattler was under it. They carefully laid the toilet back down, and Doc got a pistol from his truck.

When Doc came back, they raised the toilet, and Doc shot the snake. When they brought the toilet by the house, on their way to Gonzales, they showed me the rattler. It was about 4-feet long, as big as my arm, and had only a few rattle rings and a button (indicating that the rattles had not been broken). It was the first of five canebrake rattlers that I would see in my 22 years on the ranch.

The next was a very large rattler that a worker killed near the camp house. It was big and long, and had a long string of rattles. The third was a rattler that Al Brothers ran over with his truck as he left the camp house after a fish fry. The small canebrake was about two feet long.

The fourth was a young canebrake snake down on a ridge above the river where I had a deer feeder. I was setting the clock on the feeder when I noticed something between my feet. I look down to see a little canebrake rattler about a foot long. I put my foot next to him and pushed him away, and soon he was gone in the brush.

The fifth canebrake rattler was killed by a bulldozer operator near the camp house and close to the river. He had rousted the snake out of the brush he was pushing, and showed it to me. It was about 3-feet long with a short set of rattles.

All of these five canebrake rattlers were seen over a 15-year period on the ranch. They were all very close to the river, and within a half-mile of the camp house.

The Wreck: Suburban-Pickup Head on

In May of 2006, Dean Davis and I were on our way to the annual BBQ that was held at Al Brothers deer camp just East of Berclair, Texas. A

Jim Shipwash (R) and Horace Gore frying catfish on the Kokernot.

drizzle of rain had fallen, and about 15 miles down the road, Dean suggested that we buckle our seat belts.

About six miles North of Cuero, we were approaching a hill, when Dean said, "Gore, watch that car." I just had time to look around when the Suburban hit us head-on. My King Ranch pickup spun around and turned over twice, according to reports.

Dean and I were pinned in, with the truck on its left side. I said, "Dean, help me out." Dean replied, "I can't. My arm is broken." After that, I lost consciousness, and didn't wake up until we were landing in the helicopter on the pad of a hospital in San Antonio.

I spent four months in three different hospitals before I could get about in a wheelchair, and come back to the Kokernot. My brother Bill came back with me and stayed until I could walk and drive my new pickup to work in San Antonio. My first day out of the hospital was August 20, 2006. It was another month before Bill could drive me to the Texas Trophy Hunters office in San Antonio.

The Ranch Sells Again — Marvin Boedeker, Shiner

Every time the ranch sold, I was ready to move, but I lucked out three times. Russell Gordy, Fletcher Johnson, and Marvin Boedeker all asked me to stay. I knew the ranch well, and all the neighbors, so it was best for them that I stayed.

When Marvin Boedeker bought the ranch, things had already gone sour for me. The oil business came in about 2010, and in two years, five pads with 16 holes had been drilled and fracked, producing some 2000 barrels of oil per day. The oil was good for all the landowners who had oil, but it played havoc with the land.

Marvin was a good businessman from Shiner, and I could tell that he planned to keep the ranch for a long time. To my surprise, the deer and turkey tolerated the oil industry and did well in spite of all the activity. I was glad that Marvin had bought the ranch.

I stayed on the Kokernot for two reasons: I didn't have any other place to go, and in spite of all the oil activity, I still loved the ranch. I knew that sooner or later, I would have to leave, and I paid off Donna's house in Buda, planning to live there when I left the ranch.

The Old Diabetes Wins the Battle

In late fall of 2015, my right toes became infected, and I went to Lorena, where Donna and Bubba live, and had the toes removed at a Waco hospital. I stayed with Donna until the foot healed, and went back to the Kokernot the next May.

Things went pretty smooth until I disturbed a large wasp nest under a shed on the Kokernot in 2017, and a swarm of wasps attacked me. I jumped backward to get away from the wasps, and fell on the hard ground, cracking my left hip bone. I didn't know it at the time, but when I left the ranch that day, I was leaving forever.

> *"Biscuits and gravy has saved more lives than penicillin!"* — Goreism

The accident put me in a local rehab center, but before I could get out of there, I developed a blood clot under my right leg. Dr. Comie Hisey, my doctor in Gonzales, sent me to San Antonio Baptist Hospital, where they amputated my right leg above the knee.

That stroke of bad luck fixed me forever, as far as living alone, and doing everything for myself. I'm now living with Donna and Bubba in Lorena (near Waco), doing well and learning to live with one leg! We sold the house in Buda for double what it cost.

Today, I'm in a wheelchair, editing and writing for the TTHA *Journal*. We published a book titled "Texas Trophy Hunters — Under One Cover," and now I'm writing a book about my life. My health at 90 is good from the waist up.

Safari Club International (SCI) bought Texas Trophy Hunters in 2019, and the word is that they will move the Phoenix office to San Antonio. The TTHA crew in San Antonio is in a new office, with one or two employees commuting. I'm here in Lorena (Waco) with Donna and Bubba. We are near I-35, so travel in any direction (Dallas, Fort Worth, Houston, San Antonio) is easy. I have no idea about the future of Texas Trophy Hunters, but I have enjoyed the 29 years.

I reminisce a lot about the Kokernot Ranch; the wildlife, the hunting, the river and Peach Creek, the floods, the neighbors, and all the folks I got to know in Gonzales. The 22 years on the ranch were good — and a wildlife biologist couldn't have asked for anything better during the latter years of his life. I've been fortunate!

CHAPTER 22

Texas Trophy Hunters: A Second Career

After retiring from Texas Parks and Wildlife Department in 1993, and spending two winters guiding quail hunters at Crooked River hunting camp on the Clear Fork of the Brazos in Shackelford County, I took Dr. Brian Denman's offer to move to the Kokernot Ranch in Gonzales County. I lived on the 2,200-acre cattle ranch for 22 years, and joined Jerry Johnson at Texas Trophy Hunters only a short time after I moved to the Kokernot in September 1995.

Jerry called and asked if I would edit *The Journal of the Texas Trophy Hunters*, the "Flag" of TTHA, a very good four-color magazine that's the pride of the association. I agreed to work for TTHA in a variety of ways, but commute from the ranch to San Antonio. At the time, I didn't anticipate working for TTHA very long, but the arrangement as "extra labor" to edit *The Journal* has lasted as a second career for 28 years!

I got to know Jerry Johnston much better after my promotion in 1979 to white-tailed deer program leader for the Wildlife Division. Jerry had founded Texas Trophy Hunters around the Texas whitetail — the most popular game animal in the state, and we were both deer hunters.

Jerry and I soon became good friends as we mingled at wildlife functions across the state. We hunted together a few times, and talked about deer, but we were on different wave lengths — he with Texas Trophy Hunters, and I with Texas Parks and Wildlife. A closer relationship began after I retired in 1993, and Jerry needed an editor for *The Journal*.

I joined Jerry's team as editor sometime around mid-September of '95, and commuted from the Kokernot to San Antonio about two days each week. I was new to the job, to the employees, and to San Antonio. The office was in a quaint spot on Vance Jackson Road.

TTHA staff—Debbie Keene (left), Lauren Conklin, Jason Shipman, Jennifer Beaman, and Christina Pittman, CEO

It took a few months for me to adjust to what was required to edit the magazine. I was a hunter, writer, Boone and Crockett official scorer, and professional biologist, so it was just a matter of putting it all together and working with the two assistants. Shortly after I joined the TTHA team, Jerry moved the headquarters to a new office on Bandera Road, where we operated until he sold the association in 2006.

TTHA had three Extravaganzas — trade shows — in Fort Worth, Houston and San Antonio, and I soon became the judge and official scorer of the Annual Deer Competition at each show. I had help in scoring the whitetail bucks entered — sometimes as many as 70 in Fort Worth — and made decisions about the validity of some of the entries.

Saturday nights at the shows were special. As the crowd would wind down, we often "let our hair down" and frolicked a bit, and Jerry often took the whole TTHA Family out to dinner. Needless to say, we all enjoyed the shows.

The Fort Worth show, held in the Will Rogers Convention Center, had the biggest show and deer contest, while San Antonio had the smallest. The Houston show was at the George R. Brown Center, and the San

Antonio show at the Freeman Coliseum. In my early days at the Extravaganzas, I can remember Saturday mornings when long lines of folks went around the buildings, waiting to get into the shows, which were exceptionally popular.

The San Antonio Extravaganza was rather quaint, held inside an old rodeo arena, and required booths and activity in the rotunda above the floor area. The deer contest was situated in the rotunda, along with many other booths. San Antonio had a lot of deer hunters, and it always surprised me so few deer were brought in to the contest. I recall one show with only 16 entries, but we usually got about 25 bucks.

Jerry found early-on the Extravaganzas were the money-makers, and although the membership and *Journal* kept the association going, the Extravaganzas made the money! Jerry and the staff tried to establish more shows in Texas, as well as Louisiana and other states, but the logistics and vendor participation didn't work, and he settled for the three big shows in Texas.

Some of my most enjoyable times with TTHA were with Brian Hawkins, making television shows for Texas Trophy Hunters TV. Jerry and Brian started putting various shows "in the can" as early as 1997, but the TV shows took off with a bang in 1998.

One of the first shows where I assisted was a pronghorn-antelope hunt in West Texas starring Lee Taylor. It was a hoot, but Lee couldn't hit the side of a barn. While chasing antelope, I stumbled upon a small prairie rattler. Hawkins made the best of the snake, filming me talking about prairie rattlers and the ever-present 39 spots on the snake's back. For their size, prairie rattlers are more challenging than their

TTHA Under One Cover

As editor of *The Journal*, I write articles on hunting, Texas history, outdoor articles of interest, and Kamp Kitchen. Through the years, I have amassed hundreds of articles of interest to hunters.

About two years ago, I got the idea of putting a number of these articles in a book, and with the help of Debbie Keene and Martin Malacara, we contacted a publisher and began preparation of material for the book. The book would be used to garner memberships, and we decided to title the book, "Texas Trophy Hunters — Under One Cover."

The 282-page softcover book was set up in five separate sections — History and Management, Features, Up on a Stump, Blasts from the Past, and Kamp Kitchen. A photo section in the center was reserved for *Journal* covers, featuring several photos of white-tailed bucks by Marty Berry, a businessman, rancher, photographer and friend to TTHA. The cover is an excellent buck from Marty's collection.

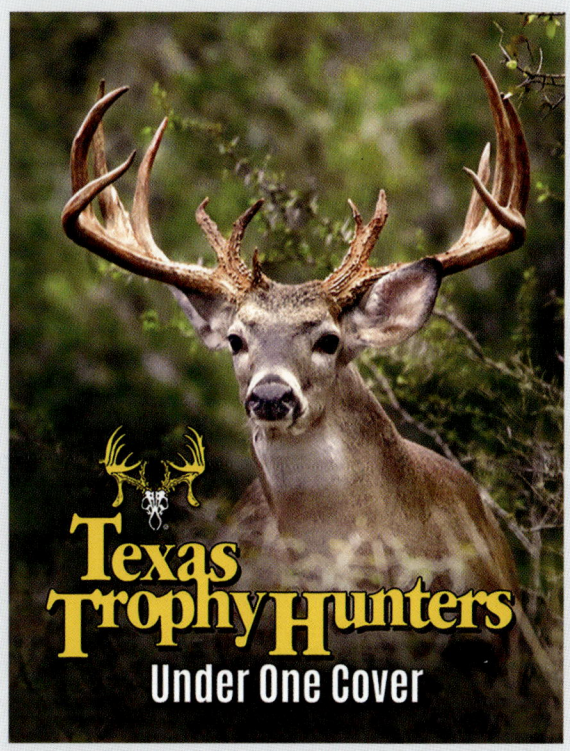

Dust Devil Publishing of Midland was contracted to put the book together and get it printed. Debbie Keene and I leaned on our friends for eight advertisements to cover the cost of publishing and printing. They are Lanny Vinson Ranches, Tina Kalig & Associates, Charco Marrano Ranch, Jason Shipman Wildlife Consulting, Texas A&M (Gore, Al Brothers, Marty Berry), G-2 Ranch, Berry Whitetails, and Texas Hunter Products. The book is available through TTHA membership or at retail cost.

Journal staff: Debbie Keene, Executive Editor and Martin Malacara, Associate/Online Editor

larger cousin, the diamondback rattler. (See the chapter on Trophy Hunters TV elsewhere in this book).

Jerry Johnston arranged several hunts for deer and dove in Mexico. On one occasion, he asked if I wanted to go to Mexico and hunt the diminutive Carmen Mountain whitetail. An advertising client and friend, Rodolfo de Los Santos, had offered Jerry the hunt in lieu of some advertising.

I accepted the hunt, and was soon on my way to Eagle Pass, where a pilot would fly me into Mexico to the ranch south of Big Bend. Rodolfo and Patricia were waiting at the spacious hacienda. Rodolfo was an influential cattleman in Monterrey, and Patricia's grandfather had been a signer of statehood for Oklahoma in 1907.

The large ranch had whitetails and mule deer, and was well known to the hunting world. I soon found out I would be hunting in the company of a deep-pocketed California hunter named Bob Woodward, who wanted a Carmen Mountain whitetail to mount full size for his wildlife museum in Palm Beach.

Bob and I hunted in separate parties for two days, and on the first day, Bob's guide wanted me to look at a muley buck that Bob had killed — maybe a mule/whitetail hybrid. I examined the deer, and was confident that the buck was indeed a hybrid. On the hunts, I saw several bunches of whitetails and mule deer running together.

Later on, my Mexican guide and I found a nice little 3-year-old six-point buck that was leaving the flats for the high country. I made a dazzling shot at about 250 yards with the .270, and Pedro almost lost his senses. In Spanish, he reveled at the shot, and we proudly took the six-point back to camp.

"California Bob" had killed a big eight-point Carmen whitetail, and we all celebrated our first Mexican whitetails. Later on, Bob asked if I would give him my six-point for his collection. I knew I would have to jump through hoops and stay another day to get the deer antlers and cape out of Mexico, due to tick fever, so I gave him the deer — my one-and-only Carmen Mountain whitetail! The hunt was exciting, but the small six-point antlers were not impressive.

Jerry and I hunted white-winged and mourning doves in Mexico on Rancho Rio Grande, also owned by Rodolfo de Los Santos. Through the years, Jerry hunted whitetails a lot in Mexico, and I'm pretty sure he killed a mountain lion on one hunt. When he established the deer contests for the Extravaganzas, Jerry included Mexico with Texas in the contest.

Jerry sold Texas Trophy Hunters in 2006, and the days of the old "family-oriented" organization were over. The new owner took steps to develop a Trophy Hunters Association in Canada, Arkansas and Alabama. As with Jerry's attempts to branch out, the logistics and hunting regulations/social atmosphere of the new locations didn't hold, and were soon abandoned.

The TTHA headquarters were moved from Bandera Road to a large building owned by the new owner on Loop 1604. When Safari Club International (SCI) acquired Texas Trophy Hunters in 2021, the office was moved east on 1604, close to US 281.

Texas Trophy Hunters is still the largest association of its kind in the Southwest. Through the 50 years since the original meeting at the El Tropicano Hotel in San Antonio, where Jerry Johnston announced the association of his dreams — Texas Trophy Hunters — more than two million deer hunters and outdoor-lovers have enjoyed the annual Hunters Extravaganzas, and many thousands have read and enjoyed *The Journal*.

The Texas Trophy Hunters Association, acquired by Safari Clubs International (SCI) in 2021, continues to serve thousands of Texas hunters and outdoor enthusiasts In Fort Worth, Houston and San Antonio, just prior to the fall hunting seasons. The well-known logo reminds folks young and old that Texas Trophy Hunters will always be "The Voice of Texas Hunting."

CHAPTER 23

Ducks, "Doc," And December

There was a time when December meant Port Aransas and redheads, airboats and waders, 12-gauges and steel shot. A time awaited for months — duck season. It was a time revered by Brian "Doc" Denman and me. I still don't know why, because every duck I killed with Doc cost me about $50, and many short nights! But we were staunch duck hunters — dogs and all.

I lived on the Kokernot Ranch, a sprawling 2,200-acre spread that covered some uplands and a lot of the Guadalupe River bottom in East Gonzales County. The ranch had been inherited by Ruth "Baby" Kokernot, from the original estate of David Lee Kokernot, who had fought with Sam Houston at San Jacinto.

Kokernot ended up with several thousand acres for his courageous adventure, and through the years, "Baby" ended up with her share of the inheritance. She had married Brian Denman during World War II, during the time when he served as a captain in the Army as a dentist.

After the war, "Doc" and Baby Denman had returned to Gonzales, where he managed his wife's Kokernot Ranch along with practicing dentistry. He and Baby were influential in community affairs, and hardly anything happened in Gonzales without their approval.

I met Doc in the '80s when I sold him a bird dog. We met south of Austin, and traded the dog for money, and since the dog turned out to be one of the best quail dogs Doc ever had, he remembered me. Later on, in 1995, my close friend Al Brothers called and said Doc wanted to talk to us about leasing the Kokernot to some deer hunters.

I met Al and Doc on the ranch, and we planned a leasing scheme for Doc and his Austin hunters. While on the ranch, I asked Doc about the big ranch house up on the hill, just out of the river bottom.

Brian "Doc" Denman and Horace Gore on a Texas Coast duck hunt

"You going to let the hunters use the house?" I asked Doc as we finished our visit and headed out of the river bottom. "Well, no." Doc said. "That's Baby's house, and it is full of family antiques. She wouldn't let hunters use it under any circumstances." Without giving it much thought, I replied, "Well, it's a shame to leave a big house like that without anybody in it." Doc stopped the truck and looked at me. "Are you concerned about the house? Why don't you move in yourself? You have retired from Parks and Wildlife, so what about it?"

I didn't know what to say. Doc had just noted that his wife was particular with the house, and now Doc was asking if I wanted to live in it! "Would Mrs. Denman let me live there?" was my next question. "I'm sure Baby would approve, if you take good care of the place." Doc said.

I knew the area pretty well, and I knew about the water east of Gonzales to the fault at Kokernot Hill. My friend, Al Springs and his wife Dorothy had property up the road, and I had visited there many times. The water was terrible. "Can we go to the house?" I asked, as Doc pulled the pickup up to the gate. We got out and went in. I went to the kitchen, found a water glass, and filled the glass at the kitchen sink. First, I took a sip, then a long drink. The water was good.

The Denmans and I cut a deal, and I moved into the ranch house in September. Al Brothers always said that it was the best thing that could have happened to Doc Denman and me. The next 22 years were some of the best of my long life.

In his younger years as a dentist in Gonzales, Doc was a dyed-in-the-wool quail hunter. As he got older and gained weight, Doc turned to waterfowl hunting — ducks and geese. I hadn't been living on the ranch very long before Doc approached me about a duck hunt on the coast.

"We could go down to Aransas Pass on Friday, kill some redheads and pintails, eat some good seafood, and be back by Sunday evening," Doc surmised. "What do you think?" I was all for it, so we loaded up in his pickup, dog and all, and went on the first of many duck and goose hunts — Doc, me, and his chocolate Lab.

Duck hunting on the coast is not cheap! There's the motel and food, the air-boat guide with his blinds and decoys, our guns and shells, and the bottles. I liked bourbon, and Doc was a Scotch man. Add it all up, and the two redheads and two pintails (the limit) per morning cost us dearly! I don't like duck meat — it's too dark — but Doc would breast out the meat and broil it. I figured that each side of duck breast was worth about $25, so the six ducks per hunt cost me $150!

Through the years, Doc and I enjoyed many duck and goose hunts, but there's one or two hunts on the coast that stick in my mind. One cold winter hunt turned out to be as strange as a $3 bill! We had arranged with our guide to go south along the shoreline to a blind with 40 to 50 decoys. It was a good spot.

We got to the blind in the dark of the morning, unloaded our gear in the dark, and got ready for a good shoot. When daylight came, we discovered we were on dry land — the water having receded with the tide. All of the decoys were on dirt, and there weren't any ducks to be seen. As I recall, the only shot of the morning was Doc downing a large pintail drake, which apparently was lost.

Another hunt involved some blue-winged teal — rare where we hunted south of Aransas Pass. Doc told the story of that hunt at least a hundred times, and the story got bigger every time.

> *"Truth is like oil — it always comes to the top." — Goreism*

On these coastal hunts, we hardly ever saw any ducks other than redheads and pintails. On this particular hunt, we were farther south than we usually hunted — down close to Corpus Christi.

As dawn broke, and ducks began to fly, I noticed a small flock of five teal coming up on the horizon. "Doc, I see some teal coming. Get ready." The five teal were doing about 60 miles per hour as they approached the blind and our decoys. Doc was shooting his Beretta automatic, and I had a Remington 870 pump. We both were using No. 3 copper-coated steel in 3-inch loads.

As the teal approached, we both began to fire, and ducks began to fall. The Lab got excited to see so many little ducks falling everywhere. As the smoke cleared, the only teal left flying was gaining altitude as I tried a long shot. The bird left the sky with a broken wing, and Doc finished it off as it hit the water.

Doc and I looked at each other in disbelief. "Did we get all of them?" Doc asked as he turned his dog loose. "I guess so," I replied. "How often do you think two hunters will kill all five teal coming by at 60 miles an hour?"

Doc couldn't get over the fact that we had gotten all of the little blue wing teal that are fast as greased lighting — he was beside himself. "That won't happen again as long as I live," Doc shouted. "Usually, you lead the first bird, and kill the last one!"

Yes, those were good days on the coast — me, Doc, the dog, and a lot of high-dollar ducks.

CHAPTER 24

Two Celebrated Squirrel Hunters

Squirrel hunting in Texas has become a lost art. Most hunters who talk about hunting squirrels with their favorite .22 rifle are over 50 years old. Oh, yes! You hear lots of talk about deer hunting, or dove hunting, or even turkey or quail hunting, but seldom do you hear a squirrel-hunting story. I guess you could say that squirrel hunting went the way of skating rinks, kite flying, moonshine, and sweet Garrett snuff.

When "Ike" Eisenhower was president, there were a lot of squirrel hunters, mostly east of the Brazos River. This story is about two squirrel hunters who have hunted together for 60 years. They grew up in very different lifestyles, one in the flat woods of Northeast Texas, and the other along the Guadalupe River in Gonzales County. One had friends and relatives to take him hunting, the other had Jim Tiller. I speak of my close friend, Al Brothers, and yours truly. I consider us to be two of the best squirrel hunters in Texas.

Al Brothers grew up hunting squirrels in the Guadalupe River bottom east of Gonzales. His folks spent a lot of time overseas with an oil company, while Al and his twin brother, David, lived with relatives and went to school in Gonzales. Their only claim to fame early in life was burning down the barn when they built a good fire on a cold, windy winter day!

Al had friends who squirrel hunted and he started floating the San Marcos and Guadalupe rivers, shooting squirrels on both banks, at an early age. He claims to have killed his first buck with a borrowed .30-30 when he was 12, but I suspect he may have killed a doe or two with his .22 when he was squirrel hunting! Al doesn't have an illegal bone in his body, but he might take advantage of a good situation.

Kokernot gate with squirrels Gore/Brothers

I grew up in Bowie County in northeast Texas, not far from the Red River. The area is generally flat with a lot of creeks and plenty of squirrels. There were no deer or turkey, and squirrel hunting was the thing. Two favorite places to go for a three- or four-day squirrel hunt were the Sulphur River bottom and Anderson Creek, just to the south of Hooks — now a part of Lake Wright Patman. Two species of squirrels frequented these two spots: fox and grays.

Jim Tiller got me interested in hunting squirrels. He was retired, and about 65 years old, and hunted squirrels with dogs. When I was about 14, I would go with Mr. Tiller and "turn" the squirrels for him, as the dog barked that a squirrel was up the tree. I made a lot of noise and shook vines or anything that would cause the squirrel to go to the other side of the tree trunk. Jim would be ready, and when the squirrel turned his way he would "roll it out." He let me shoot a few squirrels, and I can thank Mr. Tiller for getting me into the woods and teaching me how to hunt.

If you think sitting in a warm deer blind by a feeder is hunting, I invite you to go after squirrels in high timber with a .22 rifle. You'll find that this is real hunting, requiring not only patience and shooting skill, but a good knowledge of the woods and the game you're after. It may bring you to your knees! I've said many times that it takes a better hunter to kill 10 squirrels with a .22 than to kill a 10-point buck with a .30-06.

Al Brothers and I first met at Texas A&M University in 1958. He was in his second year as a wildlife-science student and a member of the Corps of Cadets. I had been out of the army for about a year, transferring from Texarkana Junior College on the GI Bill and was also enrolled as a wildlife student. We grew to be close friends at A&M, and are still close today.

Hunting and guns, along with other minor things have kept Brothers and me together as friends for all these years. At A&M, we soon found a connection that has lasted for 60 years — wildlife and hunting. We've never had an argument or a cross word — pretty good for 60 years, don't you think?

Al and I got closer with our squirrel hunting when I moved from Austin to the Kokernot Ranch in Gonzales County. The ranch house was less than a mile from where Al had killed his first buck. I lived on the ranch for 22 years, and during that time Al and I hunted squirrels on the Guadalupe River every chance we got.

Fox squirrels were most common, but right along the river, gray (cat) squirrels were a part of the game. June was a good time to hunt when the anaqua fruit was ripe. Squirrels go crazy over anaqua berries.

As a rule, a good hunt for us would be four to six squirrels in a morning hunt. Al hunted on a four-wheeler because he survived a helicopter crash in 1976. I was on foot and could cover ground not accessible to Al on the four-wheeler. However, Al was a patient hunter and could shoot a squirrel in the head at 50 yards with his Anschütz .22 and Leupold scope. He often brought in more than I did — all shot in the head!

At that time, my favorite squirrel rifle was a Winchester bolt-action 69A with a 2½ power Weaver scope. At squirrel shooting distance, it would make a ragged hole of three shots. I also killed a lot of squirrels with a Ruger 10-22 auto with a 2½ power Weaver, and a Winchester 63 auto with a Lyman Alaskan scope — both fine squirrel rifles.

> ### *It takes a much better hunter to kill 10 squirrels with a .22 rifle than to kill a 10-point buck with a .30-06. — Goreism*

I recall one spring when the anaqua was especially good and squirrels were thick as fleas on a coyote. Al came up for a two-day hunt on the neighbor ranch where Al grew up that belongs to the Turk family. Gen. Sam Turk went to A&M with us back in the day. The ranch has a lot of anaqua in a situation that was good for Al on his four-wheeler. We would hunt two mornings.

The rest of this story may make Brothers and I out to be game hogs. But let me assure you that even though we sometimes got lucky and killed a good many squirrels, not a one was wasted. We have eaten squirrels every way you can think of — fried, BBQed, stewed, dumplings, grilled, squirrels-'n-gravy, just to name a few. We never set a limit, and we did all of our hunting where there was no bag limit. We just hunted as long as the wind was still, and squirrels were jumping!

The first morning I left Al out in an open flat with lots of anaqua, and I went into a thick slough that had some anaqua around the edges. We were not too far apart, and I could hear Al's Anschütz crack every now and then. I soon found fox and gray squirrels in the slough timber, and I had a happy time chasing both. When the smoke cleared I was carrying 11 fox and gray squirrels in my bags on each hip.

Brothers had been shooting all morning, and I knew that he had a good batch of squirrels. What I didn't know was how many. When we got to the ranch house and counted, we each had 11, or a total of 22 squirrels to skin. We finally got them all cleaned and in the fridge, and sat around talking about that being our best squirrel hunt together in all the years. Al reminded me that most of his were shot in the head, while most of mine were gut-shot.

The next morning, we were back on the Turk place in generally the same areas where we had killed 22 squirrels the previous morning. Again, I chased gray and fox squirrels, while Al saw mostly fox on the flat. We hunted until about 9, when the wind got up, and met for the

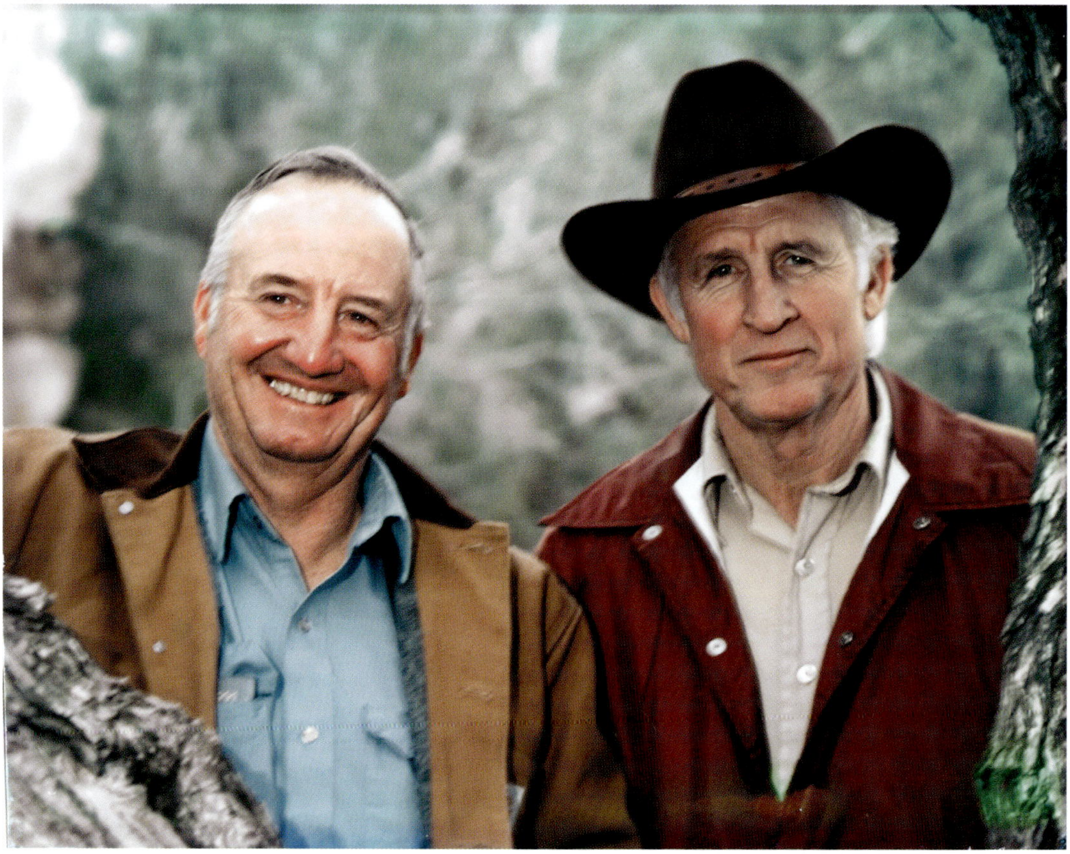

Al Brothers and Horace Gore, old Aggie hunting Compadres

count. Al had 11 squirrels scattered over the four-wheeler, and I pulled 11 fox and grays out of my bag.

We had killed another 22 squirrels for the second morning in a row —  44 squirrels in two days! "This has got to be a county record," Al said. "Yes, and maybe a state record," I replied, knowing that it was more likely a world record. And by the way, that was also our record. We killed and ate a lot of squirrels after those hunts, but never again 44 squirrels in back-to-back mornings!

CHAPTER 25

Russian Boars of the Guadalupe

When I moved from Austin to the Kokernot Ranch in Gonzales County in 1995, I knew quite a bit about feral hogs in Texas, and how they came to be. Where I grew up in East Texas, farmers and other landowners would mark their hogs and turn them loose on "open range" in the river bottoms. The marks were registered at the county courthouse, and most markings were somewhere noticeable (snout, ears, tail).

These hogs were domestic, generally spotted, with curly tails and short snouts. When farmers moved from place to place, the hogs were often left behind. By the late 1980s, wild feral hogs were practically everywhere, and I had killed a few in Burnet, La Salle and Goliad counties.

Practically all the wild hogs in Texas are "feral." However, in some isolated places, Russian-type hogs have been brought in from Arkansas, Tennessee, and other Eastern states where the Russian strain of wild hogs were brought in from Eurasia and North Africa in the 19th century. Such a place is the Guadalupe River bottom of eastern Gonzales County, where a local landowner brought in Russian hogs from Tennessee several years ago.

The hogs reproduced well, and today the river bottom and most of the Peach Creek drainage is home to these unique wild hogs. They are different in that they are a solid color — black, gray, or dark red. They have long snouts with long tusks, are big at the shoulders and narrow at the hip, and have long split hair along the back from the head to tail. The tail is long and straight, and I've noticed that Russian hogs wag their tails back and forth when feeding, and hold their tail high when they run.

I lived on the Kokernot Ranch for 22 years, and hunted wild hogs regularly. The 2,200-acre spread stretched from the upper reaches of

Peach Creek down to the Guadalupe River bottom, and was home to hundreds of Russian hogs. The boars made unique trophies with their long skulls and long, shiny tusks.

In all the years, I killed about 15-18 Russian boars that were old and trophy size. Most adult boars weighed about 200 pounds, but there were a few exceptions. Ironically, the heaviest hog killed on the ranch was a Russian sow, topping the scales at 350 pounds. My biggest boar weighed 225 pounds, and I noticed that the very old boars weighed less.

My hog hunting for 10 years was enhanced by my black lab named Belle — an excellent retriever and hog-deer trailing dog. She was the best all-around dog that I ever owned (among many), and a wounded hog or deer seldom ever got away from her.

One rainy morning I was coming from the river bottom. Belle sat in the back of the pickup and I had my .224 TTH in the seat beside me. As we left the river, I was looking at some of the black cows along the road. Suddenly, I saw they were not all cattle. There was a big black boar among them.

I stopped the truck and reached for the rifle, just as the hog saw the truck and headed for the fence into the Turk Ranch. I got off a shot at 50 yards and missed. I quickly fired again at about 75 yards, and I saw the boar sag as the bullet found its mark, but not a killing shot. The hog ran out of sight into the Turk Ranch as Belle watched it all, and got out of the truck after the boar.

I drove to the house and got on the four-wheeler with the .224 TTH, binoculars, and a knife. The rain had stopped, and I went back to where the boar had crossed under the fence. A scan of the distant terrain showed Belle and the boar about 300 yards into the Turk. I went to a gap in the fence, and on to Belle and the hog. When I got there, the hog looked as big as a mule, but later weighed only 225 pounds.

One of the biggest boars that I killed on the Kokernot was following about 15 sows and pigs across the front pasture. I had Belle in the truck, as I were driving toward Peach Creek, so I cut across the pasture and got a long shot with my .224 TTH. I hit the boar, and he left the herd, and headed in my direction.

The pasture was rather flat, and I sped to where I could get another shot. I hit the boar again as he disappeared into some tall weeds. Belle

Bubba and H.C. Schmidt hog hunting.

was in hot pursuit, and she and the boar were in and out of the weeds, while I was trying to get a good shot at the hog. Finally, the hog ran free of Belle, and I quickly shot him in the head. He was a tremendous boar, and I was disappointed that I had ruined his skull. He was big and mean, with long tusks — a good candidate for a trophy skull — but that was not to be!

Another wild chase I remember was one of the first boars that I got with Belle. She was about 18 months old, and we were riding the four-wheeler along a dim road near Peach Creek. I saw a big hog standing in the trail about 70 yards away, and I quickly stopped and took a shot with a short-barreled .30-30. The hog fell, but got up and disappeared into the timber, with Belle in hot pursuit. I waited.

In a few minutes, I heard Belle baying the hog, and I knew it was not dead. I took the .30-30 and went towards her, following the barking far ahead. When I finally got to Belle, she and the hog fought in the creek, and Belle jumped back and forth to keep from being cut by the hog's tusks. I put a .30-30 round into the boar, and he floated in the creek.

Horace Gore, "Belle", Russian boar

The boar was big, but not big enough for a trophy skull. I cut out his back straps through the thick hide on his back. With the fresh meat, we left the hog to the buzzards and caracaras (they have to eat, too). That hunt convinced me that young Belle would prove herself with hogs.

I encountered some strange boars in my 22 years on the ranch. I remember a big gray boar coming to a feeder on Peach Creek. The boar showed up, and I was up on a portable blind, cradling a .30-06. It was an easy shot at 70 yards, and to my surprise, his tusks were not long, even though he looked old. Later, he weighed a little over 200 pounds field dressed, and I wondered if he would be good to eat.

I remembered what Don Bujnoch had told me about boars:

"If you wonder if a big boar is good to eat, take a knife while the hog is still hot, and push the blade as deep as you can into the hog's hip.

> *"The varmint that needs saving, is the varmint that eats other varmints."* — Goreism

Put your finger in the cut as deep as you can and wait a few seconds. Pull out your finger and smell it. If the smell is rank like an old boar, cut out the back straps and leave. If your finger smells like hog, field dress him and take him in for sausage."

The boar passed the test, and made good Jim Shipwash "hog balls." I marinated the back strap in sweet milk and fried it for breakfast.

I learned that all hogs on the Kokernot were not wild. I had been on the ranch about three years when a friend called and asked if I wanted a little, orange-striped Russian pig about a month old. I said, "No, but my neighbor might want it." They brought the little pig, and my neighbors about a mile away were delighted to get the little female that they named "Annie." The little Russian pig grew up as a pet with two dogs.

About one year later, in November, I was in the house when I saw a big black hog coming down the gravel road. I immediately grabbed my .270, and went out the back door, and waited for a good shot.

To my surprise, the black hog came into the yard and began eating acorns under the live oaks. I couldn't believe my eyes. It was a female and she was swinging her long tail like a horse swatting flies, and grunting as she enjoyed the live oak acorns.

I walked toward the sow, gun in hand, and she came up to me. I scratched her back, and that was when I realized that the hog was Annie. I was so glad that I hadn't taken a quick shot when I first saw her on the road.

Annie stayed in the yard eating acorns until sunset. Quite suddenly, she raised her head and quit eating, went to the gate, and started up the road toward the neighbor house a mile away. As she went out of sight on the road, I thought about the incident, and that I could have killed the neighbor's pet. All hogs on the Kokernot were not wild!

CHAPTER 26

A Half Century of Texas Trophy Hunters

Jerry Johnston had a vision in 1975 for an organization that would promote interest in white-tailed deer and deer hunting in Texas. To that end, he founded Texas Trophy Hunters Association, and developed it into a household name for deer hunters and wildlife enthusiasts across the state. Texas Trophy Hunters celebrates the slogan, "The Voice of Texas Hunting," and hunters all over Texas recognize the skull logo designed by Jerry Johnston about 50 years ago. The logo is recognized by hunters and outdoors folks all across the state.

The El Tropicano Hotel in San Antonio hosted the association's first meeting, with a small attendance of dedicated deer hunters and landowners. It was a small beginning, but with the help of some friends and associates, the association took off with membership drives, a quarterly publication called *Hunters Hotline*, and a series of trade shows first called conferences, and later called Hunters Extravaganzas. These shows got folks together to see — and buy — the latest in hunting gear and deer hunting paraphernalia. Another facet of the shows was the deer contest, where hunters could bring in their deer heads and compete for prizes.

And now, in 2024, TTHA continues to promote deer hunting with a bimonthly magazine, an annual Bucks and BBQ Cook-off, and Hunters Extravaganzas held in Houston, Fort Worth and San Antonio. Texas Trophy Hunters is the largest association of its type in the Southwest.

I have been on the TTHA team for 28 years. After I retired from Texas Parks and Wildlife in 1993, I joined Jerry's team at TTHA in September 1995. My job was to edit and write for *The Journal of the Texas Trophy*

First Three TTHA Platinum Life Members: #1 Mark Herfort (L), #2 Laura Berry, #3 Owen West

Hunters, assist cameraman Brian Hawkins with television productions, assist with Operation Game Thief banquets, and be the chief judge for the Hunters Extravaganza deer contests.

At that time, the Extravaganzas were hunter-oriented, and attendees were mostly adults. The deer contest was popular, and we had few problems with "cheating" because the only prizes were a jacket and certificate for the division winners. Later, when MCMI owned TTHA, prizes increased to various expensive hunting items, and cheating became more common — hence, my job as judge of the contest.

I had known Jerry for several years, and had hunted with him in South Texas. When Jerry started Texas Trophy Hunters in 1975, I attended the first meeting at the El Tropicano hotel in San Antonio. As a wildlife biologist, and White-tailed Deer Program Leader with Texas Parks and Wildlife, I helped Jerry with matters of importance between TTHA and the state agency. When Jerry called in 1995, I was very interested in joining his team in San Antonio.

TTHA has a proud conservation history. In 1981, the 67th Legislature established Operation Game Thief to discourage game and fish violations and poaching. TTHA and Jerry Johnston organized fund-raising banquets to promote the program. The result was over $300,000 going to help fund the OGT program. During the last 50 years, TTHA has also promoted, protected, and preserved hunting, outdoor recreation, and the Second Amendment.

The bimonthly magazine, *The Journal of the Texas Trophy Hunters*, has content that encourages hunting and quality habitat and nutrition through food plots and supplemental feeding. *The Journal* has articles and suggestions for deer management and antler quality. The bottom line of *The Journal* is to promote hunting and boost hunting interest. *The Journal* also emphasizes youth hunting to keep kids off the street and in the woods!

For several years, the "Trophy Hunters TV Show," which aired on the Outdoor Channel, promoted the best in big game, upland game, and waterfowl hunting. The show was a video extension of the passion and philosophy expressed in the pages of *The Journal*. The show was also a forum for filming hunts featuring wounded warriors coming back from war.

One of the keys to the success of TTHA has been the Hunters Extravaganzas, held annually in three major cities — Houston, Fort Worth and San Antonio. These trade shows highlight the newest innovations in hunting gear, and the business of hunting in general.

A main feature of each show is the deer competition and its awards. Some of the biggest and best whitetails and mule deer taken in Texas, Mexico, and out-of-state are displayed in competition for an array of prizes. However, the original intention of the deer contest was to get trophy bucks to a venue like Hunters Extravaganzas so that attendees could view them.

The Journal has been instrumental in keeping the public informed about legislative bills that influence outdoor recreation and hunting. One is their misguided hypothesis is that a deer disease called "chronic wasting disease" is dangerous to deer herds, and the agency's publicity announcements discourage the eating of deer meat. The erroneous control measures for CWD is eroding deer hunting in Texas.

Horace Gore and the Gals at Luncheon: L to R: Sandy Pastran, Gore, Debbie Keene, Faith Pena. Top L: Jennifer Beaman, Erin Cooper, and Christina Pittman

Horace Gore, Dr. James Kroll, and Jerry Johnston at San Antonio Extravaganza

Recent research at USDA in Ames, Iowa, has shown that CWD and scrapie (a sheep disease) are one and the same, and that humans and deer herds are not affected by the disease. Deer herds are thriving, and Texans eat 15 million pounds of venison every year. TTHA has shown evidence in *The Journal* that TPWD is "barking up the wrong tree" with their control programs for the mild sheep disease that means nothing to deer or deer hunters.

Nationwide, many organizations such as Ducks Unlimited, Pheasants Forever, Coastal Conservation Association, Texas Bighorn Society, to name a few, have objectives to save or promote the existence of a species. The Millennials have been reluctant to join conservation organizations, and this attitude has caused problems with memberships.

Texas Trophy Hunter's objectives are quite different. TTHA promotes hunting recreation, and the utilization of an abundant population of game animals such as deer, wild turkey, and exotics. Without hunting and excise taxes on guns and ammunition, there would no wildlife conservation. TTHA also helps landowners realize a monetary return for their conservation efforts.

Texas deer hunting seems to be hanging in the balance. Although Texas residents have increased by 14 million since TTHA was founded, the number of hunting license sales has been constant at just over one million. Only 4 percent of the 30 million Texans hunt deer.

Texas Trophy Hunters is being courted by generational preferences, but the association has continued to grow in many ways. Several high school and college chapters have been organized to participate in activities sponsored by TTHA. In 2011, TTHA created the Bucks and BBQ Cook-off. With only 40 teams involved at the beginning, the cook-off teams now number more than 100 competing for cash prizes. The annual event is sanctioned by the International Barbeque Cookers Association.

In February 2020, Christina Pittman was promoted to president and chief executive officer of Texas Trophy Hunters. Christina had been director of sales, and also director of trade shows (Hunters Extravaganzas) for eight years, prior to her promotion. She is a rabid hunter and so is Matt, and their youngsters, Ava and Gunnar are looking at *The Journal*. Christina is now in charge of all TTHA programs, and will continue to direct the statewide trade shows.

The deadly coronavirus, that swept through the world in 2020, devastated business and pleasure in the United States. The virus was detrimental to Hunters Extravaganza attendance, and the 2020 shows were canceled. Now that the virus has subsided, the shows have continued, and TTHA is concentrating on renewing full attendance for all three shows.

In this 50th year, TTHA is going strong among several competitive organizations in the state, and some folks describe *The Journal* as the best hunting publication in the Southwest. The Trophy Hunters TV is gone, but TTHA is now experimenting with podcasts to promote the association and hunting.

The Hunters Extravaganzas have never been better as Texas Trophy Hunters get ready for another 50 years of the "Voice of Texas Hunting," the slogan of the Trophy Hunters Nation. Hunters everywhere are excited about Texas whitetails, and we hope to inspire every Texan to get into the hunt, and attend the "Granddaddy of All Hunting Shows" — the Hunters Extravaganzas.

CHAPTER 27

Hunters Extravaganzas

One of the unique facets of Jerry Johnson's Texas Trophy Hunters Association, founded in 1975, were the Hunters Extravaganzas. These trade shows were designed to give attendees an annual meeting to visit and exchange ideas, purchase hunting equipment and supplies from vendors, hear seminars on whitetail and other wildlife, and enter a trophy buck in the deer contest. Now, 50 years later, the Hunters Extravaganzas, called "conferences" in early years, held in Houston, Fort Worth, and San Antonio are a continuing popular attraction — the largest hunting trade shows in the Southwest.

Each year since 1975, the annual Extravaganzas have successfully served the association, and are a contributing factor to Texas whitetail hunting. Saturday shows would see early-morning visitors waiting in long lines to buy a ticket, and many attendees would stay all day. Since 2010, Texas Trophy Hunters has been known as "The Voice of Texas Hunting."

When Jerry started TTHA, he had a "convention" the first few years, but later named it "Hunters Extravaganza" because hunting was the cornerstone of each show. Today, with many Texans simply enjoying camping, fishing and boating, along with deer, dove, duck, and varmint hunting, the general composition of the trade shows has changed. Many youth attractions have been included, and now entire families come and enjoy everything that is outdoors.

Generational preferences affect any organization. Texas Trophy Hunters has gone through five generations since it was founded in 1975. The last of the "baby boomers" and Generation X were devout hunters. Generation Y (Millennials), also known as the media generation, are complacent to hunting and hunting organizations. Generation Z has yet to show any specific desire for anything related to hunting, and generation Alpha is only in its 10th year.

Horace and Jerry Johnston at Extravaganza Deer Contest

Individual as well as group discretion is important to a hunting fraternity like Texas Trophy Hunters, and any disregard for hunting by two consecutive generations can be critical for maintaining public interest and membership. There appears to be no connection between Hunters Extravaganza attendance and TTHA membership, but generational preferences by the eight million Texas Millennials has been felt by fraternal organizations and the business community.

TTHA has gone through many changes since Jerry Johnston founded the Association in 1975. A series of attempts to establish additional

> *"If you are prone to temptation, stay away from horse races, brothels, and gun shows."* — Goreism

extravaganzas in Texas and other states saw little success. The biggest problems with all out-of-state ventures were communication and logistics, which were insurmountable.

In the beginning, the shows always had a variety of trophy whitetails to look at and admire. Jerry even paid to have whitetail collections brought to each show. After a few years, he decided that a deer contest would serve the same purpose, and a competitive contest was developed for whitetails, and later mule deer. The free-to-members contest has been very successful for deer hunters to show their trophies and win prizes, while having a wall full of big bucks for public viewing.

The original extravaganzas had a deer hunting motif. The headquarters area had a fake-front deer camp with a screen door, and front porch, with an old hunter siting in a straight-back chair, and a big whitetail buck hanging nearby. Everything spelled "hunting," from blinds to feeders; coats to boots; and everything else from guns to knives. Attendance at any of the Extravaganzas was a hunter's dream. Of course, changing times brought the shows to a more modern scene with many outdoor additions.

In 2006, after Johnson sold TTHA to Dr. Jim Leininger and his company, MCMI, attempts were continued to establish associations in Canada, as well as Arkansas and Alabama. These attempts were soon discontinued, with the entire focus placed on three major Extravaganzas in leading Texas cities. In relation to attendance, Fort Worth is first, followed by Houston and San Antonio.

The coronavirus pandemic of 2020, which affected business and pleasure all across the United States, had a detrimental effect on Hunters Extravaganzas. All three shows were canceled in 2020, but were resumed in 2021. Attendance to the popular trade shows was disrupted, and will take some time to recover. However, the two seasons since the pandemic have shown a good comeback by the thousands of hunters and outdoor enthusiasts who have been regular attendees for many years.

Each Extravaganza has a wide array of educational, entertaining, and competitive attractions for young and old people. Seminars on deer management, camping, cooking wild game, and varmint hunting are annual events, while attendees can check out the vendors for a variety of goods and services.

The annual deer contest might be the backbone of the shows, where trophy whitetails and mule deer are displayed. Winners of various divisions receive awards in the form of clothing, hunting gear, and certificates, and the large array of trophy bucks is always a center of attention.

Horace Gore and Judy Jurek are all smiles.

The alligator show is a popular attraction for all ages. The event features all sizes of live gators, and performers go through routines with the reptiles that thrill the large crowds. In many cases, the alligator show is the only time some attendees get to see a real alligator!

Another popular event at all shows is the Fish Tank, where youngsters pay a small fee to fish for channel catfish in a large, round tank of water. For some, the fee for fishing includes a trophy, shaped like a jumping black bass. During each show, the fish tank area is crowded with youngsters, anxious to catch a fish and win a trophy prize.

Other events for youth is the Bubble Runner, where kids get into a large bubble and try to stand or run. Another youth event is the Lone Star Bowhunters booth, where kids (and adults) can try their luck at popping a balloon with an arrow. Both events are popular, and usually have a long line of kids waiting to participate.

Of course, the hundreds of vendor booths are the key attraction for the thousands of attendees at each show. Folks can look and buy a variety of gear for hunting, fishing, camping, cooking, shooting, and any other activities done in the wild. There are things to eat, to cut, to shoot, to cook, to hunt, to fish, to wear, to camp, to store, and to photograph. In general, there is hardly anything an outdoors person can't find at the Hunters Extravaganzas.

In the past, many celebrities have attended the shows — stars from football, basketball, baseball, and pro-fighting have been on hand to greet visitors. Hunting personalities for big game, ducks, predators, and continental safaris have also been show attractions.

Representatives of Safari Club International, *North American Whitetail*, *Sports Afield*, *Outdoor Life*, National Rifle Association, Lone Star Bowhunting Association, Texas Wildlife Association and Texas Parks and Wildlife are both formal and casual show guests.

The location of the three Hunters Extravaganzas are as follows:
- Houston, the NRG Center
- Fort Worth, the Convention Center
- San Antonio, Freeman Coliseum and Expo Hall

All shows are held annually in August, when the sun is hot and the Extravaganzas are cool! Also, all shows are held just prior to dove season, which is the first of several hunting seasons during fall and winter. The popularity of the Hunters Extravaganzas can be seen by all of the Texas Trophy Hunters Logo skulls and other TTHA insignias on vehicle windows, doors, highway signs, and belt buckles. The TTHA logo is almost as recognizable as the Dallas Cowboy's logo!

Mark your calendar for August, and plan a day or weekend trip to a Hunters Extravaganza in Houston, Fort Worth, or San Antonio. You'll be glad, and the kids will want to go back, year after year!

CHAPTER 28

Trophy Hunters TV: A Memorable Video Experience

My tenure with Texas Trophy Hunters was in its second year, when Jerry Johnston approached me about assisting videographer Brian Hawkins with a new television show. Brian would direct and conduct all videography, while I would do the interviews and actions related to making a 30-minute show. Production began in 1998, and Brian, Jerry and I produced some excellent shows for the series. In 2004, the show won the Outdoor Channel's "Golden Moose" award for two productions depicting the fiasco of chronic wasting disease in Wisconsin.

Some of the early productions involved pronghorn hunting in West Texas, as well as ranch oddities, as well as whitetail, hog, and varmint hunts. Many of the shows emanated from the McLemore Ranch in Shackelford County, operated by Lanny Vinson of Abilene. Lanny was a good friend who also owns and operates Abilene Ag, an agriculture supply and retail store in Abilene. He was also the instigator of the Legends Dove Hunt, which has raised 4.2 million for a children's wing of Hendrick Hospital in Abilene.

The McLemore Ranch rests on both sides of the Clear Fork of the Brazos, and has a thriving population of white-tailed deer, feral hogs, and Rio Grande turkey. Many of the TV shows involved hunts by both commercial and family hunters, and celebrities often attended the hunts.

I lived on the Kokernot Ranch in Gonzales County during all of the TV production days, and some of the shows were videoed on Peach Creek and the Guadalupe River, which forms the south boundary of the scenic cattle ranch. However, the majority of the TV series were videoed on the McLemore and Cutbirth ranches, and other places in the Texas Panhandle.

Brian liked to include unusual incidents with the shows, like the time we were doing a pronghorn antelope hunt in West Texas, when I stumbled upon a prairie rattler in the short grass. Brian videoed the small rattlesnake, and it was a unique part of the show. I added a few biological remarks, including the coloration of the snake, and its ever-present 39 round spots from head to tail, or should I say, "rattles."

Brian Hawkins, Trophy Hunters TV Director and videographer

The making of a hunting show usually goes through the same routine. The first is the hunt, where the kill shot is filmed. Once the target animal or bird is dispatched and filmed, the hunt situation is created to correspond to the kill shot of the hunted species. As expected, there is a lot of fakery in movie and TV productions.

When Ralph Lermayer of New Mexico and I developed the "Wildcat" .224 TTH (Texas Trophy Hunter) to commemorate the 25th anniversary of Texas Trophy Hunters, Brian Hawkins and I, along with some others, did a few TV shows to demonstrate the hunting qualities of the .224 TTH cartridge.

I recall a hog hunt that Brian and I did on the McLemore, when we were "discovering" the hunting attributes of the .224 TTH. I picked up a trailered ATV in San Antonio, and met Brian on the ranch. Later, we corned a dim road near the river that was home to feral hogs. We went back to the spot, hoping to get some video of me shooting a big pig. As we went into the brush, Brian spotted a group of hogs eating our corn.

I glassed the hogs while Brian got the camera ready. He gave me the go-ahead, and I took careful aim at a big red boar. At the shot, the hog went down in a heap. We went to the dead hog and finished the videoing, when Brian noticed that the 300-pound hog had no ears or tail! All that was left of both ears were the earholes, and about an inch of what once was a foot-long tail — strange for a hog that lived and died in the wild!

On a pronghorn antelope videoing spree north of Amarillo, Brian and I drove up in the truck, while Jerry Johnston and Marty Berry flew up in Marty's plane. A guide had been looking for a good pronghorn, and when we all got to Amarillo about 2 p.m., the guide called and said he had found a good trophy for Jerry. We all went to the ranch, and Jerry glassed the 16-inch pronghorn across a canyon about 400 yards away.

Jerry got his .300 Win. Mag. ready and steadied himself against the pickup. He had bragged about how good he could shoot milk jugs at 600 yards, and Brian and Marty were ribbing him about the pronghorn at some 400 yards. Brian had the camera rolling as Jerry squeezed the trigger, and the .300 roared. After what seemed like several seconds, the bullet hit and the pronghorn went down.

We all congratulated Jerry for the good shot, and then wondered how we were going to get to the animal. A dim road went down the canyon for a few hundred yards, where we could cross and get to the pronghorn. While we made the trek, Marty asked Jerry where he hit the antelope. "I was aiming for the shoulder," Jerry said. "But he fell so quick, I may have hit him in the head!"

We got to the animal, and I went over to look for the bullet hole. Nothing up front — then I saw blood on the pronghorn's rear end. "Jerry, you shot him in the ass!" I chided as Jerry came over. "Well, it was a long shot," Jerry said, and changed the subject. He had hit the antelope high in the hip, breaking the spine.

Later, Marty passed up a shot at a big pronghorn that we jumped from the brush, and stood broadside at 100 yards. "I didn't come to the Panhandle to murder an antelope," Marty said, and went home empty-handed.

We were filming a whitetail hunt in Mexico with the .224 TTH, and were guests of Dr. Polo of Nuevo Laredo. His family owned a big ranch about 20 miles west of Highway 1, which followed the Rio Grande. We

> *"For years I tolerated Porter, just to hear Dolly."* — Goreism

were hunting in mid-February, and a cold front had blown in, with strong north wind and freezing temperature.

We needed a good 8- to 10-point buck for the TV show, but all the bucks had broken antlers. On the third day, we hunted a blind just northwest of the ranch house that was dilapidated, with the cold north wind cutting us to the bone. Who would have thought it could get so cold in Mexico?

We got to the blind early, and endured the cold wind all morning. We were deciding whether to stay that evening when a lone buck came up the dirt road toward us. The cold air was exasperating, and we were glad to see the buck, which looked like a 10 pointer with an 18-inch spread.

The .224 TTH was loaded, and the camera was ready. The buck was slowly walking into the cold wind as I squeezed the trigger. The deer fell like a rock in the middle of the road. We vacated the blind fast, and finished the camera work. The cold had us chilled, and I didn't want to carry the rifle back to the house. I laid it on the buck, hoping that no one would steal it before we returned for the deer. We hustled the half-mile as fast as we could back to the house, and the warm fire. Our cold Mexico TV hunt was over.

The Texas Trophy Hunter TV show lasted about eight years with Jerry Johnston, and another six years after Jerry sold Texas Trophy Hunters to Dr. Jim Leininger of San Antonio. The original filming of the shows for eight years was good experience for me, and I enjoyed all of the excitement and camaraderie that went with Brian Hawkins and playing the "hunter" for Trophy Hunters television.

CHAPTER 29

The .224 Texas Trophy Hunter

Our 25th anniversary cartridge is a real winner

In 2000, Texas Trophy Hunters introduced the .224 TTH, a "wildcat" cartridge that was new to most shooters. Ralph Lermayer and I simply picked up on an old idea that was ready for its time. Back in 1964, Kenneth Clark of Madera, California, came up with the idea of reducing the neck diameter of the .257 Roberts case down to .224. We used the 6mm Remington, which is simply the .257 Roberts necked down, with the shoulder changed from 17 degrees to 26 degrees. The .257 Roberts was created years ago by necking down the venerable 7mm Mauser. Reducing the neck of a cartridge case to take a smaller bullet, at usually a higher velocity, is commonplace with the national shooting clan.

Mr. Clark had a good plan back in '64, but he didn't have the right powder and bullets to back up his idea of a 1-in-8 twist of rifling to shoot a heavy 82-grain .224 bullet. He had to make his own bullets, but the slowest powders available at that time were not adequate to accomplish his goals, and the wildcat load never developed a lot of interest. In 1999, Ralph Lermayer of New Mexico called me with the idea of an anniversary cartridge. I was all for it.

Ralph, who wrote for *The Journal*, and I are both self-professed "gun nuts." We discussed several cartridge cases and finally settled on the 6mm Remington necked down to .224. We eventually named it the Texas Trophy Hunter. The cartridge design was good, and Texas hunters needed a souped-up .22 cartridge that would be ideal for deer-sized game.

We knew that it would require a good rifle with a 26-inch barrel and a bullet of 75 to 80 grains that would take the centrifugal force of a 1:8

twist at a velocity of over 3,500 fps. We're talking about 1/3 million revolutions per minute! The rifle was no problem, but the bullet was. In 2000, there were only two or three factory bullets that would take that kind of rotation without coming apart. They were the 75-grain Hornady A-Max, the 64-grain Winchester Power Point, and the 60-grain Nosler Partition.

Now, I know a lot of you are thinking, "Why another cartridge — especially a heavy .22? We've got more fat-cased deer cartridges than you can shake a stick at." You're right, and we apologize again for coming up with a good idea that was ready for its time. If rifle manufacturers had been as anxious to bring out new ammo back in the '60s as they are today, the .224/6mm would be a factory load of some name today. But that didn't happen because there were no powders for such ammo at that time. Today, slow-burning powders are available that make cartridges like the .224/6mm really shine if you use the right bullets and a long barrel.

The introduction of the .224 TTH was not intended to replace any other cartridge, nor are any claims made that it's in any way superior to some other good .224 cartridges. However, it does offer better performance than anything else currently on the shelf. It's a dual-purpose high velocity varmint/deer cartridge that is mild of recoil, flat shooting, and inherently accurate without taking a toll on the shooter or rifle. As a rifle shooter and hunter for more than 60 years, I have never seen a cartridge that will take deer-sized game dead in its tracks like the .224 TTH with good 75-grain bullets.

I've killed a lot of game during the last 10 years using the .224 TTH. During that time, new bullets have been developed to give the hunter a choice of explosive or deep penetrating loads. I personally have settled on two bullets that will satisfy the most discriminating hunter. The 75-grain Hornady A-Max kills deer-sized animals like a time bomb, but seldom exits the animal. The Swift Scirocco in 75 grain is a terrific

.224 TTH rifle, serial no. 1

Gore and Dr. "Polo" with Mexico whitetail taken with .224 TTH for TTHA TV Show

killer, and usually exits to leave a blood trail. I shoot both at 3,650 in a 26-inch barrel using 46.5 grains of reloader .22 and a Magnum primer.

The last pronghorn I shot in the Panhandle in the fall of 2008 fell like a sack of feed when hit at about 175 yards with the Swift Scirocco. A whitetail buck fell within 20 yards when hit behind the shoulder at 90 yards with a 75-grain Swift Scirocco. He was a big eight-point that grossed 153 B&C — one of the best bucks I've ever killed.

The spectacular, one-shot kills this cartridge makes on pronghorns, deer, and hogs lead me to believe that there's something about these super-fast, heavy .224 bullets that has been overlooked. Perhaps it's the fast rotation of these bullets; or maybe the knife-like entry of a long bullet that delivers all its energy internally with tremendous hydrostatic shock — we don't know. But experience and field-testing have shown that this combination is very deadly on Texas game.

After shooting the .224 TTH for 10 years at all manner of game, you can rest assured that it *has* been tested. Nearly all game shot with a variety of bullets have stood at less than 200 yards, which is rather common for Texas hunting. I'd guess that most big game in Texas is shot as less than 150 yards. And most coyotes fall at less than 200. Laura Berry of Corpus Christi has killed a pickup-load of hogs with the .224 TTH from her deer blind.

I've seen some long shots with the TTH. Ralph Lermayer killed a half-grown aoudad on the Y.O. Ranch at 325 yards. I saw Michael Riser of

George West kill a whitetail doe at 305 yards. Bill Benton of Austin shot a doe out of a top-drive on the Gates ranch near Catarina. She fell so fast we lost her in the high grass. I walked to where she fell and Bill put the range finder on me at 278 yards. Deb Cleverdon of Houston killed a sika buck on the Y.O. at 191 yards. I've killed several good whitetail bucks and big hogs at up to 180 yards, and one big eight-point whitetail fell to a 75-grain Scorocco at 275 yards!

Not all animals shot with the .224 TTH were small. We killed bull elk, aoudad rams, a nilgai cow (head shot) and some BIG hogs with the rifle. All fell in their tracks, but some had to be finished off. The hydrostatic shock will put an animal down in a hurry, but they are not always dead. And we are not recommending the .224 TTH for nilgai, elk and aoudad!

Long coyote shots have been common with the .224 TTH, but they seem to be harder to kill instantly than some of the larger animals. I like to sight in the .224 to 1½ inches high at 100 yards. It shoots very flat and is only 1 inch low at 250 and 3 inches low at just over 300 yards. At 300 yards, it still has 1,300 foot-pounds of energy — plenty to kill anything the size of a deer.

"How do I go about getting a .224 TTH rifle?" you ask. Well, you have to have one made by a competent gunsmith. You can re-barrel an existing rifle in your battery, or you can buy a new rifle and have it re-barreled. The cost will vary, depending on the brand and type of barrel you want, and whether you want to use the stock that is on the rifle. Aftermarket triggers add to the expense.

Now that you know about the .224 TTH, let me leave you with a few tips. If you get a rifle made, keep the barrel clean. The quick twist rifling will shoot much better if you buy a Bore Snake and pull it through the barrel about every 12-15 shots. Also, the new barrel should be "shot in" so that the rifling will adjust itself to your bullets and loads.

There is an old saying: "Don't knock it 'til you've tried it." I feel that way about the .224 TTH. Every animal that I've shot at fell immediately or sooner. Shoot the right bullet and you'll walk away a believer.

CHAPTER 30

The Kokernot Mockingbird

I've been around mockingbirds all my life. Yell County, Arkansas, where I lived with my grandmother for five years — from age 7 to 12 — had a lot of mockingbirds. Maude Gilmore gave me strict warning about shooting mockingbirds with my slingshot.

There are 16 species that are called "mockingbirds," but only the Northern mockingbird lives in the United States. They are found in nearly every state, and in Canada and Mexico. The mockingbird is the official bird of Texas, and can be found almost anywhere in the state. It is one of the few birds that often sing on a moonlit night.

Every Arkansas boy that I knew at school had a slingshot, and our favorite "ammo" was glass marbles that we played marbles with at school. We played "keeps" when the teachers weren't looking, where we kept all the marbles that we knocked out of the ring with our steel balls. I was a pretty good marble player, and kept quite a few glass marbles to use in my slingshot.

Maude made hard rules for my bird shooting: "No mockingbirds, wrens, cardinals (red birds), and blue birds." Sparrows, black birds, shrikes, robins, blue jays, and meadow larks were fair game. My grandmother was especially fond of mockingbirds and cardinals.

When Maude and I moved from Briggsville to Bluffton (the Philips Place), my cousin Charles Edward Daniel and I shot at a lot of birds and wasp nests with our slingshots, using mostly thumb-nail size stones that we found in the gravel roads. We seldom ever hit a bird, but we shot at a lot of sparrows and blackbirds.

When I moved to Hooks in northeast Texas (Bowie County) in 1945, we had a lot of birds in that area, including mockingbirds. The same was

Northern mockingbird

true with my Mother, when I got a .22 single shot for my 12th birthday — no mockingbirds, wrens, red-headed woodpeckers, or cardinals. I spent a lot of time chasing blue Jays, meadow larks, blackbirds, crows, and cottontails in the fields and flatwoods north of hooks.

We had several mockingbirds in the neighborhood, and I knew their nesting habits and the color of their eggs. I watched many young birds leave the nest and go through the first dangerous days of being on the ground, unable to fly. I say all of this, because I was not new to mockingbirds when I moved to the Kokernot Ranch in East Gonzales County in September 1995.

The Kokernot ranch house sits on a big, flat hill, overlooking the pastures to Peach Creek and the Guadalupe River. The house area includes the cattle pens, the big barn, a small barn and the house. The yard has live oak and cedar elm trees, and there are no other residences for a mile in any direction. The summer birds around the house were cow birds, wrens, cardinals, scissor-tailed flycatchers, meadow larks, finches, an occasional painted bunting, humming birds, and one mockingbird.

I first saw the mockingbird in the spring of 1998. He may have been there before, but I hadn't noticed him. What caught my eye about the bird was that his right wing was drooped noticeably, and once I recognized this, I saw him around the house each summer. Another unusual thing about this bird — he was a literal virtuoso! I've been around mockingbirds most of my life, but I had never heard a bird sing as much as "Mr. Mocker" — the Pavarotti of Peach Creek!

The ranch house had an old tall TV antenna attached to a little storage shed behind the house, which had about three long veins sticking out from the main pole. The dilapidated antenna was the favorite place for the "mocker" to sit and sing — and I mean SING! I suspected the bird was a male, because he sang his heart out each summer for at least five years, and I never ever saw another mockingbird with him or around the house. The ranch house was so isolated that his singing never did get him a mate.

After the first year or two, I began to watch for his arrival each spring. Along about late March or the first days of April, I would hear him singing from his high perch on the TV antenna. He was a regular visitor for at least five years, and maybe more. I would always look for the drooped wing, but I got to know him by his singing habits on the antenna. He never sang anywhere else — just on top of the antenna.

If you've ever watched a singing mockingbird, you have noticed that during his singing, he will suddenly fly straight up for two-three feet, and turn a flip in the air — coming back to where he left his perch. The Kokernot Ranch bird did the same thing — up off the antenna and back again, never missing a note.

I noticed that the bird sang mostly in mid-morning and late evening, but he was always close to the house. Like all mockingbirds, he was territorial and ran a lot of little birds away from the yard. His only rivals were the cardinals, and they usually kept their distance!

One summer evening just before sundown, I was sitting in a lawn chair having a cool drink, when the old bird flew to the antenna and began to sing. I went into the house and got a scrap of paper and pen, and came back to my chair. The old bird had been singing all the

> *"We are known by the company we keep."* — *Goreism*

while. I waited until he mocked a sound that I could remember — the "bobwhite" of a quail. With that, I started counting his songs and making notes.

After a long spell of singing, he came back to the bobwhite call, and I counted the many different calls he had made: 34! I was so amazed that I googled up the mockingbird, to see if anyone else had counted their calls during a long singing session. The report noted 35 different calls, but my count was good. I guess my old bird may have forgotten one of the many songs in his repertoire.

There has long been debate about mockingbirds — do they mock other birds, or is their many bird imitations a natural inheritance? Experts point out that the birds repeat the songs of other birds that do not exist in their locale. I personally think the mockingbird has an inherited vocabulary, and doesn't mock anything.

I enjoyed this mockingbird for about 5 or 6 years — then one summer he didn't come back. He may have decided to change his singing spot, since he had never called in a mate. Or, he may have just died somewhere in his travels — I'll never know. However, I enjoyed his long vocabulary of melodious bird calls for a long time.

All male "mockers" don't sing like the Kokernot bird. Where there are several mockingbirds in one area — both male and female — the male birds hardly ever sing. But when an old bird is all alone on a hill in Gonzales County, perched on a high TV antenna, he will sing his heart out, hoping that some far-away female will hear him and join his company. Woe is the life of a lonely Kokernot Ranch mockingbird!

CHAPTER 31

The Boar of Long Lake

A short story

I lived, and hunted on the Kokernot Ranch in eastern Gonzales County for 22 years. The ranch had hundreds of Russian-type hogs, hogs that had been brought in to the Southeastern states from Eurasia and North Africa in the 19th century. The hogs on the Kokernot were from Tennessee, brought to the Guadalupe area by a neighbor rancher across the river. One of the oldest, meanest Russian boars on the ranch lived at Long Lake, a wet-weather, shallow lake on the Shiner side. This story is about that old boar, and a memorable chase with the dogs.

The Russian strain on the Kokernot Ranch is quite different from the spotted, curly-tailed feral hogs (domestic hogs gone wild) in other parts of Texas. The Russians are tall at the shoulder and narrow at the hip, with long snout, long straight tail, small ears, and big tusks. The hair, which is solid red, black or gray is thin, with a line of long hair running down the center of the back, from head to tail. Adult boars look big, but seldom weigh over 225 pounds. Sows may weigh up to 175.

After retiring from Texas Parks and Wildlife in 1993, and spending two winters guiding quail hunters in north Texas, I moved to the Kokernot Ranch in September 1995. The owners were leasing the hunting for the first time, and wanted the advice of Al Brothers and I about price and a contract. Al and I met with Brian "Doc" Denman, and while we were on the ranch, I asked if the deer hunters would be using the ranch house. "Oh, no," Doc said. "Well, it needs to be used," I said, knowing I had

> *"When gas, oil and coal are gone there will still be electricity. But where is the miracle of science that can restore an extinct bird or animal, or devise means of rejuvenation for Man such as is found only in the chase."* —Anonymous

said the wrong thing. Doc looked over at me and replied, "Well, If you are so concerned, why don't you move in." I was surprised at his offer!

I had worked in the TPWD Wildlife Division as a wildlife biologist for 33 years, and I took Doc Denman's deal, and moved to the ranch. I had known Doc for several years, and had sold him a good quail dog. He wanted me to help in getting deer permits for the hunters, and watching over the hunting operation. I thought about all the wildlife on the ranch — especially the squirrel and hog hunting.

I would move from Austin to the vacant ranch house for a pittance of rent, and keep an eye on things. And having been on the ranch nearly two years, I was still getting familiar with all of the uplands and river bottom areas on the 2,200-acre cattle ranch. With two miles of river on the south side, and Peach Creek meandering down the middle of the ranch, there was a lot to see on the Kokernot, one of the oldest and finest ranches in Gonzales County.

The ranch house was big, and old. Although eastern Gonzales County was known for bad water — sulfur and iron — the Kokernot house had usable water. The first time Doc Denman mentioned me moving into the house, I went to the kitchen sink and took a long drink — the "acid test" for moving in.

The Austin deer leasers brought a double-wide camp house to the "Hog Pasture" on the river, about a mile down from the ranch house. The camp house was on the highest point of the river bottom. Near the house were two large trees — a big cedar elm, and an ancient bur oak. The camp house sat near the high bank of the river, which was lined with cypress and cottonwood trees.

Most of the lease hunting involved deer, hogs and turkey, and hunters killed coyotes on sight.

The deer were a subspecies called "Avery Island" whitetails that were native to the ranch. Deer and hog hunting were good, and hunters sometimes killed a turkey gobbler from the large flocks along the river.

Spring-fed Peach Creek runs through the ranch from the north, and empties into the Guadalupe, which formed the ranch's south boundary. The creek and Long Lake are water sources for cattle and wildlife.

The Kokernot is a haven for wildlife and hunting. White-tailed deer and hogs were dominant, with waterfowl, eagles, caracaras and buzzards, horned and barred owls, pileated woodpeckers, sandhill cranes and white ibis, gray and fox squirrels, coyotes and bobcats, a plethora of songbirds, and a few beaver, alligators, canebrake rattlesnakes, copperheads and cottonmouths. Dove hunting was good in the uplands when we scattered a little milo, and let water troughs run over during dove season.

On the north side of Long lake, a big patch of mesquite, hackberry, elm scrub timber and brush made a perfect hideaway for wildlife because the brush and timber were not easily accessible from the dim road on the south side of the lake. I had suspected that some animal, a whitetail buck or an old hog, used the quiet spot as a hideout during the day. On a warm evening in September 1997, my suspicions were confirmed when I first saw the big black Russian boar.

I was on a four-wheeler just at sundown with my young black lab, "Belle," and as I got to the lake, I got a glimpse of something coming from the thick brush into the shallow lake bed. I could see it was a big black hog.

I had a scoped rifle in a rack, but by the time I stopped and got the rifle up, the hog had crossed the lake and was about 20 yards from me, running at a fast clip. I managed to fire a .270 shot that missed because the hog was close and the 3-9X Leupold was on 8-power. All I could see through the scope was black hair, as the bullet went over the hog and kicked up dirt. Belle jumped off and took after the hog, and in short order, the dog and hog had disappeared.

I sat on the four-wheeler in complete surprise, knowing I had broken my own rule — keep the scope on lowest power until you get ready to shoot. Belle had chased the hog out of sight, and while I was studying the situation, she came back with a slight cut on her left shoulder. Belle was a retriever — not a fighter.

I kept after the big, black hog, and I would hide near the lake on the four-wheeler, with Belle behind me. I hunted several times from sundown until dark, cradling the .270 on 4-power, but I never saw the hog. I suspicioned that the warm weather had him moving after dark. The boar became an obsession, but I got interesting in other things, and forgot about it until squirrel, duck, and deer seasons ended.

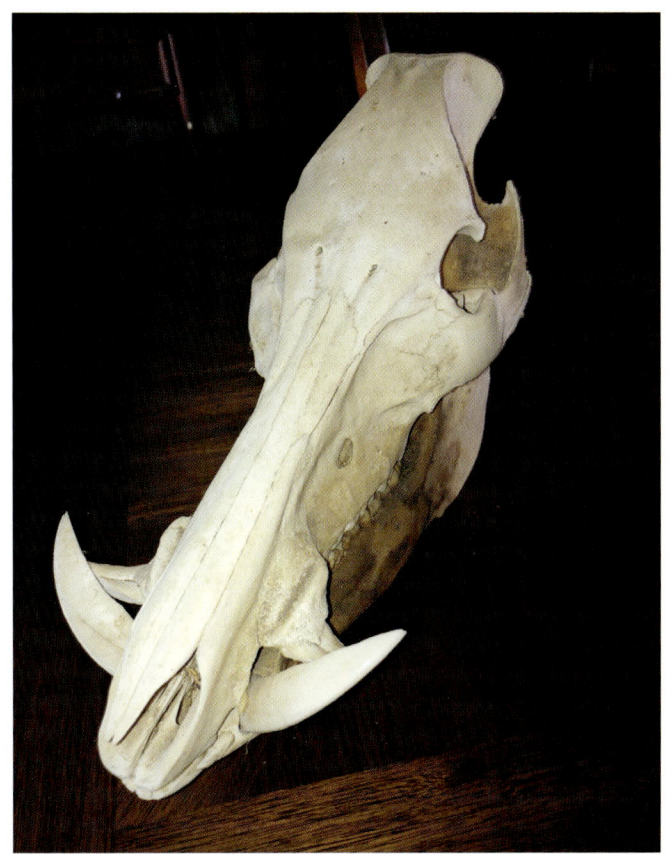

Russian boar skull

The next spring, my mind went back to the black boar at Long Lake. I had heard a local fireman in town had a pack of hog dogs, but I had never met him. On a summer day in June, I passed by the fire house and stopped to see if he was working. I inquired about a man with hog-dogs, and the lady in the office directed me to Bob Reynolds.

I found Bob and another fireman washing a fire truck, and introduced myself and said, "I live on the Kokernot, and was wondering if you have ever hunted hogs in that part of the County." "Oh, so you are the fellow who moved into the Kokernot ranch house a year or so ago?" he asked. "Well, I've hunted Peach Creek some, but the hogs on the creek and where you live are tough on dogs." I told him I'm a retired wildlife biologist, working for Texas Trophy Hunters Association in San Antonio, and that I had killed and eaten several of the younger Russian hogs on the ranch. They were all lean, but good eating.

"Old boars are scarce — I've killed only two boars that were old enough to boil out for trophy skulls," I remarked. "Those boars, with long sharp tusks, would have given a hunter with dogs a hard time."

"You say Russian hogs?" Bob asked, as I sat down. "Yes, all the hogs on the Kokernot are Russian-type hogs, I guess you know," I said. "Well, all I know is that they are solid color — no spots, and are tough on dogs," the fireman replied. "I've caught several sows and pigs on Peach Creek, and they don't look or act like the spotted, curly tailed hogs on the San Marcos. I never caught a boar, though."

"I hear that you have some hog dogs. What kind of dogs do you use," I inquired, as Bob turned off the water hose. "I like black-mouth curs for strike dogs and for chasing hogs, but I take along a bulldog-cross of some kind for a catch dog. If the curs can bay a hog, the bulldog will catch it in a hurry. I have two female black-mouth bitches, and a big bulldog catch dog named Rowdy."

I asked Bob, "Have you ever lost a dog in a hog fight?" Bob smiled and replied, "I've had young dogs cut up, but if they live a year or two, they get smart. I use wide leather collars to protect their neck and throat, which are the most vulnerable places. Dogs can survive cut bellies and legs, but they don't get over a boar tusk deep in the neck."

I asked Bob what kept his cur dogs from getting killed. He replied, "A good catch dog. If you have a good bulldog of some kind that will hold the hog, it will keep your other dogs from getting cut up in a fight." I thought back at the size of the black boar on Long Lake, and figured it would take a big bulldog to hold him down.

Bob could tell that I was interested. "Have you ever hunted with dogs?" His question reminded me of the hog hunts on the Clear Fork of the Brazos in Shackelford and Throckmorton counties, when I went several times with Jim "Barefoot" Richards. Jim was a rare individual, and would hunt barefooted in the summer. We would laugh, and say, "If Barefoot stepped on a nail or thorn, he wouldn't know it."

All of the hogs on the Clear Fork were feral, and easy to catch with good dogs. "Oh, I've hunted a few feral hogs with dogs," I told Bob. "But chasing Russian hogs with dogs will be new to me."

One morning in early July 1998, I met Bob in town at the Taco Hut, and asked, "Have you caught a hog lately." Bob replied, "I haven't hunted much lately. One of my bitches got a bad cut and I'm letting her heal up." I didn't want to push Bob too much, but I said, "I was just wondering, do you think your dogs can catch a big Russian boar?"

Bob took my comment as a challenge. "My dogs can catch any hog, Russian or not." I knew I had stirred Bob up a bit, and I said, "Well, I know where a big boar hangs out, and wondered if you'd like to go after him sometime." Bob quickly changed the subject, as he looked at his watch. "I'm late for a meeting at the fire house." He drove away and left me standing on the sidewalk.

A few days later, Bob called the ranch. "I've been thinking about the boar you claim to know so much about. Susie is healed, and I'm about ready for a hunt." I agreed, and suggested Bob bring the dogs any time. "I go to Texas Trophy Hunters in San Antonio a couple days a week," I said. "Give me a day or two notice, and I'll be ready. We planned a hunt for Wednesday, July 22, one of the hottest days of July.

Wednesday came, and Bob showed up in his pickup about 5 p.m. He had three dogs in dog boxes and parked his pickup in the cedar elm shade. The wind came out of the south, meaning we needed to go into Long Lake from the north.

The main road east through the ranch passed north of Long Lake. We could cross the creek, go through the pasture gate, and turn south toward the lake. Bob planned to turn a strike dog out when we got to the lake brush.

We left the ranch house just before sundown, with me driving Bob's truck. I didn't carry much gear — my folding Buck knife, binoculars, a gallon milk jug of water, a small 35mm camera, and some Red Man tobacco.

The house well water was drinkable, but the taste of sulfur and iron got stronger in the summer. Bob and the dogs would do all the work, and we would need water to salve the July heat. The camera was just an afterthought. "Should I take a gun?" I asked. Bob didn't answer.

As we crossed the low water crossing on the creek and headed up toward the Shiner Pasture gate, Bob asked, "How far are we from the Guadalupe." I estimated a little more than two miles, as the crow flies.

Russian boar in mudhole

Photo courtesy Wikimedia Commons

"Why?" Bob was looking out the pickup window toward the lake. "We don't want a hog to get to the river. It's dangerous, especially after dark." I didn't think of the river as being dangerous, but I said, "If the hog crosses the river we will let him go."

Bob opened the wire gap going into the pasture, and I told him to leave it open. The thick brush along the lake was just a few hundred yards ahead, and the bumpy trail down the fence line caused the dogs to get excited. They were well seasoned on hunting hogs.

Bob carried the two female curs in one box, and the bulldog-cross in the other. All of the dogs had some age. The curs, "Susie" and "Jane," were four and five years old, and the bulldog, "Rowdy," was three. Bob claimed they had caught a lot of hogs.

I stopped the truck and Bob got out on the right side and turned Susie loose. She had a wide leather collar, just as Bob had described. Susie went directly toward the timber along the lake's edge. I could see Bob expected to follow the dogs because he had high leather boots laced up over his Wranglers, and a long-bladed knife on his belt. I expected to see a pistol of some kind, but I remembered Bob saying, "I don't need a gun with my dogs."

As we sat in the truck, I asked Bob what kind of knife he liked best for sticking a hog. "What about a wooden-handled butcher knife?" Bob grimaced a little, and said, "No! We are sticking a hog — not butchering it!" With that, Bob reached back and took his knife out of the sheath. It had a leather handle and a clip blade about 5 inches long, with a small blade guard. "This is a Western brand knife that I have had for years," Bob said. "It has a sharp point, and has caused the demise of many hogs." We sat waiting for Susie to strike hog scent.

"Is sticking a hog in the heart difficult?" Bob knew that I had hunted hogs with dogs and a knife, and asked, "Don't you know how to stick a hog?" I commented that Barefoot Richards had always stuck the hog and I just watched. "Well, you don't stab the hog — you stick it. That means you pull the hog's front leg up, and place the knife point inside the leg and simply push the blade into the heart. That kills the hog instantly."

Even in the hot weather, Bob had on a long-sleeved shirt and wore a bill-cap. He had followed dogs through thick brush many times. He also had a water bottle in one hind pocket, with a small flashlight in the other. I could tell he thought we would be out after dark, and that the chase might be long and hard.

As he walked by me, I noticed a nylon cord hanging out of his back pocket. "What's the cord for?" Bob looked over and replied, "You never know when you'll need to stop the bleeding — on me or one of the dogs."

I laid out the property for Bob. "If you follow the dogs on this side of the creek," I said, "you will have to cross over to the west side when you come to a wire gap on a fence line. The creek is the Bouldin property boundary from there to the river."

Bob asked, "When I cross the creek at the Bouldin property, how far is the river?" I answered, "About half a mile or more." We both knew if Susie struck a hot hog trail, or jumped the hog out of his bed, the hog would likely head toward the river.

We planned what I would do. If Bob followed the dogs, I would go back across the creek and go to the river with Rowdy. "I will holler you in if you lose the hog, and if he goes down the creek, he will be close enough for me to turn Rowdy loose when we hear or see the other dogs." It was hot in the truck, and I planned to part under the bur oak at the camp house.

Susie was working the brushy timber as I looked over at Bob. "You ever think of dying?" I asked. "You know that sticking a hog with a knife is dangerous, especially if you have a big boar with 3-inch tusks as sharp as a razor." Bob looked surprised, and replied, "No, I have never thought about it. When Rowdy catches a hog by the ear and latches on, it's not that difficult. I've never thought much about dying over sticking a hog."

Bob looked out the truck window, as I said, "What if the dog loses his hold on the hog just as you are about to stick it. I think the hog we are after could cut you pretty bad, and you would bleed to death going to the doctor." Bob replied, "Well, that's why I carry the cord, and I doubt that death is all that bad. I blacked out once when we were building a fence in July, and didn't come to until we were at the hospital. That's a whole lot like dying."

A few minutes later, Bob said one final thing about dying. "I'd as soon be cut by a hog and bleed to death, as die in the river." We changed the subject, and I thought to myself, "If either of us dies on a hog hunt, it won't be in the river."

Part II

The female cur Bob Reynolds called "Susie" let out a loud howl, and Bob, who had dozed off, jumped from the truck and yelled, "Yeow, get 'em, Susie." The cur continued to bark, and Bob let Jane out of the box. She immediately went to the sound of the other dog, as Bob said, "Susie has found some hot scent. I think they have your big hog on the run." With that, he checked his gear and the sheath strap around the knife handle. The chase was on.

Both curs had crossed the lake, and Bob said excitedly, "I'll follow the Susie and Jane. You go back across the creek, and I'll see you somewhere near the river. Blow the truck horn when you get to the river, and when we get close enough for you to hear the dogs, turn Rowdy loose." With that, Bob started trotting towards the lake, looking for a place to cross the low water and mud. The last time I saw him, he was following the barking dogs.

I was in no hurry to go back across the creek and go to the river bottom. I left the pasture, and closed the wire gap. When I got to the creek, I stopped the truck for a few minutes to listen for the dogs. The silence meant that Bob and the dogs were far away down the creek. I took a chew of Red Man and sat in the shade, listening for sounds from the creek. I heard nothing but the rapping of a pileated woodpecker on a dead hackberry.

After crossing the creek, I turned south toward the river camp house. I would wait with Rowdy under the big, shady bur oak. I expected the black-mouth curs and hog to come out of the creek bottom somewhere near the camp house, because I had seen hogs coming from the creek to the river through the hog pasture. It was a gamble, but it might pay off.

Bob was trying to keep up with the dogs, and could hear them fighting the boar when he would stop and charge the dogs. The fights didn't last long, and the hog would run again, toward the river. Bob had caught up just long enough to see that the two curs were being challenged by a full grown, black Russian boar. Bob figured that the big hog would tire and try to whip the dogs before they got to the river.

Everything went in favor of the Russian boar. Bob didn't know exactly where he was; the dogs didn't know the terrain, and the hog was on familiar ground. The boar knew all the twists and turns between Long Lake and the river, and he had been up and down the creek many times.

The cur dogs were fast, and could catch up with the hog about every hundred yards. A short fight would occur, and the boar would run again. Bob figured he was getting close to the fence that led into the Bouldin property, and started looking for a good place to cross the creek. He thought the creek might be deep and cold.

Bob got to the Bouldin fence line, and turned right towards the creek. The creek bank was high, but he jumped in and waded waist-deep to the west bank, taking a scoop of creek water in his hand and into his mouth. He immediately spat it out, and continued after the dogs.

The boar knew the trails to the river. The creek meandered a long way to its convergence with the river, where it made a big bend close to the camp house. The boar knew this, and was headed to the hog pasture, and safety across the river.

Bob's wet Wranglers and sloshing boots felt cool. He had found a good trail to follow, as he heard the honking of the pickup horn from the west. I had arrived at the big bur oak near the camp house, about a quarter mile from the creek, and was blowing the horn to let Bob know where I was. I opened the pickup door to let in some hot wind, and sat watching the creek. The bur-oak shade felt good — a reprieve from the hot sun setting over the river. The air was already getting tolerable.

In the dim light of evening, I could see to the creek. I had my binoculars and was watching, hoping to see the hog or dogs. I thought I could hear them, but I wasn't sure. Rowdy was whimpering in the truck, wanting to get in on the chase. I figured he could hear the barking curs on the creek.

I finally heard Susie and Jane chasing the boar. As I glassed the pasture, the hog emerged from the creek, headed across the Middle Pasture in my direction. The two curs were close behind, barking and nipping at the hog as he was tiring — slowing down — trying to get to the river. I could see if the boar kept his course, he would come close to the bur oak.

When the boar slid under the barbed wire fence into the hog pasture, I got out of the truck and opened the bulldog's box. Rowdy nearly knocked me down as he jumped from the truck, knocking his water pan out on the ground, and heading in the direction of the barking curs. I noticed Rowdy didn't have a wide collar — just a plain leather collar, and I wondered why.

I looked again, and the boar and curs were not more than 150 yards away, and coming toward the river. Bob had come out of the creek and into the pasture, trying to catch up. I watched him through the binoculars. He appeared washed out from the long chase.

The running bulldog was trying to intercept the other dogs and hog. The hog would stop momentarily, and turn to fight. The curs would be in and out, nipping at the hogs nose or tail. Both dogs were quick in dodging the charging boar's maneuvers, but it was evident they were tiring from the chase. I could see they were getting careless, and likely to get cut from the boar's slashing tusks if the chase continued.

The boar stopped for a quick fight about 100 yards from me, as Rowdy left the ground and caught the hog's ear in mid-air, clamping down and throwing the boar on his side. Rowdy's weight was too much for the tired boar that laid squealing, with the curs going back and forth, biting anything they could see.

Black mouth Cur hog dog

In the wild melee, Jane bit Rowdy, but he didn't turn loose of the ear as a tired Bob Reynolds finally got to the fray. He carefully dodged the excited curs, while Rowdy had the squealing boar by the ear — both of them flat on the ground. As Bob arrived, the boar tried to stand, but fell back down, with his head on the ground.

Bob didn't hesitate, as he pulled the long knife, and grabbed the boar by a front leg. The hog was squealing as Bob slid the knife blade into his heart. Suddenly, all was quiet, as the bulldog let go of the ear, and the curs began to chew on the hog's flank, and lick the thick, red blood on the ground. Bob pulled his knife out. The chase ended.

I ran to Bob and the dogs just as darkness set in. After Bob had caught his breath and sat down on the ground, he looked over and said, "Damn, I'm tired. How far is it back to Long Lake from here?" He wiped the hog blood from his knife blade with a handful of grass, and put it back in the sheath. I thought for a minute, and said, "A little over two miles." I went to the truck and got the jug of water, and Bob drank his fill. His water bottle had gone empty a long way back in the chase, and he couldn't take the rank creek water.

I took a long drink from the jug, and screwed the lid back on. Some folks didn't like the well water at the Kokernot ranch house, but it sure tasted good on a hot July day. As I put the jug back on the pickup tailgate, I remembered the first time I made a bourbon and water at the house, and chuckled about how black my drink was.

Glancing over at the dogs, I was looking at the biggest Russian boar I had ever seen on the Kokernot. Both females were licking their wounds, and Rowdy lay stretched out, very close to the boar, as if to claim it for himself. He weighed about 70 pounds, but was small in comparison to the big hog.

Bob sat cross-legged on his rear, sweating like a sinning Democrat. His long-sleeved shirt was ripped in two or three places, and he had a bad briar cut on one cheek that was bleeding. His pants were still wet from the creek crossing, and his wet boots were oozing water. "The creek was cold. I was out of water, and took a handful of creek as I crossed. It is worse than your well water." I knew what Bob was talking about. The spring fed creek that flows all the way from Bastrop to the Guadalupe gets pretty smelly in late summer.

Darkness was setting in, and I could tell that Bob had put everything he had into the long chase. He just sat there on the ground, still breathing hard, and wiping the blood off his bleeding cheek. "Damn, what a chase! The longest one that I can remember," he exclaimed as he sat flat on the ground, with Susie licking his bloody cheek, and growling jealously at Rowdy.

We thought about photos, and I had my cheap camera in the truck, but darkness overtook us, and the camera didn't have a flash. "I should have taken a picture of you and the dogs, with the boar." Bob said. "We'll have the skull as proof that the hog was big, and the long tusks will show that he could be mean." That ended the discussion about pictures.

I looked the two curs over for bad cuts. Both had a few deep gashes on their upper parts, and a lot of blood on their heads and shoulders, but nothing that wouldn't heal in a week or two. They had run the boar more than they had fought, and that kept them from getting more deep cuts. The boar was more interested in getting to the river than turning and fighting the dogs. He was a smart old hog, but his time ran out!

Susie's collar had a few — what looked like new cuts — in the leather. I looked close and I thought she had caught some tusk marks on the wide collar. Jane's collar also showed some new, light colored rakings in a place or two. It was clear to me the wide collars did protect each dog's neck and throat.

"Rowdy doesn't have a wide collar," I said to Bob. "Why the difference in him and the curs?" Bob pulled Rowdy over to him, and the dog liked the attention. "Rowdy don't need a wide collar," he explained. "He goes in fast and grabs the hog by the ear or nose, or whatever he can hang on to. He won't let go, and so he don't need protection from cutting tusks. The other dogs do."

I put each dog back into their boxes, along with Rowdy's water pan, and gave them the rest of the water from the milk jug. Bob and I sat on the pickup tailgate for a while in the dark, talking about the hog, and how much he might weigh. Bob guessed more than 200 pounds, and I guessed close to 250. Russian hogs are tall at the shoulder and little at the hip. They don't weigh as much as they look, but a big, heavy Russian boar resembles a dead mule when they are stretched out on the ground.

The old boar almost made it to safety. Bob followed him and the dogs for more than two miles; crossed the creek, and the hog got to within 100 yards of the Guadalupe, before Rowdy overtook him and pinned him down. Different circumstances would have given the boar a chance to escape. If I had not gone to the camp house with Rowdy — if I had stayed up by the well house near the hog pasture gate — the boar would have made it to the river.

Bob and I had already agreed that if the hog got to the river, we would let him go. Neither of us were up to swimming the river after a hog. But that was "water under the bridge" because Rowdy had caught the boar, and Bob had given the boar a coup de grâce.

The boar was old and tough, but in the headlights of the truck, I rolled him over on his belly to stabilize him so that I could slip my knife blade upside down under the gritty skin along the backbone, from the shoulder to the hip. As Bob held the flashlight for better light, I peeled out the two back straps, which were nearly two feet long, and put them on top of a dog box in the bed of the pickup. They would be good marinated in sweet milk, tenderized and fried in small slices, with cream gravy and biscuits.

We marveled at the boar's long, split black hair down his back and inch-thick shoulder pads that were hairless from the boar fighting and plowing through the brush. His long tail had dried mud on the end, but most had washed off when he crossed the creek.

Both of the hog's upper and lower tusks were long and shiny but one lower tusk had been chipped on the end. The upper tusks turned up, and the lower tusks rubbed against them, making the long bottom tusks very pointed and sharp—formidable weapons for a big boar.

"Well, what do you think of our Russian boars," I queried, as Bob was beginning to breathe easier. He looked around at the boar, with 3-inch tusks shining white from his bottom jaw. "They are a lot of hog." Bob replied, as he put his finger on one of the tusks, and quickly pulled it back. "Sharp," he quipped. "These hogs are not anything like the spotted, curly-tailed feral hogs on the San Marcos."

"Why do you prefer the knife instead of a rifle or pistol," I asked, because I knew a couple of hunters at Cotulla who had dogs, and shot the hog with a rifle — mostly .30-30s and .44 Magnums. Bob didn't hesitate with his answer. "I have two reasons for the knife. Guns are dangerous when there's more than one hunter in the chase. If a greenhorn has a gun when the dogs catch a hog, and tries to shoot the hog, there is always a chance the bullet might hit a dog — or me!"

"Then, there is the noise of a gunshot. Sometimes a hog will go to a property where I don't have permission to hunt. I can follow the hog and stick it, with only the barking of the dogs. A loud gunshot could arouse someone close by, and I might be in trouble. A knife is the silent way to kill a hog." I thought about Bob's reasoning, and it made good sense. However, I know some hunters would prefer to shoot a hog, than stick it with a knife.

I took my folding Buck knife out of the sheath, and started cutting the boar's head off. I cut to the bone all around with the knife blade, and Bob helped me twist the head, and break the neck bone. "I'll take his head to the house, peel all the meat off, and boil it out. After the skull dries, I always pull the tusks out a little and glue them to make a better trophy skull for you to show your friends at the fire house." Bob just smiled.

As we gathered everything up, I thought to myself, "He'll put that hog skull where everyone will see it, but I doubt that he will ever come back to the Kokernot again to chase another Russian boar. He'll stick to the spotted feral hogs with short noses and curly tails on the San Marcos."

I wiped the knife blade on my pant leg, and slid my thumb across the blade's edge. The dirt in the hog's skin had dulled the knife, but my whetstone would cure that. I closed the blade, and put the knife back in the belt sheath. "I need your cord to drag this hog off."

Bob handed me the nylon cord from his back pocket, and I tied one end to the boar's hind leg and the other to the truck bumper, as Bob shined his flashlight. I started the truck and pulled the hog away from the camp house and left it in the open Hog Pasture. There would be a dozen or more caracaras and buzzards on it soon after daylight.

I went back to Bob and handed him the nylon cord, glad that he hadn't had to use it on himself, or one of the curs. I made sure I had everything: my binoculars, my Buck knife back on my belt, the empty water jar, the back straps, the hog head, and turned the truck towards the hog pasture gate.

As the pickup lights shined on the gate — I had left it open — and Bob had closed it, we drove by the well house and on up the mile to the ranch house. I thought back to when I had first seen the boar at Long Lake, and had shot at it, and missed. If I had made a lucky shot, the boar would have been dead — not having the chance to try to elude the dogs on the chase; not getting to fight the dogs and die a quick death from the knife blade, while providing a thrilling chase for a fireman who likes to hunt hogs with dogs.

The hunt had been a fitting end for a Russian boar that had lived a long, undisturbed life in his favorite haunt at Long Lake. He would take no more acorns and pecans from the deer and turkey, or eat another week-old fawn. And above all, the caracaras and buzzards would be taking hog meat to their fledgling young, and the young coyote pups would get their first taste of pork. Me? Well, I'd be at the ranch house with Belle, boiling out an impressive Russian boar skull for a hog-hunting fireman.

SECTION 4:

EPILOGUE

The Head-On Wreck and Afterward

CHAPTER 32

Was That Trip Necessary?

A short story about a Saturday BBQ trip that went awry.

On May 5, 2006, Dean Davis called about nine o'clock in the morning, asking when I was going to pick him up to go to the BBQ in Berclair. "I'll be there about 10," I replied, and went about getting ready to go to the annual gathering of friends for the 22nd Wayne Spahn cookout. Berclair is an hour and a half drive from Gonzales, and festivities started at noon. About 80 old friends met at the annual event to celebrate the good times and plan for more. The trip was not necessary, but Dean and I thought it was.

In my line of work as a wildlife biologist for 33 years, I traveled a lot. Many were the nights when I would get home at late hours from long drives after working all day. I didn't like motels, and I didn't like camping out in lonely places, so I always tried to make it home, which sometimes meant driving 200-300 miles.

At the peak of my wildlife career, I was driving as much as 30,000 miles a year, and more than once I thought of the chances of a wreck for someone who drove so much. In my mind, it was not a matter of "if", but a matter of "when." I always shunned the thought as meaningless because I was a good driver, and most of the roads were paved.

I made many trips that were not necessary. Trips to quail hunt; trips to parties and gatherings; trips to make gun trades; trips to dances; and trips to simply enjoy life. Most of the trips could have been avoided, but then, life would have been a bore. Therefore, I made many unnecessary trips in my time, and enjoyed every one of them.

I am not superstitious, but I am a student of common sense. In my mind, I knew that sooner or later, someone who traveled as much as I did would meet with some accident on the highway. I had already made it through some pretty hairy incidents in the past — a wreck or two during my army days, and when I lived in Waco. I ran a car through a barbed wire fence while driving home from a retirement party — in the pasture and out of the pasture — without a scratch except for the vehicle.

Then there was the antelope hunt west of San Angelo, when Nelson Franklin and I had a near-deadly blowout of a front tire and ran down the midway between a four-lane highway, and almost crashed into a concrete culvert. That one was close! We backtracked the incident and decided that we had ruptured the tire while going through some rocky terrain to retrieve a dead pronghorn. Up to my retirement from Texas Parks and Wildlife, that was the closest I had ever come to meeting the Grim Reaper!

Not all of my close calls have been in vehicles. During the fall of 1956, shortly after I had gotten an early discharge from the army to go to Texarkana College, a friend and I were in a home-made wooden boat on Lake Texarkana, trying out a new Wizard 7½ horsepower outboard that I had bought. We were somewhere close to the middle of the lake, when I noticed the transom of the boat was pulling apart, and water was coming in.

I didn't know whether to go slow, or to speed up as fast as we could, to get to the shore before the boat sank. I decided to speed up, and we got to the bank just as the back end of the boat came completely off, leaving us in knee deep water. That was a very close call, because we had no life preservers, and the November water was very cold. It was a good case of bad judgment.

After I retired from state employment and moved to Gonzales County, I continued to travel extensively with Texas Trophy Hunters and my own personal pleasure trips. I thought all of them were necessary, even though many were simply choices. I didn't know it, but time was running out on my commonsense observations that sooner or later the "axe would fall." That day was May 5, 2006.

"Better buckle up," Dean suggested after we had gone about 10 miles out of Gonzales. A light drizzle had fallen early in the morning — not

Berclair BBQ—Bottom: Al Brothers (L), Horace Gore. Top; Rex Kelly (L), Buddy Wood, Rex Spahn

enough to use the wipers, but enough to make the roads slick. I didn't like to wear seat belts in the King Ranch pickup because I thought they were too tight on my chest. Dean pulled his around and buckled up, and I did the same.

We continued the 30 miles across the Guadalupe River on 183 that would take us to Cuero, then on to Goliad and eventually, Berclair on Hwy 59. On this fateful trip, however, we would not make it to Cuero. The eventful occurrence that I had thought of so many times for the woeful traveler would soon happen near a creek below a curvy hill on the highway. A Chevy Suburban driven by an employee of a funeral home in Victoria would try to pass a pickup on the hill, lose control while passing, and hit our King Ranch pickup head-on at speeds close to 60 miles per hour.

The collision caused the pickup to leave the highway near the creek, and roll over twice and land on the left side. In the collision, I never lost consciousness, and I said, "Dean, help me get out." Dean was slightly above me, and said, "I can't. My arm is broken." That was the last thing I remembered until I was in the helicopter on the way to Memorial Hospital in San Antonio. I came to, and the nurse said, "We'll be there in a few minutes." Then I remember the chopper setting down on top of Memorial Hospital, and my daughter taking all of my personal items as they hauled me to emergency. I didn't know where Dean was, but apparently he was in the helicopter with me.

The wreck did not damage my upper body because of the seat belt and air bag, but my legs were a shamble. When the emergency room and a few more days were over, I had steel rods in my left leg, which was in a cast up to my knee, and my right leg was under suction treatment for gangrene. I was on a drip regimen of morphine for several days, and I took many trips into fantasy land. The entire fiasco was a horrible ordeal, and I wouldn't wish it on anybody.

I stayed in San Antonio hospitals through May, June, and most of July. I got some relief when they took me by ambulance to Brackenridge

Berclair BBQ crowd

> *"In today's world, technical genius is on every street corner, but common sense is as rare as hen's teeth."* — Goreism

Hospital in Austin for rehab treatments. While in Brackenridge, they removed my gall bladder, and I spent about a month in rehabilitation. Many of my friends came by to visit in Austin, and I was glad when they released me to go back to the ranch on Aug. 20, 2006. From the helicopter trip to the day I got out of Brackenridge Hospital in Austin was 107 days spent in a hospital bed.

My brother Bill was there to help me through the next two to three weeks at the ranch, and a county care worker came in two or three times a week to help me recover and get back on my feet. After a time, I was able to go to Texas Trophy Hunters with Bill as my driver, and by the first of the year (2007) I was walking and driving, and getting back to my regular routine.

Can we ever predict when a trip is necessary? Had Dean Davis and I backed out on that trip to Berclair, I would have avoided a miserable hospital stay, and years of problems with my legs. Was the trip necessary? Of course, not. We could have stayed home and gone squirrel hunting — the anaqua was getting ripe, and squirrel go crazy over anaqua berries. Or, we could have stayed home and shot turtles in the river. A high bank near the camp house was an excellent spot to sit and try to shoot turtles in the head.

We could have done many things, but instead we went to the BBQ at Berclair, and the story of miles of travel, whether necessary or unnecessary is history. The wreck has haunted my health for years, and activated a diabetes problem that had laid silent until I got all of the leg and feet injuries. But I was lucky to survive the crash. In days of yore, I would have been dead as a mackerel, but life goes on.

CHAPTER 33

My Last Whitetail

The deer season was almost over in 2016. I hadn't killed a buck because the old diabetes had me taking short steps and staying close to home. I wanted to try out my new Jack O'Connor Commemorative .270 Super grade rifle on a good eight-point that would score about 150 gross. Marty Berry and I had talked about a hunt, and I was in no hurry because I expected him to call any day.

Sure enough, Marty called early in the week, wanting to know if I could come down and hunt for a big 8-point that he had seen on his Gloriosa Ranch in Live Oak County. We talked about my health — and my new rifle — and finally planned a hunt during the next week. I would meet Jason Shipman in Lytle, and he would drive me on down to the hunt. I needed a little help, and Jason was there to assist me in getting about. We got to Marty's camp about noon, before he arrived from Corpus Christi. We made ourselves at home in the nice camp house. We had been there before.

Jason had been with me when I bought the rifle from Gary Machen at the Los Cazadores store in Pearsall. We had all been to a wildlife meeting near town, and after the meeting we went to the store with Gary to look at some guns. The Jack O'Connor .270 was among them, and I looked it over with keen interest. The price was high, but the quality was good. I wanted the rifle because I have been a fan of Jack O'Connor since my first days in high school, when I would read everything I could find that had Jack's name on it. He was a great outdoor writer and an expert on guns — especially Winchester Model 70s. I must say I idolized Jack O'Connor.

Gary and I haggled over the price, and when the deal was over I carried the rifle out in the box, and my bank account had suffered. I took the gun back to the Kokernot Ranch and put a 3-9X Leupold scope on it and adjusted the trigger to 2½ pounds. With my handloads of Winchester brass, 130-grain Hornady over 60 grains of H4831, the rifle put

Horace Gore's last whitetail buck, with Marty Berry on his Gloriosa Ranch

three shot into a group the size of a quarter. I was satisfied, and ready for a good buck.

At the camp, Marty showed up about 2 p.m., and we all got into his truck for a tour of the ranch and a look at some nilgai. All the time, Marty was talking about a plan to get the big eight-point that he had seen a couple of times near the front gate. "He'll go close to 150." Marty said as we got back to camp. "I'm going to go entice the deer with some corn where I saw the buck last," Marty said as he left camp and headed south. Jason and I got ready to go, and when Marty came back about 4:30 p.m., we all got into his truck to do a little safari hunting over near the lake. I slipped three 130-grain Hornady cartridges into the .270, leaving an empty chamber.

We hadn't gone far, when a big 10-point with a couple of long drop tines came into view by the lake. "Can I substitute that drop tine buck for the eight-point? I asked. "Not hardly," Marty replied, and we went on our way. Marty wanted to get on to where he had seen the eight-point, and as the sun was getting low, we were getting close to the front gate. All eyes were looking for the big eight.

"Is that gun sighted in?" Marty asked as we watched for the buck. "It'll put three into close to an inch," I replied. "I think I can kill the buck if you can find him." Jason sat in the back seat, taking all of the smart talk in, and looking for the buck. Marty pulled the pickup over near some brush and said, "Let's sit here for a few minutes." As we waited, several does came out on the road looking for the corn. They were all slick heads, but Marty figured the old buck was hiding back in the brush.

"You know that we would be out in the brush rattling if your health could stand it," Marty uttered with a quaint smile. "I can't help it if I'm old and crippled up," I answered. We watched the does and suddenly Jason punched me in the shoulder from the back seat. "You ready for the buck?" I turned toward the window of the truck and asked, "Why, do you see him?" "He's on the right side of the road, about 80 yards in the brush." I put the glass on the spot, but saw nothing. "He went back in the brush," Marty said, and we all kept watching. The sun was getting low, and we figured that the buck would come out soon.

I put the barrel of the .270 out the truck window, and got as comfortable as I could. The scope was on 4-power — plenty for this kind of a hunt. We watched the does — they would tell us when the buck was coming. We all sat quietly, not saying a word as the does started moving about, looking toward the brush down the ranch road. Marty said, "I see his outline in the brush. Gore, get ready."

As if being punched in the butt with a sharp stick, the buck quickly came into the road as the does gave plenty of room. The buck paid no attention to the corn — he was looking at the does. I looked at the buck's big antlers and asked, "Marty, are you sure that's the right buck?" Marty quickly replied, "I'm sure — just shoot." I slipped a

> "My tomorrows are getting fewer every day." — Goreism

round into the chamber, pushed the safety off, and took a rest on the rear-view mirror. It was a chip shot with the Winchester, and I waisted no time in pulling the trigger. The .270 roared, and the Hornady bullet hit the buck right between his neck and shoulder. The 80-yard shot put him down quickly, as Jason slapped me on the back.

We could see the buck on the ground, so we were in no hurry to go to him. We got out of the truck, and Jason gave me an arm as we walked up to the buck. He had massive antlers, with eight long times. I saw Marty rubbing on the antler base, as he counted 10 points. Too our surprise, the old buck had two short kickers on the base of his left antler — a 10-pointer.

"Well, I know that you like eight-points, and I thought he had eight points," Marty said as we studied the antlers. "I guess we'll just have to chuck him and look for another eight." I looked at the buck, which would easily gross 150 — maybe more than that. "No, we'll take him to the shed." I replied. The old buck was a beauty, and I was sure that Jack O'Connor would have approved.

We took the buck back to camp and field dressed him and hung him up to drain. The next day, Jason and I took the buck back to the Kokernot, and later, put him in Jimmy Turk's cooler. I got Dean Davis to mount his antlers with a shoulder mount, and for days I just looked at the mount, and the big 10 that was supposed to be an eight. He would be my farewell to the whitetail — a buck fitting to be the end of a long career of deer hunting. It was also fitting that I finished my hunting with two dear amigos — Marty Berry and Jason Shipman, and a commemorative rifle for my long-time idol and mentor — Jack O'Connor.

CHAPTER 34

The Kokernot Finality

Hospital rooms all smell the same. The nurses look the same, and the doctors all act the same. I was in bad shape, with a cracked hip and nowhere to go except the local hospital in Gonzales. The doctors were there, and their prognosis was several weeks — maybe months — in the local rehab center where cracked hips don't heal as well. Little did I know that my long years on the Kokernot Ranch would soon end.

Diabetes runs in the Gore family, and several of my relatives had suffered from diabetes amputations. I knew I had high blood sugar, and was taking a weekly shot for the malady. My situation got worse in early 2016 when my right foot became infected and I went to Waco to have the toes amputated, and spent a recoup period with Donna and Bubba.

In June 2016, I returned to the Kokernot in time to go to the annual BBQ at Berclair. The right foot was healed and I used a stuffing in the toe of the right shoe. Walking was not easy, but I managed and got back to normal on the Kokernot, and at Texas Trophy Hunters. I did a pronghorn TV show for Trophy Hunters in August, along with the three Extravaganzas in Fort Worth, Houston, and San Antonio. Things went well until November 2017 when I met with a big nest of red wasps and broke my left hip.

The whole thing was a farce. I had gone from the house to the pickup shed to get a metal ladder so that we could replace a few light bulbs in the high ceilings. Donna and Bubba were down for a deer hunt, and Donna had just come in with a nice eight-point buck. The weather was lovely, and we were all enjoying the fall deer season on the Kokernot. I had no idea that a wasp nest as big as a feed-store cap would spoil the weekend.

The ladder hadn't been used for some time, and I was having a hard time getting it out of the junk stashed in the off side of the shed. I

Kokernot ranch house — a last look, 2017

leaned over the riding mower and used both hands to pull the ladder high enough to clear the rubble. Out of nowhere came hundreds of red wasps, ready to sting any intruder who disturbed their nest.

My reaction was to jump away from the swirling wasps, and I fell backward toward the pickup, on the hard caliche floor of the shed. I immediately felt the pain in my left hip, and I was surprised that I could not stand. The mower was close, and I reached for the steering wheel to pull myself up to the seat. The pain was intense, and I was still in awe as to what had happened.

I didn't know exactly what to do — my hip was hurting, and I could not get off the mower seat. I sat there for a good while, when Donna came out of the house, and I told her what had happened. "You need to call Hisey," I said, and she went into the house for her phone. Donna came back, telling me that Dr. Comie Hisey was waiting for us at the hospital. We managed to get me into the truck, and on to the Sievers Hospital in town.

Comie Hisey was my personal physician who I had known for 20 years. After checking me out, Comie suggested that we get the hip fixed, and that I should spend a few weeks in rehabilitation. It seemed a logical venture for the shape I was in. So, I was out of it for a while, and woke up in the local "Get Well Center" of Gonzales. I figured on being back on the Kokernot in a few days.

I was in a wheelchair for all the time I was out of bed. The private room was satisfactory, but the food was terrible. Doctors, nurses and friends came and went, and the folks at rehabilitation came calling. I did not take well to all their exercises, because I was hurting like hell. Between the food and the exercises, it was a miserable existence. After a short time, Dr. Hisey brought me back to the hospital for further tests.

While in the hospital, the doctors found a blood clot under my right knee. The situation was serious, because the clot could break and send bad material to my heart. I ended up in Baptist Hospital in San Antonio, where the doctors amputated my right leg above the knee. I don't remember much about the amputation because I was under sedation for some time before and after the operation. I have to assume that the doctors were right in removing my leg, but when you lose a leg, it is gone forever and so is your previous lifestyle.

Being shy a leg meant a long time in the hospital in rehab, and I got to know a lot of nurses in Baptist Hospital. The routine was the same — in bed all the time except for about two hours each day in the rehabilitation area where I used everything from my fingers to my left leg, in preparation for leaving the hospital and going to Lorena with Donna and Bubba. The hospital "sent me away" when the insurance ran out, and Donna came to get me.

In Lorena, with Donna and Bubba, I had weekly care from county health workers, and before long I was up and walking with a walker from the living room to the kitchen, and back. Things looked good for a "peg leg", and we began to make preparations for the artificial limb. Then, things turned sour when my left foot and toes showed infection. I went to the hospital in Waco where the toes were removed. All plans for a peg leg were off the table, and there was little chance that I would ever get out of the wheelchair.

I'm lucky in one respect — Bubba's house is big; it's out in the country; it has good parking for my pickup with a special seat to put me in

> *"You can tell a lot about people by looking at their butter dish."* — Goreism

and out, and has a long porch that allows me to get out and feel the summer breezes, winter winds, and watch the cattle, horses and wildlife. It certainly beats living in an apartment in town!

I've quit hunting, and sold most of my gun collection — many rifles, shotguns and pistols that I have collected during my long life. It was difficult to let them go, and I only sold them to my close friends. Some I will keep — my Winchester Model 12 20-gauge quail guns of 40 years, and the Winchester Model 97 hammer gun that I used to take a truck-load of turkey gobblers. I'll keep some rifles and pistols that were engraved by Tommy Kaye, a master engraver and close friend. I still get invitations to go hunting, but my days of chasing wild birds and animals are over.

The only thing I can do now is write. Writing and Texas Trophy Hunters is a blessing when each day is wheelchair and computer — writing for books and *The Journal*. I don't drive, and my usual outings are the yearly Hunters Extravaganzas, doctor visits, and an occasional restaurant dinner — not a lot to look forward too. However, the good thing about writing from your experiences is that you get to go back through those times, and by writing about them — experience the good years all over again.

CHAPTER 35

Requiem for a Tiger in a Cage

After five years of existence in a wheelchair, and generally being confined to three rooms in the house, I have come to feel like a tiger in a cage. My thoughts about confinement go back a long way, ever since I read "Bring'em Back Alive" by Frank Buck (1930) when I was in the 9th grade in Hooks, Texas. The idea of catching a wild animal in Africa and putting it in a zoo for public viewing was very new to me at the time, but now it comes back to reality since I'm now like a wild animal in confinement.

When I look back at the 89 years of my life, I can readily compare my days to those of a tiger. I was always on the prowl, living on the edge, looking for something to achieve — something exciting — and feeling subjective to those whose attributes were superior to mine.

I always liked the freedom of the wild, the hunt, and sometimes dreamed of being put in jail for something I didn't do. Later in life, I found myself to be estranged from some of the rules of society, and landed in jail once when alcohol got the best of me — when I used poor judgment. I didn't like jail, and don't recommend it.

I've always been a hunter, but not always after game. I've hunted for love; for money; for the excitement of the chase; for fame; for professional achievement, and success in life. We all hunt for something.

My idea of life comes from a philosophy that a person's existence is nothing more or less than the total of all of their experiences. The more experiences — the richer the life. If I compare my life to that hypothesis, I must admit that I have had a very rich life — one that should be celebrated, and in some ways, copied. A rich life is more than advancements to piety — there must also be bad times, when contributions to society are contrary to the good. I've made payments to both.

> *"The only difference in life and death is waking up in the morning."* — Goreism

A tiger does not have thought processes that separate good from evil. It relies on three things for a good life — food, cover and replication. These necessities are entwined with staying alive and fighting for dominance. If I look at my life, it has been no different than that of the tiger. I came from a humble beginning, and have taken on the task of marriage, children, and the military, and spent years obtaining an educational parameter that would make me dominant in a particular field. The difference in me and the tiger is that I have the ability to discern good from evil, as stipulated in our Christian society. We must live by The Golden Rule, and the Ten Commandments.

I've had a good life. I've accomplished most of the things that I've wanted to do. Just like a tiger, I have prowled and conquered. My home range has included education, marriage and divorce, fatherhood, personal achievements, professional success, and now all I can do is write. But I'm thankful for the ability to use words to express my thoughts about hunting and living.

I've stood at death's door twice. A head-on wreck, and when my blood sugar suddenly went down to about 40 while the folks were away, and I sank to oblivion at my computer. I dodged death in the wreck, and I came back to reality when the emergency crew pumped sugar back into my veins. If I did taste death in either case, it was very quick and quiet — no trumpets or angels — just nothing, and not bad at all if it were not so permanent.

I'm reminiscent of Frank Buck's catching of animals for zoos, a tiger in a cage. No more roaming; no more combat; no more conquests. Like the tiger, I get good food and care, with few challenges. And, as we hear from the Christian brethren — It's all over but the shouting! I will die peacefully in confinement — a tiger in a cage.

ACKNOWLEDGMENTS

Texas A&M University

Texas A&M University is acknowledged for their excellence in education, sports, and character building in the student body.

Gig 'em, Aggies!

Texas Trophy Hunters Association

Texas Trophy Hunters Association (TTHA), an organization of Safari Club International, is acknowledged for being the "Voice of Texas Hunting," and presenting to Texas a series of Extravaganzas that promotes hunting and the Texas outdoors. TTHA is recognized for their Journal excellence, which provides a setting for wildlife information, hunting stories, and a recognition of wildlife values to the hunting public.

Safari Club International

Safari Club International (SCI) is acknowledged for protecting the freedom to hunt and to promote wildlife conservation worldwide. SCI advocates, preserves, and protects the rights of all hunters, and promotes safe, legal, ethical hunting and related activities. Safari Club International Foundation is acknowledged for its 20-year history of being a leader in science-based solutions to real problems facing wildlife conservation and sustainable use of wildlife resources.

ACKNOWLEDGMENTS

This Texas Trophy Hunters 50th Anniversary book was published with generous contributions from these Friends of Texas Trophy Hunters:

Walter and Donna Athey
Lorena, Texas

The Berlanga Family
Hugo, Laura and Omar
Mustang Ranch, *San Diego, Texas*

Marty Berry
Platinum Life Member #189
Gloriosa Ranch
The brush country of South Texas

Marvin and Cathy Boedeker
MC Boedeker Agriculture
Shiner Premium Whitetails
Shiner, Texas

Joe and Kathryn Coleman
Richmond, Texas

Don and Sandy Gilchrist
G2 Ranch, *Pearsall, Texas*

Horace Gore
Wildlife Biologist,
Outdoor Writer
Platinum Life Member #273
Lorena, Texas

Mark Herfort
Platinum Life Member #1
Rosenberg, Texas

Barry and Liz Hogan
Hogan Wilderness Retreat
Caldwell County, Texas

Phil and Jackie Hunter
Charco Marrano Ranch
Cotulla, Texas

Bobby and Sue Schmidt
Platinum Life Member #149
Schmidt Ranch,
Niederwald, Texas

Jason Shipman
Certified Wildlife Biologist
Shipman Wildlife Consulting
Lytle, Texas

Lanny Vinson
Vinson Ranches, *Abilene, Texas*

Brian Hunter Welker
CEO and Chairman, Welker Inc.
Platinum Life Member #6
Sugar Land, Texas

Modesta Williams
Clayton Williams Companies
Midland, Texas